MW00764709

CREED and CULTURE

Jesuit Studies of Pope John Paul II

CREED and CULTURE

CULTURE

Jesuit Studies of Pope John Paul II

EDITED BY

JOSEPH W. KOTERSKI, S.J.

AND

JOHN J. CONLEY, S.J.

SAINT JOSEPH'S UNIVERSITY PRESS

PHILADELPHIA

Copyright © 2004 by Saint Joseph's University Press
All Rights Reserved. No part of this book may be used or reproduced in any manner
whatsoever without written permission.

Printed in the United States of America at Saint Joseph's University Press,
on the campus of Saint Joseph's University, Philadelphia.
Book design: Carol McLaughlin
Cover design: Jon Kostesich
Cover photo: Servizio Fotografico, *L'Osservatore Romano*, 00120 Città del Vaticano

Library of Congress Cataloging-in-Publication Data

John Paul II Jesuit Symposium (1998 : Georgetown University, Washington, D.C.)
  Creed and culture : Jesuit studies of Pope John Paul II / edited by Joseph W. Koterski and
John J. Conley.
     p. cm.
  Includes bibliographical references.
  ISBN 0-916101-45-2 (paper over board : alk. paper)
  1. John Paul II, Pope, 1920---Congresses. I. Koterski, Joseph W. II. Conley, John J. III. John
Paul II Jesuit Symposium (2000 : Xavier University, Cincinnati, Ohio) IV. Title.
  BX1378.5.J548 2004
  261'.092--dc22

                                    2004000923

Published by:

SAINT JOSEPH'S UNIVERSITY PRESS
5600 City Avenue
Philadelphia, Pennsylvania 19131-1395
www.sju.edu/sjupress/

Member of the Association of Jesuit University Presses

Contents

Creed and Culture: An Introduction

Pope John Paul II leaves no one indifferent.

Since the beginning of his pontificate, John Paul II has provoked the admiration and the consternation of the world. On abortion and on war, he proclaims the unvarnished gospel. When democracies promote religious freedom, he praises them. When they destroy the child or the elderly, he denounces them. If the left commends his condemnation of the war in Iraq, the right applauds his defense of the traditional family. The most ecumenical of popes, serenely presiding over interreligious conferences at Assisi, John Paul II simultaneously insists that outside the Church there is no salvation.

In the late 1980s a group of American and Canadian Jesuit scholars founded the John Paul II Jesuit Symposium. The Symposium's purpose is to sponsor scholarly discussion on the teaching of John Paul II. Interdisciplinary, the Symposium welcomes Jesuits from different fields: theology, philosophy, law, social science, physical science, the fine arts, history, and literature. Pluralist, the Symposium encourages debate on different interpretations of the meaning and the pastoral implications of the pope's thought. Open to all Jesuits, the Symposium attempts to place the scholarly resources of the Society of Jesus at the service of the papacy, which Jesuits have defended with particular fervor since their order's birth in the Catholic Reformation.

The major work of the Symposium has been the sponsorship of a biennial conference devoted to the teaching of John Paul II. The following conferences have already been held: "The Thought of John Paul II" (Loyola-Chicago, 1990); "The Ecclesiology of John Paul II" (Fordham-New York, 1992); "The Fundamental Moral Theology of John Paul II" (Canisius-Buffalo, 1994); "The Applied Ethics of John Paul II" (Georgetown-Washington, D.C., 1996); "Priesthood, Religion and Culture in John Paul II" (Georgetown-Washington, D.C., 1998); "Pope John Paul II on Faith, Culture, and the New Evangelization" (Xavier-Cincinnati, 2000).

The members of the Symposium gratefully acknowledge the support provided for their 1998 and 2000 conferences from the following benefactors: The

Homeland Foundation; Mr. and Mrs. Roger Miller; Dr. and Mrs. Arthur Kunath; the Maryland Province of the Society of Jesus; the New York Province of the Society of Jesus; the Jesuit community at Georgetown University; the Jesuit community at Xavier University.

The Symposium has also sponsored the publication of the conference proceedings. Two previous books based on the conferences have already appeared. *The Thought of John Paul II*, ed. McDermott (Gregorian University Press, 1993), presents papers from the 1990 and 1992 conferences. *Prophecy and Diplomacy: The Moral Doctrine of John Paul II*, ed. Conley-Koterski (Fordham University Press, 1999), provides papers from the 1994 and 1996 meetings. The present volume incorporates papers from the 1998 Georgetown and the 2000 Cincinnati conferences.

The focus of this book and of recent conferences on the relationship between faith and culture was an obvious one. The longstanding dispute over church-state relations has broadened into a debate over the proper relationship between religion and culture. Many of the Church's most anguished pastoral questions concern the degree to which the gospel can be adapted to a particular culture. What of African polygamy or of Asian arranged marriages? On what points should the Church commend or contest North Atlantic feminism? Where is the line between idolatry and legitimate inculturation when non-Christian terms and practices are incorporated into Christian worship?

Nor is this discernment of cultural orthopraxis confined to the Church's relations *ad extra*. The internal life of the Church, especially since Vatican Council II, has been agitated by questions on her own religious culture. To what extent should the human rights defended by the Church in the political forum be operative in her conduct *ad intra*? How can the exercise of authority be altered without damaging the Church's hierarchical constitution? Where is the frontier between divine institution and cultural convention in how the Church worships, teaches, and sanctifies?

From the beginning of his pontificate, John Paul II has explored how the Church can critically engage contemporary culture. In the pope's perspective the human person is not a generic *homo sapiens* distinguished by powers of intellect and will. The human person shapes and is shaped by the concrete networks of language, religion, politics, economics, family, work, art, and science that constitute a particular culture. It is this encultured person, not an abstract individual, who is the focus of the Church's mission to evangelize:

> All human activity takes place within a culture and interacts with
> culture. For an adequate formation of culture, the involvement of

the whole person is required, whereby one exercises one's creativity, intelligence, and knowledge of the world and of people....The way in which one is involved in building one's own future depends on the understanding a person has of himself and of his own destiny. It is on this level that the Church's specific and decisive contribution to true culture is to be found. The Church promotes those aspects of human behavior which promote a true culture of peace, as opposed to models in which the individual is lost in the crowd, in which the role of one's initiative and freedom is neglected, and in which one's greatness is posited in the arts of conflict and war. The Church renders this service to human society by preaching the truth about the creation of the world, which God has placed in human hands so that people may make it fruitful and more perfect through their work; and by preaching the truth about the Redemption, whereby the Son of God has saved humankind and at the same time united all people, making them responsible for one another.[1]

The Church's mission to human culture is not one of simple respect. It entails a courageous critique of the moral worth of different cultures according to the criteria of the gospel. The gospel decenters culture by revealing its origins in God's creative gift, not in its own initiatives, and by proclaiming its final end as a gift of God's redeeming grace, not a result of its own achievements. Paradoxically the Church's supreme service to human culture is to defend the human person's transcendence of culture by proclaiming the divine sovereignty that creates and saves us in our cultural relations.

Cultural preoccupations permeate many of the works of John Paul II that are not primarily focused on the concept of culture. Numerous works on ethical controversies study the social conflicts fueling contemporary moral dilemmas. *Familiaris consortio* (1981) examines the disparate cultural traditions surrounding marriage which render the Church's wisdom on conjugal life so contested and so necessary. Devoted to the issue of work, *Laborem exercens* (1981) analyzes the challenges to human dignity presented by the rise of now technological cultures in the workplace. *Letter to Families* (1994) dissects trends in contemporary culture that contest "the civilization of love" that is the social ideal of family life.

The pope does not limit himself to a simple description of divergent cultural tendencies that form the background to current moral and religious conflicts. He trenchantly analyzes how certain ideologies turn particular cultures into stony ground for the proclamation of the gospel. Written on the eve of the collapse of European communism, *Sollicitudo rei socialis* (1987) condemns the totalitarian cultures that systematically deny the human person the right to political expression and that destroy the rights of intermediate bodies, such as the family and the guild. *Veritatis splendor* (1993) examines how individualism and materialism have shaped the resistance of Western culture to religious conversion. *Evangelium vitae* (1995) diagnoses how liberal democracy's cult of freedom has nurtured a grim culture of death.

The Jesuit contributors to this volume study the relationship between faith and culture in the writings of John Paul II from different perspectives. Cardinal Avery Dulles, S.J., analyzes how the dignity of the human person operates as the keystone in the pope's theory of society. Martin Tripole, S.J., explores the current clash between gospel and world, reflected in the culture wars surrounding the pope. Raymond Gawronski, S.J., describes the distinctive Polish background which shapes John Paul II's theory of culture, while John Haughey, S.J., argues that the Vatican itself possesses a particular culture with its own limitations. Arthur Madigan, S.J., studies how certain cultural traits of the postmodern West create serious obstacles to the "new evangelization." Mitchell Pacwa, S.J., warns that various "New Age" currents in American culture often foster counterfeits of the gospel. Joseph Bracken, S.J., explores the resources of process theology for the intercultural problems raised by the Church's interreligious dialogue. John Conley, S.J., analyzes how in practice and theory the pope treats the cultural contributions of art. In his paper on priesthood, Cardinal Avery Dulles, S.J., underscores the functionalist cast of contemporary religious culture, which makes adherence to John Paul II's theology of priesthood problematic.

The final papers focus on two particular papal documents dealing with urgent problems of contemporary culture. In his analysis of *Letter to Families* (1994), Peter Ryan, S.J., argues that John Paul II's treatment of the destiny of the family raises the broader question of the ultimate history and beatitude of the human person. In his discussion of the encyclical *Fides et ratio* (1998), Stephen Fields, S.J., analyzes the effort of the pope to revive Christian philosophy in contemporary culture. In this document John Paul II pays close attention to cultural movements eroding both philosophy and theology: postmodernism, pragmatism, and nihilism.

If these Jesuit studies on the pope's theory of creed and culture indicate John Paul II's sensitivity to cultural pluralism, they also underscore the pope's critique of contemporary culture. They document the pope's refusal to countenance a distortion of human rights that reduces burdensome groups to the status of non-persons. The papers echo John Paul II's critique of the libertarian and the materialist creeds of postmodern culture, which promote an illusory freedom. Recognizing the pope's efforts to reconcile religious freedom in the civic order with doctrinal integrity in the religious order, they signal his refusal to import the conventions of liberal democracy into the internal life of the Church. If the world and its myriad cultures are a gift of God's creation, they remain under the judgment of the Church summoned to proclaim the gospel of conversion to every creature and to every cultural system.

John J. Conley, S.J.
Fordham University
New York City

NOTES

1. John Paul II, *Centesimus annus* (1991), n. 51.

The Enrichment and Transmission of Faith in the Theology of John Paul II

Cardinal Avery Dulles, S.J.

From his early years the future Pope John Paul II had a lively interest in the topic of faith. As a young man, he found a spiritual guide in a remarkable layman, Jan Tyranowski, who trained him and other young men to be attentive to the presence of God within them and to grow in the ways of prayer. According to an associate of Wojtyla in Tyranowski's circle, the young men were taught to understand progress in prayer as a matter of "experiencing with one's whole being the presence of God within us. It is not the intellect but the will and feelings that have to be trained so that, with the help of grace, we may perfect ourselves in the theological virtues of faith, hope and charity, and be capable of receiving the gifts of the Holy Spirit."[1] John Paul II reports that Tyranowski introduced him to the great Spanish mystics and in particular to St. John of the Cross. Reading the poems of the great sixteenth-century Carmelite, the pope recalls, "was a very important stage in my life" (*CTH*, 3).

ST. JOHN OF THE CROSS

In 1946, when the young priest Wojtyla arrived in Rome for doctoral studies, he quite naturally chose as the topic of his dissertation, *The Doctrine of Faith of St. John of the Cross*.[2] In this dissertation he evinces a familiarity with, and an acceptance of, the teaching of St. Thomas Aquinas. Faith, for Thomas as well as for John of the Cross, is a *habitus* in the intellect whereby it assents to revealed truths on the authority of God the revealer (53-55, 237, 265). Faith comes by hearing (80), and more specifically by hearing the proclamation of the Church, "which alone has received the total revelation to which the intellect must assent by believing" (181). "Revealed truths," writes Father Wojtyla, "must be believed in the sense defined by the Church and proposed by the Church for belief and not because of any private revelation or interpretation" (127). "It is in this way that the Church intervenes in

1

every act of faith" (181).

The dissertation focuses on the question whether and how faith effects union between the believer and God. Following John of the Cross, Wojtyla distinguishes between two levels of faith and two kinds of union. At the lower level, he declares, faith may be considered simply as an act or habit of the intellect (264-65). It assents to God's revelation as conveyed by words or propositions (180, 208). The words or propositions are not themselves the objects of faith but are means whereby the mind adheres to the divine reality they signify (270). The supernatural light of faith directs the assent of the mind beyond the propositions to God himself, who is the primary object of faith. Because faith brings the mind into an intentional union with the divine reality, it effects what Wojtyla describes as an initial ontological union between the soul and God (263).

The heart of the dissertation deals less with the ontological relationships just described than with the psychology or phenomenology of the life of faith. By itself alone, Wojtyla maintains, faith produces some elements of union but lacks the capacity to effect a properly psychological union with God (247, 255). The words and concepts by which faith is mediated belong to the created order and therefore fail to represent the divine reality they signify (94, 241, 247).

This psychological shortcoming, however, is remedied by the supernatural gift of charity, which is the virtue that properly unites the soul to God and tends by its own force to transform the lover into a participation in the Beloved (50-52, 249). When faith is animated and rendered operative through charity, it becomes capable to uniting the soul to God, even to some degree psychologically (250-51). This union of love is still imperfect in the present life because the intellect is still deprived of proper knowledge of the reality in which it believes. Only the infused light of glory, to be given by God in the life to come, removes the disproportion by immediately communicating the divine reality itself (65, 243).

The major portion of the book is taken up by tracing the psychological progress of the believer who is guided by love. In tracing the passage from meditation to contemplation, Wojtyla, following John of the Cross, explains how love weans the mind from reliance on created representations and thus brings about "dark nights" of the senses and of the spirit (183-201). Paradoxically, faith gives light precisely by blinding the soul (71-72). "The more darkness it causes, the greater light it gives" (95). In what mystics call "the passive night of the spirit," the divine comes to be understood not through intentional representations but through the redundance of love (260), which prepares for the transformative union described by authors who have undergone mystical experiences. The soul suffers intense pain, being deprived of any comfort or support from the natural light of the intellect. Love, though it brings about a union of the heart with God, is not a replacement for faith. Loving contemplation presupposes faith, whereby the mind accepts the truths revealed by God (224, 258). Even in this life charity imparts a certain participated likeness to God. Faith animated by charity is therefore the proper and proportionate means of union with God (18, 33-38, 137).

The treatment of faith in Wojtyła's Roman dissertation is individualistic, even monastic.[3] It deals with the lonely progress of the individual withdrawing from social contacts and seeking solitary union with God. After studying modern personalism and participating in Vatican II, Wojtyła will put much more emphasis on the dignity of the person as a self-determining agent and on the participatory character of faith as taking place within the community of believers.

In some respects, however, the book on John of the Cross provides a platform for Wojtyła's later development. He will never cease to give attention to faith as an acceptance of revealed truth and to the importance of the testimony of the Church as the authorized custodian of revelation. He will also insist on the mystical dimension of faith as involving an intimate union with God, who through the infused virtues of faith and charity calls the soul to himself. Never satisfied with a merely doctrinal concept of faith, he will ceaselessly explore the individual person's growth in faith as a grace-given existential response to God himself.

AT VATICAN II

In his interventions as a young bishop at the Second Vatican Council, Karol Wojtyła spoke on a great variety of topics, including faith, in ways that seem prophetic of his later work.[4] In his interventions on the "people of God" and on the lay apostolate, for example, he made the point that lay persons do not have a merely passive possession of the faith. The grace of faith itself gives them the right and duty to engage in witness and apostolic activity. The lay apostolate, therefore, is a personal actualization of the faith and a vocation of which lay persons should be conscious.[5] In these declarations Wojtyła was perhaps thinking of laypersons such as Tyranowski, who had so influenced him in his youth.

SOURCES OF RENEWAL

In the decade following Vatican II, Wojtyla further developed his thinking on faith, as may be seen from his *Sources of Renewal*, a book composed as a guide to the teaching of the Council in connection with his archdiocesan synod at Kraków.[6] The central question put by the Council, as he explains it, was: *Ecclesia, quid dicis de te ipsa?* (36, 39, 203, 420). The presupposition of the question was that the Church is a subject, and is therefore capable of expressing its corporate self-awareness (112-21). The answer proffered by the Council was that the Church is a community of men and women responding to the word of God in faith. The implementation of the Council, according to Cardinal Wojtyla, requires an enrichment of faith on the part of the whole Church and its individual members.

The enrichment of faith, as the Cardinal explains it, has two aspects. It means, objectively, a better understanding of the content of faith and, subjectively, an acceptance of faith with greater courage and personal responsibility (22).

Although Wojtyla's interest focuses on the subjective or existential dimension, he by no means ignores the objective. Faith for him still means (as it did in his doctoral dissertation) a firm acceptance of what God has revealed (19, 53). Its central content is the Paschal mystery of Christ crucified and risen "as it was announced from the beginning" (83). That content is something to be assimilated through personal reflection; it can always be more fully and precisely understood within the scope of the truth already given (27).

The objective aspect, however, is not the whole of faith. "Perhaps the traditional formula 'to accept as true whatever God has revealed and what the Church teaches us to believe' implied a rather passive and mainly receptive notion of 'acceptance,' which was more or less identified as the basic element of a profession of faith" (206-07). Besides being seen as a profession of belief, faith must be recognized as a vocation to be followed (58).

Vatican II, as a pastoral council, looked especially to the subjective enrichment of faith (18). Emphasizing that aspect, Wojtyla insists that faith is a "fully personal" participation in an encounter with God (22). The act of faith is by its very nature free (21; cf. *DH*, n. 10). The proper response to God's self-revelation is not just an acceptance of a set of propositions, but a total self-commitment to the God who reveals (20).

If the approach to faith in Wojtyla's work on John of the Cross seems unduly individualistic, the deficiency is corrected in *Sources of Renewal*. In this work faith is held to relate the believer in a new way not only to God but to all fellow human beings

(38). Even the relationship to God is emphatically trinitarian, and therefore social, since it looks always to God as a *communio personarum* (121). Belief is an act of the Church itself, and of individuals insofar as they participate in the belief of the Church (36, 38).

The social character of faith, manifestly realized within the Church, goes outward to embrace all men and women, for all are in some way included in God's plan of salvation (36). "If in the past there was a tendency to use the method of separation to preserve the purity of the faith," writes Wojtyla, "Vatican II has indicated a different way of enriching it" (29). The new way is that of dialogue, which both expresses a certain maturity of faith and contributes to its further maturation (32-34). In the global situation of the present day, attention should be paid to every group outside the Church, with full respect for the human personality and conscience of their individual members (29). Interreligious and ecumenical dialogue may be seen as two forms of the dialogue of salvation which Paul VI described so memorably in his encyclical *Ecclesiam suam* (30-31, 208).

A further property of the theology of faith in *Sources of Renewal* is its historicity. Wojtyla sees the Church as advancing in the course of centuries toward the plenitude of divine truth (15; cf. *DV*, n. 8). The enrichment of faith therefore demands a mature response to revelation that is adapted to the reality of our times (422). The Council's whole concept of *aggiornamento* (or in Latin, *renovatio accommodata*) is "above all an expression of historical consciousness." Such updating requires a careful discernment of the signs of the times in the light of the word of God (173; cf. *GS*, n. 44).

Although the Cardinal attaches great importance to the historical development of faith and of its expressions, he is careful to avoid the pitfalls of historicism. He speaks of the "principle of integration," which requires that the whole patrimony of faith coming down to us from the apostles be integrated into the consciousness of the Church today. According to this principle, the teaching of Vatican II must be grasped in continuity with the teaching of all previous councils and popes (39). Faith is an organic whole, all of whose parts are interdependent (40). The entire creed is mirrored in the mind of the Church, and conversely, the mind of the Church embraces the entire creed (41).

Having dealt with the "consciousness of faith" in the major portion of *Sources of Renewal*, the author goes on in the third and last part to discuss "the formation of attitudes" (201-418). Wojtyla defines an "attitude" as something intermediate between consciousness and action. The enriched awareness of faith, he holds, results in an active relationship which is not yet action (205). Faith, as a total commitment of the self to God who reveals, demands a continual readiness to act accordingly. "Faith without works," writes the Cardinal, "is dead (cf. James 2:26); it cannot consist merely of knowledge or the content of consciousness. Essential to faith is an attitude of self-commitment to God—a continual readiness to perform the fundamental 'action' which corresponds to the reality of revelation" (206).

Inasmuch as revelation is God's testimony to himself, faith and witness are inseparably connected. The believer must be prepared to bear witness to the gospel (209). Mature faith therefore expresses itself in testimony (211). The Christian bears witness to Christ not "from outside" but "from within," on the basis of participation. Thus Wojtyla can write: "Faith, in all the wealth of its personal and communal characteristics, is essentially and basically a participation in the testimony of Christ" (219).

In a more general way, we may say that faith is connected with mission. Since the revelation to which faith responds is given through the respective missions of the Son and the Holy Spirit, it follows that the Church is always in a state of mission and that individual members of the Church must be committed to that mission so that revelation may become a reality in the world (207). More specifically, members of the Church participate by faith and baptism in the threefold mission of Christ as priest, prophet, and king (219).

Wojtyla devotes some fifty pages to a discussion of the ways in which various groups and orders within the Church share in each of the three offices. The threefold office of Christ, he concludes, informs faith and guides its development in the Church as a whole and in each member. An attitude of participation in the mission of Christ as priest, prophet, and king "should be seen as both a touchstone and an expression of man's supernatural maturity 'in Christ'" (270). Each Christian "in a certain sense rediscovers himself in Christ so that he may recognize Christ and Christ's mission in himself and in the dimensions of his own life and his own vocation" (271).

Sources of Renewal is Wojtyla's most thorough exposition of his postconciliar theology of faith. It anticipates the major themes that will resound in the encyclicals and apostolic exhortations he will write as pope. Composed in the flush of enthusiasm that followed Vatican II, it may be in some respects overly optimistic about the achievements of the Council and about the possibilities of communicating its delicately nuanced teaching to the rank and file of the clergy and laity.

Speech to European Bishops' Symposium

In October 1975 Cardinal Wojtyla delivered an important address on faith to a symposium of European bishops held in Rome. His topic was "Bishops as Servants of the Faith."[7] Consistent with *Sources of Renewal,* he here defines faith as a response of the whole person to the Word of God—a response given to God in the community of the Church. Faith therefore has a communal character; it is a participation in the *credo* of the whole Church (264).

Faith, as Cardinal Wojtyla here explains, is the object, content, and purpose of all episcopal ministries (263). Each bishop in his threefold role as priest, prophet, and pastoral ruler is called to be a servant of the faith of the people to whom he ministers (266). Bishops must arouse, form, and deepen the faith of the People of God (267). To be capable of that service, they themselves must believe wholeheartedly in Christ (263).

In exercising his prophetic office the bishop is first of all a preacher. The announcement of the gospel is the primordial service that he can render to faith. Such proclamation should render faith actual and authentic, making room for the action of the Holy Spirit (269). Among the prophetic ministries of the bishop, the magisterium has special importance because it is directly concerned with the safeguarding of the truth of God's word (267). The magisterium of the bishop is exercised collegially, in union with the whole body of bishops and with the pope as successor of Peter (268).

Wojtyla's Writings as Pope

I have dwelt at some length with these early works of John Paul II because they treat more specifically of faith than anything he has composed since his election as pope. As occupant of the see of Peter, he has been concerned to mediate and protect the established teaching of the Church, giving less prominence to his personal perspectives, which he would not wish to confuse with obligatory Catholic doctrine. Only in unofficial works such as *Crossing the Threshold of Hope* does one find him indulging in free theological speculation.

Notwithstanding this reservation, one can find in his papal pronouncements echoes of many of the themes already noted in his earlier work. Three of them seem particularly important. He continues to emphasize the intensely personal or interpersonal character of faith; he distinguishes between various degrees and stages in the maturation of faith; and he insists that faith shines forth in witness. In the remainder of this paper I shall discuss each of these three salient features.

PERSONALISM

The word "faith," in daily usage, has a double reference, both to a person and to an objective reality. "'I believe you' means that I trust you, and I am convinced that you are telling the truth." In other words, I believe "that the content of your words corresponds to objective reality" (*God*, 31).

The objective aspect of faith, for John Paul II, depends on the subjective. Faith differs from other forms of cognition insofar as it arises within a relationship of loving trust and a commitment to the reliability of a witness (*FR*, n. 32). From this it follows that divine faith is never a purely intellectual act. It involves a total submission of the whole person to God who reveals (*God*, 46). God, in making himself known, guarantees the credibility and truth of his own word (*FR*, n. 13).

Theologically, then, faith has two dimensions. On the one hand, it is an assent to the truth attested by God and on the other hand, more fundamentally, it is "a decision involving one's whole existence. Christian faith is an encounter, a dialogue, a communion of love and of life between the believer and Jesus Christ" (*VS*, n. 88).

As a personalist, John Paul II dwells repeatedly on the freedom of the act of faith, as taught in Vatican II's *Declaration on Religious Freedom*. Freedom, he points out, is in no way opposed to firm commitment. On the contrary, it actualizes itself in deeds whereby we commit ourselves. The fundamental decision of entrusting oneself to God is a consummate exercise of the believer's freedom (*FR*, n. 13). Because authentic faith is by nature free, it is never permissible to coerce a profession of faith (*RM*, n. 8; *CTH*, 190). One of the historic mistakes for which the Church has been asking pardon since the jubilee year is the improper use of violence by Christians in the service of religious truth (*TMA*, n. 35).

The structural freedom of faith should not be interpreted as though it implied that faith is optional or that one would be justified in refusing God's gracious invitation. Every human person is bound to seek the truth about religious matters and to adhere to it once it is seen to be credibly attested (*God*, 56). Although we have the power to say "No" to Christ, we are not morally entitled to do so (*RM*, n. 7).

It would also be a mistake to imagine that the freedom of faith implies a moral right to dissent from binding magisterial teaching. The ecclesiastical magisterium, according to John Paul II, derives its authority from Christ and the

Holy Spirit (*VS*, n. 116). "Opposition to the teaching of the Church's pastors," he writes, "cannot be seen as a legitimate expression either of Christian freedom or of the diversity of the Spirit's gifts. When this happens, the Church's pastors have the duty to act in conformity with their apostolic mission, insisting that the right of the faithful to receive Catholic doctrine in its purity and integrity must always be respected" (*VS*, n. 113). The general principle enunciated in this quotation might have to be nuanced to do full justice to the pope's thinking on the situation of theologians who are convinced that the magisterium has overlooked some aspects of truth. He is concerned, above all, to exclude public dissent and contestation.

STAGES OF FAITH

Consistently with his earlier positions, John Paul II as pope teaches that faith is not a static given. On the contrary, he maintains, it is a journey forward in which every believer, like Abraham, is moving toward a destination not yet seen (*RM*, n. 14). Like the Magi, believers follow the guidance of a star that points the way to the realm where God dwells in inaccessible light (*CT*, n. 60).

The journey of faith begins with the aspirations and desires that are rooted in our spiritual nature. The pope alludes frequently to the statement of St. Augustine: "Our hearts are restless until they rest in you."[8] We are disposed for faith by the realization that nothing finite and created can fully satisfy the hungers of the human spirit (*God*, 46-47). So deep is the inbuilt longing for transcendent truth that the human being can be defined, according to the pope, "as the one who seeks the truth" (*FR*, n. 28). Pascal, following Augustine, profoundly remarked that God is already present and active in the hearts of those who seek him. "You would not be searching for me," he wrote, "if you had not found me."[9]

Building on this insight, Pope John Paul II maintains that "God is already at work in the depths of the person who searches for the truth with an honest effort and who willingly accepts it as it becomes known to him" (*CTH*, 194). If faith is necessary for salvation, then, the earnest seeker meets the qualification. "In the very search for faith an implicit faith is already present, and therefore the necessary condition for salvation is already satisfied" (*CTH*, 193).

These insights are crucial for John Paul II's appraisal of non-Christian religions. In religion, he contends, man seeks answers to the unsolved riddles of the human condition. "The various non-Christian religions especially express this quest on man's part, while the Christian faith is based on revelation on God's part" (*God*,

77). In the many religions the pope finds signs, reflections, and hints of Christ who alone is the way, the truth, and the life. Quoting Paul VI, he states that the religions are "impregnated with innumerable 'seeds of the Word' and can constitute a true preparation for the Gospel" (*God*, 78, quoting *Evangelii nuntiandi*, n. 53). To the best of my knowledge, John Paul II does not speak of non-Christian religions as revealed or as containing revelation.

Faith in the biblical and Christian sense of the word goes beyond this attitude of searching. It is a welcoming response to revelation. "In Christ, religion is no longer a 'blind search for God' (cf. Acts 17:27) but the response of faith to God who reveals himself" (*TMA*, n. 6). Since faith in this sense presupposes revelation, John Paul II can say that "logically and historically revelation comes before faith. Faith is conditioned by revelation" (*God*, 32).

Revelation, as we know, developed gradually in the economy of salvation history. It reached its culmination in the Incarnate Word, who surpassingly fulfills the hopes and expectations contained in all the religions, including Judaism. In a number of texts, therefore, the pope declares that "to believe in a Christian way means to accept God's self-revelation in Jesus Christ, which constitutes the essential content of the New Testament" (*God*, 75). Christian faith may therefore be defined as "the conscious and free response of man to God's self-revelation which reached its fullness in Jesus Christ" (*God*, 86). The original deposit of faith continues to be made available in and through the Church. "The living transmission of divine revelation, contained in Tradition and Sacred Scripture, remains integral in the Church, thanks to the special service of the Magisterium, in harmony with the supernatural sense of the faith of the People of God" (*God*, 63).

Concerned to protect the objectivity and universalism of faith, John Paul II warns repeatedly against subjectivism and religious relativism. Too many Christians suffer from a tendency to adhere only to "what pleases them, to what corresponds to their own experience, and to what does not impinge on their own habits" (*PDV*, n. 7). When they find themselves in religiously pluralistic social situations, such persons tend to fall into religions relativism. "While respecting the beliefs and sensitivities of all," the pope admonishes, "we must clearly affirm our faith in Christ, the one Savior of mankind" (*RM*, n. 11). Only in Christ, he asserts, "are we set free from all alienation and doubt, from slavery to the power of sin and death" (*RM*, n. 11).

Evangelization is a complex process involving two major phases: initial adherence to the word of God and further instruction in the profound meaning of that word. Primary evangelization leads to a full acceptance of the person of Jesus

Christ as the one Lord, to whom one lovingly submits by a sincere conversion of heart. At a second stage, known as catechesis, evangelization seeks to impart a fuller knowledge of the "mystery" of Christ, including the contents and requirements contained in the gospel message (*CT*, n. 20). Since faith bears on God, who is ultimately mysterious, the data of revelation admit of ever deeper exploration (*RH*, nn. 18-19).

Although the development of faith has an cognitive aspect, it is not simply a matter of intellectual understanding. Conversion, says John Paul II, "gives rise to a dynamic and lifelong process which demands a continual turning away from 'life according to the flesh' to 'life according to the Spirit' (cf. Rom 8:3-13)" (*RM*, n. 46). Faith needs to be constantly rekindled and intensified through fresh encounters with the living Christ (*Amer*, n. 28). Prayerful encounters with the Lord through the Scriptures and the sacraments can contribute greatly to the process of maturation by which Catholics arrive at a strong, lively, and active faith (*Amer*, n. 12).

Collectively the entire Church possesses a "supernatural sense of the faith" which, according to Vatican II, is protected against error in matters of belief (*God*, 61; *RH*, n. 19; cf. *LG*, n. 12). Although this sense of the faith is not proper to the laity alone, they share in it and are called to discern the signs of the times in its light (*CL*, n. 14). Pastors must promote this sense of the faith, authoritatively judge the genuineness of its expressions, and educate the faithful to an ever more evangelical discernment (*FC*, n. 5).

As an example of faith brought to its highest degree of intensity and maturity, the pope turns to the Blessed Virgin Mary (*MR*, nn. 13-19). Elizabeth's exclamation, "Blessed is she who has believed" is a kind of key that unlocks for us the innermost reality of Mary (*MR*, n. 19; cf. Lk 1:45). At the Annunciation she responds to the divine invitation with a full submission of intellect and will, believing that what the angel announced would be fulfilled. By her *fiat* she entrusts herself to God without reserve, and throughout her life she unfailingly conforms herself to the ways of God, inscrutable as they are. Her pilgrimage of faith leads her to the foot of the Cross, where she unites herself perfectly to Jesus in his self-emptying. Her fidelity at this terrible moment is, in the phrase of John Paul II, "perhaps the deepest 'kenosis' of faith in human history." He quotes St. Irenaeus to the effect that "The knot of Eve's disobedience was untied by Mary's obedience; what the virgin Eve bound through her unbelief, the Virgin Mary loosened by her faith" (*MR*, n. 19)[10]

EXPRESSIONS OF FAITH

As in his writings as archbishop and cardinal, so also as pope, John Paul II insists that faith never remains a merely individual possession. Persons who believe strongly in Christ, he observes, will regard faith as their most precious possession and will seek to share it as widely as they can (*RM*, n. 49). A living faith seeks to communicate itself in witness. The entire Church, and each of its members, is called to be missionary.

Missionary activity, then, is the sign of mature faith (*MR*, nn. 11, 49). To be effective, it presupposes a vibrant faith, nourished by prayer and contemplation, by liturgical worship, and by the example of fellow believers (*Asia*, n. 23). Missionary activity, in turn, redounds to the benefit of churches that engage in it. It "renews the Church, revitalizes faith and Christian identity, and offers fresh enthusiasm and new incentive. Faith is strengthened when it is given to others" (*RM*, n. 2).

Missionary activity takes place through deed and word. "The witness of a Christian life," writes the pope, "is the first and irreplaceable form of mission" (*RM*, n. 42). Faith, as a lived knowledge of Jesus Christ, connaturally expresses itself in action. It possesses a moral content and inclines believers to observe the commandments of God. "Through the moral life, faith becomes confession, not only before God but also before men: it becomes witness" (*VS*, n. 89). By living according to the gospel we give a kind of silent testimony that makes a deep impression if it is connected with an explicit profession of faith (*RM*, n. 42; *Asia*, n. 42). The saints and martyrs are the most credible witnesses to Christian faith (*VS*, nn. 93, 107). Mission, however, would be incomplete without verbal proclamation in which Jesus is explicitly confessed as the Savior of the world (*RM*, n. 44). Such proclamation is aimed at conversions in which people's hearts are opened so that they can draw near to Jesus in faith and boldly confess him (*RM*, n. 46).

In the perspective of Vatican II, John Paul II makes it clear that evangelization should always take account of the close relationship between faith and culture. "A synthesis between culture and faith," he writes, "is not just a demand of culture, but also of faith.... A faith that does not become culture is a faith that has not been fully received, not thoroughly thought through, not faithfully lived out."[11] To be vitally present in a given locality, the gospel must be brought into contact with the existing culture, enriching it and liberating it from evil, so that that culture, in turn, may enrich the life of the Church (*SA*, n. 21). In the delicate process of inculturation, bishops, as guardians of the deposit of faith, must see to it that the objective requirements of the faith itself are respected (*RM*, nn. 53-54). Syncretism is on all accounts to be avoided (*Africa*, n. 62).

Missionary activity, conducted with due respect for the authentic patrimonies of other churches and religions, gives rise to dialogue, in which all parties humbly and frankly express their points of view. Dialogue, by overcoming prejudices and stimulating self-scrutiny, can be advantageous to all participants. But it does not dispense the Church from the task of proclamation. Insofar as dialogue includes an ingredient of witness, it may be said to constitute a dimension of missionary activity itself (*RM*, nn. 55-56).

In all that John Paul II writes about faith, he never loses sight of the advances of Vatican II. He is as convinced as he ever was that the Council was "a historical and prophetic event" (*RP*, n. 1), marking "a many-faceted enrichment of the Church's consciousness" (*DM*, n. 1), calling for a reawakening in the Church's self-awareness, and arousing a fresh missionary impulse (*SA*, n. 16). There is no evidence that the pope has given up his conviction, expressed in *Sources of Renewal*, that the Council constituted for the Church and all her members an epoch-making summons to an enrichment of faith. In his writings as pope, John Paul II has continued to emphasize the need for existential encounter with the Lord, humble submission to God's word, recognition of religious freedom, respectful dialogue, and unceasing growth in faith. While he is careful not to isolate this one council from the whole tradition of the Church, John Paul II, in his postconciliar writings on faith, as on other matters, is emphatically the pope of Vatican II.

ABBREVIATIONS

Africa – John Paul II, Apostolic Exhortation *Ecclesia in Africa*

Amer – John Paul II, Apostolic Exhortation *Ecclesia in America*

Asia – John Paul II, Apostolic Exhortation *Ecclesia in Asia*

CL – John Paul II, Apostolic Exhortation *Christifideles laici*

CT – John Paul II, Apostolic Exhortation *Catechesi tradendae*

CTH – John Paul II, *Crossing the Threshold of Hope*

DH – Vatican II, Declaration *Dignitatis humanae*

DM – John Paul II, Encyclical *Dives in misericordia*

DV – Vatican II, Dogmatic Constitution *Dei Verbum*

FC – John Paul II, Apostolic Exhortation *Familiaris consortio*

FR – John Paul II, Encyclical *Fides et ratio*

God – John Paul II, *God: Father and Creator. Catechesis on the Creed*, vol. 1 (Boston: Pauline Books & Media, 1996).

GS – Vatican II, Pastoral Constitution *Gaudium et spes*

LG – Vatican II, Dogmatic Constitution *Lumen gentium*

MR – John Paul II, Encyclical *Redemptoris mater*

RH – John Paul II, Encyclical *Redemptor hominis*

RM – John Paul II, Encyclical *Redemptoris missio*

PDV – John Paul II, Apostolic Exhortation *Pastores dabo vobis*

RP – John Paul II, Apostolic Exhortation *Reconciliatio et paenitentia*

SA – John Paul II, Encyclical *Slavorum apostoli*

TMA – John Paul II, Apostolic Letter *Tertio millennio adveniente*

VS – John Paul II, Encyclical *Veritatis splendor*

NOTES

1. Mieczyslaw Malinski, *Pope John Paul II: The Life of Karol Wojtyla* (New York: Seabury/Crossroad, 1980), 20.

2. Published in English as Karol Wojtyla, *Faith according to St. John of the Cross* (San Francisco: Ignatius, 1981). Page references to this work are indicated in parentheses in my text.

3. For present purposes I do not think it necessary to determine whether Wojtyla's treatment of St. John of the Cross departs from the views of his mentor, Réginald Garrigou-Lagrange. Gerald McCool, writing on "The Theology of John Paul II" in *The Thought of John Paul II: A Collection of Essays and Studies*, ed. John M. McDermott (Rome: Università Gregoriana, 1993), 29-53, at 35, emphasizes the continuity. Rocco Buttiglione in his *Karol Wojtyla: The Thought of the Man Who Became Pope John Paul II* (Grand Rapids: Eerdmans, 1997), 47, holds that Wojtyla, by his attention to the subjective experience of the mystic, goes beyond his master.

4. For an overview of Wojtyla's interventions, see Avery Dulles, *The Splendor of Faith: The Theological Vision of Pope John Paul II*, 2nd ed. (New York: Crossroad, 2003), 6-9, 21-22.

5. Karol Wojtyla, speech of October 21, 1963, on the Church and the lay apostolate, in *Acta synodalia* II/3, pp. 154-57, at 156. See also his speech of October 8, 1964, on the lay apostolate, in *Acta synodalia* III/4, pp. 69-70.

6. John Paul II, *Sources of Renewal: The Implementation of Vatican II* (San Francisco: Harper & Row, 1980). Page references in parentheses will be to pages of this edition.

7. Karol Wojtyla, "Bishops as Servants of the Faith," *Irish Theological Quarterly* 43 (1976): 260-73.

8. Augustine, *Confessions*, I,1; quoted in *God*, 47.

9. Blaise Pascal, *Pensées*, 553, quoted in *CT*, n. 60. In printings that follow the Louis Lafiuma edition (Paris: Luxembourg, 1951), this appears as Fragment 919; see, e.g., London: Penguin Classics ed., 1966, p. 314.

10. The quotation is from Irenaeus, *Adv. haer.*, III.22.4 (PG 7:959).

11. John Paul II, Letter to Cardinal Agostino Casaroli, May 20, 1982, establishing the Pontifical Council for Culture, *L'Osservatore Romano* (Eng. ed.), June 28, 1982, pp. 19-20, at 19. For further discussion, see Avery Dulles, "Faith and Culture in the Thought of John Paul II," in *Prophecy and Diplomacy: The Moral Doctrine of John Paul II*, eds. John J. Conley and Joseph W. Koterski (New York: Fordham University Press, 1999), 175-89.

A Response to Cardinal Dulles

John M. McDermott, S.J.

Daunting is the task that has fallen to me: to criticize the presentation of Avery Dulles, America's foremost theologian, a man renowned as much for the balanced nuances of his theological positions as for his appreciation of the pope's theological project. Let me say from the beginning that his presentation of the pope's understanding of faith is excellent. But I have to earn my bread as a commentator, and I must do something more than applaud and disappear. So I intend to put the pope's understanding of faith in a wider theological context, attempt a few small expansions on Father Dulles's presentation, hazard a small criticism of the pope's interpretation of implicit faith, point out a persistent tension in the pope's position, and indicate briefly how that tension may be explained with appeal to the pope's understanding of person and freedom.

THE THEOLOGICAL CONTEXT[1]

Dulles has noted the clear shift of emphasis from Karol Wojtyla's doctoral thesis to *Sources of Renewal*, from faith understood as an assent to propositions to faith understood as a personal response to the self-revealing God. This transition seems at first to mirror the transition from the theological dominance of conceptual Thomism before Vatican II to the primacy of transcendental Thomism after the Council. The former, holding that being (that is, all of reality) can be conceptualized, consequently identifies as the material object of faith conceptual propositions revealed by God. Since faith's object is supernatural, exceeding the grasp of the natural intellect, the truths of faith cannot be intuited nor proven rationally. They have to be accepted on the authority of the revealing God who employs a divine legate, or messenger, to communicate them in human language. The veracity of this divinely chosen witness is guaranteed by the prophecies fulfilled and the miracles effected. In order to ensure the promulgation and proper interpretation of supernatural truths, Jesus Christ, the divine messenger, established an authoritative Church. Clearly the Church, like Christ, serves as the mediator of God's truth and, in the sacraments, of His grace.

Despite the clarity of this theology, many difficulties were raised. A few may be mentioned. First, the apologetic arguments supporting the act of faith, the *praeambula fidei*, are rational, perceptible to natural reason: either they are sufficient to motivate faith's assent, thus reducing faith to a natural act, or they are insufficient, thus rendering faith's act irrational and immoral. Second, since the revealed truths surpass human intelligence, it is hard to see how they can be understood, interpreted, and dogmatically defined; even pope and bishops cannot in theory understand what has been entrusted to them and what they may be called upon to define definitively. Third, history shows the development of dogmatic formulae: the truths of faith did not fall entire from heaven but were elaborated and defined by human intelligence under grace through the centuries.

Transcendental Thomists thought to resolve such problems from a different philosophical starting point. Locating truth, that is, the correspondence of mind and reality, in the judgment, these Thomists understood man's knowing as dynamic, stretching beyond the concept, which is only a part of a judgment, toward reality itself. Ultimately, since nothing finite can satisfy the mind's quest for truth, man is referred to the infinite God as the source, goal, and motor of his intellectual movement. Since the direct intellectual possession of God is the beatific vision, a supernatural gift, St. Thomas's "paradoxical" doctrine of the natural desire to see God in Himself is granted a central place in this theology.[2] Moreover, because the judgment involves a subjective, reflexive act, knowledge can no longer be understood as the passive reception of an abstracted form representing the object; knowledge involves the subject's activity. There is no objectivity except over subjectivity. Finally, since the intellect is conceived primarily as a dynamic faculty oriented to the true as its good, the traditional distinction between intellect and will in terms of their formal objects, the true and the good, is overcome. Man's quest for truth involves his freedom as well as his intellect. As Karl Rahner wrote, "The deepest truth is the most free."[3]

Conceptual thought distinguishes clearly one reality from another, for concepts provide clear, formal abstractions. Dynamic judgments, though presupposing distinctions, always provide their synthetic unity in the *conversio ad phantasma*: concept and judgment, essential and existential orders, form and matter, subject and object, God and man, natural and supernatural. These dynamic unities in diversity supply a subtle flexibility whereby various conundrums of conceptualist

Thomism are overcome. In the act of faith, for example, the arguments of credibility are not seen as persuasive in themselves but are interpreted as signs of a greater meaning which illuminates them even as they point to it. There is a mutual causality between sign and signified. Thus the supernatural meaning is synthesized with the natural sign and the act of faith results. For the dynamic judgment is a natural act with a supernatural end. The material object of faith consequently is not a conceptual proposition but God Himself, the term of the intellectual dynamism, who is present through the attraction of His final causality at every step in the process. Usually this act of faith is deemed "personal" because its object is God—in contrast to the "propositional" material object in conceptualist theology. Actually its object is not a person as such, but the infinite nature of God, which terminates the natural intellectual drive of man.[4] But by postulating the infinite nature of God as faith's material as well as formal object, transcendental Thomists allow for dogmatic development. The initial act of faith comprehensively affirms the full reality of God, and subsequent thematization (or conceptualization) spells out what was implicit in the initial affirmation. Thus more detailed dogmas can be legitimately derived from the original unthematic experience of faith.

However appealing this analysis of faith may be at first reading, it contains real difficulties. For example, if objectivity is known only over subjectivity, it is impossible to speak of a natural sign in itself since the sign is perceived only in the subject's supernaturalized dynamism. The paradoxical doctrine of the natural desire for the supernatural either permits everything natural to be understood as supernatural or has supernatural revelation reduced to natural knowledge. Again, since God is implicitly affirmed in every judgment as its term, anything, even a blade of grass—such is Rousselot's opinion—can serve as the occasion or sign for a supernatural act of faith.[5] Hence, faith's historical anchoring in Jesus Christ is lost and one arrives at the absurdities of anonymous Christianity and of Jesus as merely the greatest realization of grace offered and accepted in time, indeed as another believer like the rest of us.[6] These novelties in the Catholic tradition contradict Scripture and ignore the basic personal distinction between the Second Person of the Trinity and men.

Clearly both the conceptualist and transcendental interpretations can easily be driven to extremes. The greatest theologians in both camps have recognized the need for a sane balance between essential and existential orders, abstractions and judgments, object and subject, will and intellect, nature and grace, man and God.[7] Both the unity and the diversity have to be respected. The Fathers of Vatican II affirmed that God not only reveals Himself (*DV*, nn. 2, 6) but also "tells the inmost realities about God" and the "eternal decisions of His will" (*DV*, nn. 4, 6).[8] Vatican II's compromise between the two theologies maintained the balance which was given to the Church by Christ Himself. For Jesus not only revealed Himself and the Father (Mt 11:25-27; Jn 12:45; 14:9), calling for faith in Himself as in the Father (Jn 14:1), but He used also human words in that revelation and required that men believe and hold fast to His words (Mk 8:38; Jn 3:11f., 32-34). Without words meaning something intelligible to men, He could not have revealed Himself. For meaning is always mediated through finite, intelligible signs.[9] The notion of analogy so basic to Catholic theology preserves the balance between the finite world's intelligibility, which cannot be absolutized, and the infinite mystery of the free and loving God, who in His goodness does not destroy the finite meaning of the reality He created and redeemed. For if the finite did not possess a certain intelligibility, human choices would become arbitrary and lose their freedom.

SOME EXPANSIONS

Karol Wojtyla's initial understanding of faith certainly has to be classified as conceptualist. Since he wrote his thesis under the direction of Reginald Garrigou-Lagrange, the foremost proponent of conceptualist Thomism, hardly anything else could be expected. He clearly held for a distinction of spiritual faculties: faith is located in the intellect while the mystical experience depends upon supernatural charity, which is located in the will. On this point it may be possible to propose a small correction in the terminology of Dulles, who writes: "By itself alone . . . faith produces some elements of union but lacks the capacity to effect a properly psychological union with God. The words and concepts by which faith is mediated belong to the created order and therefore fail to represent the divine reality they signify." Dulles is correct in following Wojtyla's distinction between the ontological and psychological unions effected in faith. But he exaggerates, I suspect, the inability of words and concepts to "represent the divine reality." Certainly they cannot represent God *adequately*; hence there results a psychological lack of clarity. "God is present to the intellect through faith, but the intellect never fully comprehends or possesses him through faith."[10] "Although the divine essence is truly united objectively to the intellect through faith as the 'substance of revealed truths as understood,' psychologically the intellect lacks that 'substance as understood'" (247). This lack of clarity does not, to Wojtyla's mind, utterly prevent all intellectual grasping of the truth mediated through concepts. Even if "propositions and concepts concerning revealed truth" hide God from the intellect, "they truly give God to the intellect . . . and what they give is nothing other than the divine substance, but received in an intentional mode." The divine substance "can be expressed in certain particular revealed concepts and, thus expressed, can retain its intentional identity with the divine reality—an identity of the intentional form contained in those concepts with the form of the divine reality as it is in itself." Consequently the intellect is united to the "substance of revealed truths ontologically," but not psychologically. "The divine substance is truly present in the revealed concepts in an intentional mode; the intellect adheres to those concepts and through the power of the divine infused light it also adheres to the 'substance' contained in those concepts, but in an intentional mode of adherence" (207-09; cf. 71f, 86f, 89f). Faith in a revealed proposition effects a true, intentional, metaphysical union between the mind and God, mediated by the propositions, even if the divine substance infinitely transcends the created intellect (244-46, 252, 267). As St. Thomas wrote, "Actus autem credentis non terminatur ad enuntiabile, sed ad rem" (*ST,* II-II, 1, 2, 2).

For Wojtyla, the psychological union pertains primarily to the realm of the will (or of the good) since mysticism occurs in faith enlivened by charity (249f, 255). Somehow the will's charity overflows and is perceived by the intellect (212f, 216f, 219f, 260); it seeks to influence all the other faculties, indeed to penetrate the entire substance of the soul. It transforms the soul, effecting a real likeness and union with God, and provides "a dark and loving knowledge" (198f, 212-17, 222, 240, 249f). In the first phase of his development, Jacques Maritain also explained mystical experience in terms of the overflow of the will's love so that it passes into the condition of an object and so is perceived by the intellect.[11] The difficulty remains that such knowledge is not mediated by the external senses, man's normal way of knowing, and conceptualists resist acknowledging any intuition except sensation and the beatific vision. What is interesting in Wojtyla, where he goes beyond the early Maritain, is his recognition that mystical union penetrates not only the will and the intellect but also what John of the Cross called the substance of the soul (247).[12] There the "spiritual feelings," moved by God's "touch," are apparently located; thence they overflow into the intellect: "apprehension and knowledge and understanding overflow from them to the intellect" (214). The soul's substance, called also its apex, or peak, by Baroque Scholasticism, is apparently St. Thomas's *essentia animae,* the central, unified and unifying point where the soul is most concentrated in itself and whence emanate the diverse spiritual and material faculties (*ST*, I, 77, 4-7). For Wojtyla, the charity vivifying faith results in contemplation, also described as an "obscure and general knowledge," and in contemplation there is a unity of the spiritual faculties (148f, 156-59, 164, 166-68, 177). This would seem to occur in the soul's essence. But if this point represents the source of knowing and willing as well as supplies the unity to the knowing process, can it be less than conscious and free, even if the knowledge is not fully conceptualized?

The answer to that question is not unambiguously positive. In his doctoral thesis Wojtyla notes Labourdette's opinion that in John of the Cross's writings the soul's "substance" is not a philosophical term opposed to the soul's potencies but "simply designates in a general way that part of the soul in which mystical knowledge and love are experienced and perfected" (214). Yet, for various reasons he does not seem to agree totally with that opinion. First, "that part of the soul" is not further identified. Second, he had earlier (57f, note 50) noted that Labourdette's remark refers to Book II, chapter 16 of *The Ascent of Mount Carmel* and certainly not to chapter 5 of the same where "'substance' is strictly a Scholastic term." So he restricted Labourdette's opinion to one text, and not the one discussed in our present consideration. Third, immediately following the later reference to Labourdette's opinion, Wojtyla continues: "Yet, in chapter 24 of *The Ascent*, the Mystical Doctor declared his intention of treating the union of the soul with the divine substance." The quotation of that text leads him to distinguish the "'touch' of the divine substance in the substance of the soul" from "the operations of the Holy Spirit through the gifts and charity." Whereas the latter operate in the order of efficient causality, the former deals with "the material cause of the mystical experience" (215f; cf. 128, 166f, 192, 196f). Thereafter he opposes the "touch of the virtues of the Beloved" to the knowledge of them in the intellect (216). Thus Wojtyla seems to recognize a type of knowledge of God in the "substance of the soul." Nonetheless, even after admitting the restrictions on Labordette's opinion, one might argue that Wojtyla is still committed to a psychology emphasizing different spiritual faculties: mystical contemplation occurs in the intellect, specifically the passive intellect, in which the divine form is received intentionally through the redundance of love (218-21). The intellect as a separate faculty seems to be the receptor of mystical union through the medium of faith (217-23). Obviously the locus of mystical knowledge is not unambiguously identified, and Wojtyla is probably aware of the tension between the knowledge acquired by the intellect and the touch felt in the substance of the soul. Although the passive intellect may enjoy a type of simple, general intuition of the divinity apart from the workings of the active intellect, it is not "a particularized intentional knowledge as could be obtained through the senses" (218) or which the "touch" of the spiritual feelings provides.

Wojtyla's interest in mysticism reflects that of Garrigou-Lagrange and as such need not lead to conflict with his director. But it would lead to a deeper, more personal appreciation of faith. Already in the doctoral thesis Wojtyla stresses St. Thomas's doctrine of the natural desire for the supernatural. Conceptualist Thomists generally interpreted that doctrine as a conditional, inefficacious desire depending for its fulfillment on God's will to elevate the soul beyond its natural powers, or as a mere natural velleity that recoils from its desire as soon as it recognizes knowledge's natural tie to the phantasm, or as an indication that the beatific vision is not absolutely impossible for man, who possesses "some capacity" for it, or as an elicited desire "naturally" arising after the message of faith had been received.[13] With them Wojtyla affirms the soul's passive, obediential potency for faith (72f), which involves "an antithesis between the natural and supernatural" orders and the "absolute separation" of natural and supernatural lights (107f, 75, 217). Hence, the believer should not desire mystical experience; otherwise it would become "the object of a natural desire, and since the measure of faith is participation in divinity, such a desire is alien to the virtue of faith" (146). Despite these affirmations Wojtyla also stresses the continuity between natural and supernatural orders. The intellect is so oriented to God that its natural desire is for the divine object, so as "to possess the divine essence in an intentional mode." The intellect has "a capacity and a natural desire" for "an unlimited and infinite form"; the desire, however, is impeded both by the soul's union with the body and because its natural light is insufficient to know the substance of the divinity. "The intellect, therefore, by reason of its very nature, should unite with God, but perfect union with the infinite and unlimited form is attained only through the beatific vision, which requires a change in the subject, namely, the separation of the soul from the body" (243; cf. 60, 65, 75, 217). But already in faith the intellect's "natural tendency to the essence of revealed truths" is not destroyed but adapted through its union with the divine essence, even if full clarity is lacking insofar as the intentional species of the divinity still remains to be given (160, 164, 267).

One cannot but notice certain tensions in Wojtyla's early understanding of faith. On the one hand, faith is given once and for all ontologically in the assent that both introduces the habit of faith and is the first expression of that habit; on the other, it is dynamically oriented toward growth psychologically. Psychological faith oscillates between the intentional, metaphysical union attained in the assent to revealed propositions mediating truly the divine essence and the final intellectual intuition of God to which it is oriented (238, 240-43). The same light is operative in faith, in the whole process of mystical union, and in vision (190). More fundamentally, psychological faith is caught in the tension between *fides ex auditu*, that arrives through the senses, and the interior experience of the divine substance, which comes with the excessive light of infused faith, can result in the highest type of spiritual mysticism, and maintains continuity with the beatific vision (244f, 260f). But is there not a danger of a disjunction? If God can let Himself be perceived interiorly by the soul, is not the necessity of preached faith relativized?

Wojtyla is well aware of the possible tension between preached faith and spiritual experience of the divine substance not mediated by definite historical circumstances. J. Baruzzi alleged such a distinction between "dogmatic faith" mediated through external authority and "mystical faith," and Wojtyla deliberately rejects that opinion (181f). He dedicates a long section of his thesis (172-82) to a singular expression of John of the Cross: "the Son of God, who is communicated to the soul in faith," and builds his argument upon it. Faith does not just establish a relation between the divine substance and the soul so that the soul through the infused light participates in the divinity and is made like to God. The specificity of Christian faith concerns Jesus Christ. The participation in divine wisdom is actually a participation in the Wisdom of God, God's only Son: "The Word appears as the *terminus* of the knowledge in which God, knowing himself exhaustively and comprehensively, expresses his own infinite perfection in the person of the Word. . . . sharing through faith in a knowledge that is essentially divine—the wisdom of God—the intellect in some way likewise shares through faith in the generation of the Word" (172; cf. 190).

This entrance through faith into the eternal Trinitarian life and self-knowledge, to which the blessed are admitted and which "terminates *ad intra* as the Word" (179), does not occur for us through a leap outside of time. For Wojtyla, the revelation to which faith responds culminates in the Son's Incarnation. "Because God has manifested himself fully and definitively in his incarnate Word," it is no longer permissible to look for any private revelation outside the Incarnation. This historical revelation involves much more than the revelation of propositions. "Revealed truths are given to the intellect, but Christ himself is given as the life of Christians." The Incarnation involves "the personal manifestation of God in the person of Jesus Christ." Since this personal revelation can never be exhausted, "there will always be an infinite number of ways to imitate Christ and to know him more intimately, and through the knowledge gained by love and imitation of Christ there will always be more revealed." Through faith in the incarnate Word "we possess the divinity in its entirety." Indeed faith's "general and dark knowledge" is grounded in the incarnate Word. "Faith is identified with the knowledge that God has in himself and of himself and to which he gives expression, not so much by reason of the revealed truths precisely as received by the intellect, but by reason of the person of the Word revealed in the Incarnation." Consequently faith's transformation into God is really transformation into "the simple and pure wisdom that is the Son of God" (173-77, 128, 190f).

The soul's participation in the Word's generation, or in His generative light, never excuses men from the need of obedience to the Church. They need it in order to overcome their spiritual weakness and ignorance. For the mediation of the Church's authority is based on the analogy of the mediation of Christ's humanity. Common to both is the principle: "God wills that everything supernaturally communicated to us should be received through other men so that we may perform a true act of faith, which would be lacking if we were to accept those things through a private and personal revelation" (180). Whereas "the body of revealed truth is concentrated principally in Christ, to whom is attributed the personal manifestation of divinity," the Church "alone has received the total revelation to which the intellect must assent by believing" (180f). So Wojtyla insists repeatedly on the necessity of obedience to the Church established by Christ (126f, 130, 179-82, 237). There is no opposition between *fides ex auditu*, accepted on the Church's authority, and the interior experience of faith, but total correspondence and continuity. The real God is the Trinity of which the Second Person became man. So mystical union presupposes *fides ex auditu* or articles of faith (203, 206f, 209f, 219, 224f); only through faith does the mystical union occur (224f). Even when the natural intentional species, in which the articles of faith are expressed, are not employed, faith still adheres to "'the substance as understood' contained in revealed truths" (221f).

By now it is clear that the foundations for the later shift in emphasis in Wojtyla's understanding of faith are laid in his doctoral thesis. And the personalist understanding is oriented not to the Trinity nor to the divine nature but to the incarnate Word. Moreover, the social aspect of faith could be easily developed from understanding faith as a sharing in the personal life of the Trinity in and through the incarnate Son. For the institutional Church which proposes propositions of faith is also the community that shares and lives the divine life. Indeed in the doctoral thesis there is more emphasis on the growth in faithful love to mystical fruition than on propositional faith. What happens in *Sources of Renewal* and thereafter is an awareness that faith is primarily personal from the beginning and that this faith involves a total self-commitment to God. The whole person responds to the God who reveals Himself.

A CRITICISM

The pope's personalist understanding of faith will lead to some tensions. Although he insists on the centrality and necessity of Christ and His Church, John Paul II proposes in *Crossing the Threshold of Hope* an "implicit faith" whereby in the honest search for faith "the necessary condition for salvation is already satisfied" (193, 93, 140f). As support for his position, he cites *Lumen gentium,* n. 16, which affirms that those who with the help of grace follow God's will in the dictates of conscience "can attain eternal salvation" (*CTH*, 81, 78). But if implicit faith, which is really the quest for the truth about man (cf. *FR*, nn. 1f, 13f, 17), suffices for salvation, why is there need of Jesus Christ? When the pope affirms a common destiny for all men and postulates through the *semina Verbi* mentioned in *Lumen gentium,* n. 13 "a kind of common soteriological root present in all religions," one must asks how he avoids relativizing Christ and the Church. Is a type of anonymous Christianity or even anonymous theism being proposed? When *Redemptor hominis* announces that Christ "fully reveals man to himself" (*RH*, nn. 8, 11) and that man "is the primary and fundamental way for the Church" (*RH*, n. 14), it seems as if theology were in danger of being reduced to anthropology, as in Rahnerian theology or even in Modernism.

In order to resolve these difficulties some distinctions should be made. First, *Crossing the Threshold of Hope* is not a magisterial document; it contains personal reflections of John Paul II designed to help spread the gospel to all who wish to hear it (viii). Second, the interpretation of *Lumen gentium*, n. 16 is not quite accurate. Although Karol Wojtyla played an important part in the final redaction of *Gaudium et spes*, he was not so directly involved in *Lumen gentium*. Despite the fact that many theologians cite n. 16 to ground the affirmation of salvation outside the visible Church, whoever reads that paragraph in context must note that it is concerned not with the question about salvation outside the Church, but with the question how all men are related to the Church, the "Catholic unity of the People of God" (n. 13). It deals in turn with Catholics (n. 14), non-Catholic Christians (n.

15), and finally "those who have not yet received the gospel" (n. 16). Among these latter are mentioned Jews, Moslems, and "those who, without blame on their part, have not yet arrived at an explicit knowledge of God, but who strive to live a good life, thanks to His grace." In each case *Lumen gentium* points out elements of common belief, and with regard to the last mentioned group notes that "they also can attain to eternal salvation" and "divine Providence does not deny them the help necessary for salvation." Years ago Cardinal Alois Grillmeier, who was involved in the composition of n. 16 and wrote the commentary on the text for the Herder Commentary on Vatican II, pointed this out to me. He also related that Karl Rahner, one of the editors of the Commentary, returned the future cardinal's contribution several times in the effort to have him write that *Lumen gentium* affirms the salvation of men of good will outside the Church. Grillmeier refused doggedly since such was not the intention of the authors.[14]

Later Vatican documents will refer to *Lumen gentium,* n. 16 to affirm the possibility of salvation for all, but without specifying the means whereby Christ's mediation of salvation is effected. *Redemptoris missio,* however, apparently goes beyond the learned ignorance of the previous tradition. Discussing the universal offer of salvation mediated through Christ, the encyclical treats the case of people educated in other religious traditions who do not explicitly receive the gospel and enter the Church because of impeding "social and cultural conditions." For them the possibility of salvation outside the visible bounds of the Church is apparently recognized. "Christ's salvation is accessible to these people through a grace which, while having a secret relationship (*arcanam necessitatem*) to the Church, does not lead them into her formally (*formali relatione*), but enlightens them in a way accommodated to their interior condition and the circumstances of times and events" (10). But one magisterial pronouncement does not make a binding tradition, and it remains to be seen if subsequent popes will continue to recognize the novelty of an official teaching about this "secret relationship."[15]

That men of good will might attain salvation under God's grace has never been denied by the Church. Traditional theology saw God's grace given to all pagans in order to move them to salvation. But this grace was considered to be actual grace, which prepares for the sanctifying grace ordinarily given in baptism, upon whose bestowal God Himself, uncreated grace, comes to dwell in the soul. So the affirmation that men of good will may attain salvation by following their conscience can easily be interpreted in traditional categories—and the overwhelming majority of the bishops were trained in the traditional, conceptualist theology—to mean that by following the promptings of grace such men might come to explicit faith and baptism. With Rahner, of course, the presuppositions of interpretation change. Given his hypothesis that man naturally desires the vision of God and granted God's universal salvific will, grace is understood primarily in terms of God's gift of Himself, uncreated grace, which effects sanctifying grace as the condition of its acceptance, and then works itself out in particular actions as actual graces.[16] Furthermore, given Rahner's hypothesis that being is self-conscious, God's presence in the soul must be somehow, unthematically, perceived as God's self-revelation; man's acceptance of that grace is equivalently faith.[17] So an implicit faith is given wherever man acts in accord with his conscience under God's grace. One sees therefore why Rahner wanted to interpret *Lumen gentium,* n. 16, as affirming salvation outside the Church, but there is no reason to suppose that the authors of the text had the same interpretation; indeed, it seems that they had a different interpretation. But has John Paul II accepted Rahnerian theology?

I do not think so. As Dulles notes, nowhere does the pope hold that non-Christian religions are bearers of revelation or mediators of salvation. They express man's quest, to which Christ's revelation is the response. Moreover, after the doctoral thesis Wojtyla no longer speaks of the natural desire for the intuitive vision of God, the thesis at the center of transcendental theology. Augustine's and Paschal's vision of the restless heart is rather interpreted as a personal desire for a vision of the personal God. Not only are all the drives of nature taken over and integrated into a personal dynamism that is constituted in moral freedom and in relation to others,[18] but also the natural desire for truth is transmuted into a desire for a relation with the personal God that involves faithful self-giving.[19] For "truth and freedom . . . go hand in hand" (*FR,* nn. 90, 105). The basic questions about life, which go beyond the abstractions of philosophy and with which wisdom has perennially grappled, can only be answered by Christ. The origin and solution for evil and suffering, man's immortality, God's personal nature, etc., are conundrums which belong to human nature and existence and which philosophy alone cannot answer (*FR,* nn. 13, 15, 20, 26, 33f, 76, 80; *SD,* nn. 2f, 9f, 13, 15). Although natural philosophy cannot explain the cross, the cross alone can justify philosophy. Its deeper wisdom, which is possessed in faith alone, makes sense out of human existence (*FR,* nn. 23, 43). The ultimate truths about human life man cannot attain from a merely natural philosophy nor from his own experience. The answers must be revealed by God in Christ's *kenosis* of love and in His call for faith and in suffering for others in union with Christ (*FR,* nn. 13, 81, 93; *SD,* nn. 14-24, 26f).

Certainly there is no "anonymous Christianity" in the pope's doctrine. That nonsensical term was attacked very strongly by von Balthasar, de Lubac, and others who said that such a theory is contrary to Scripture and tradition and that any institutional bearer of revelation outside Christianity would relativize Christ's claims and lead to contradictions in revelation.[20] In response to attacks, Rahner himself recognized the "ambiguity" in the term "anonymous Christianity" and indicated that he did not understand it as an institutional presence. In view of God's universal salvific will manifested and effected in Christ, he continued to employ "anonymous Christians" while maintaining the justness of the content of his opinion.[21] That the pope should allow that the grace of salvation is offered to all even as he insists on the definitive revelation in Christ as well as on Christ's and the Church's unique salvific mediatorship[22] need not imply an incompletely digested transcendental Thomism. There are other ways of interpreting the polarity between the universal offer of salvation and its historical actualization only in Jesus Christ. Indeed that same tension is manifested in 1 Tm 2:3-7, where St. Paul juxtaposes God's universal salvific will with the "one mediator, the man Jesus Christ." As we have shown elsewhere, this tension between universality and particularity is essential for the task of preaching and, more deeply, reflects the sacramental structure of love that is the Christian mystery: for love involves absolute commitment to a concrete limited instance, boundlessness and limitation.[23] To this structure the pope is faithful because it is also the structure of freedom, and like no other modern thinker Karol Wojtyla has insisted on freedom as the characteristic defining man as God's image.[24]

THE REMAINING TENSION: TOWARD A SOLUTION

Before advancing to a consideration of freedom and person, it may be appropriate now to give a slightly different nuance to another aspect of Dulles's interpretation. In explaining how faith is a journey, he contrasts it with another view: "the pope teaches that faith is not a static given." Though one can agree with Dulles's view of a growth in the virtue of faith as well as of a development in its thematic formulation and admit the possibility that faith may be lost, the emphasis on development or change should not overlook the complementary truth that as God's gift faith in the full mystery of Christ is entirely given in baptism as an infused virtue. Through the sacraments the baptized really participate in the divine life mediated and revealed by Christ. This plenitude bestowed in baptism is grounded in the objective order of revelation and salvation. There is no further public revelation to be awaited beyond Jesus and the apostolic age (*DV*, nn. 2, 4, 7; *DS*, nn. 1501, 3070, 3421). As John Paul II proclaims, "In and through Christ God has revealed Himself fully to mankind and has definitively drawn close to it" (*RH*, n. 11). Christ is the full, definitive self-revelation of God and the universal savior (*RM*, nn. 5f). One may come to a better understanding of the mystery (*RH*, n. 19; *FR*, n. 73), but Christ is known personally or unthematically in His fullness (*DV*, n. 8).

Moreover, since God's gifts are without repentance (Rom 11:29), faith cannot be lost without fault on the part of a believer (*DS*, nn. 3014, 3036). From God's point of view, faith is permanently given as a virtue and its object is to be permanently possessed. As with the kingdom of God, there is a tension in faith: it is objectively fully present, yet it has to grow to its fullness in believers. This tension persists until the end of time because man, the image of God, is a creature of freedom and is called to be perfect as his heavenly Father is perfect and to imitate Jesus Christ, the plenitude of grace and love. Although God is infinitely close, there is always more room to grow into God's infinity.[25]

The pope's understanding of freedom is not primarily that of an independent power in man nor as a will dynamically oriented to limitless good (or God). He understands man as freedom actualized in self-giving. Freedom is a gift that has to be given back in responsible love: "In reality, freedom is a great gift only when we know how to use it consciously for everything that is our true good. Christ teaches us that the best use of freedom is charity, which takes concrete form in self-giving and in service. For this 'freedom Christ has set us free' and ever continues to set us free. . . . The full truth about human freedom is indelibly inscribed on the mystery of the Redemption."[26]

In a world of sin and suffering, the mystery of evil perplexes the mind and heart of man and causes him to fear losing himself. Christ is the one who gives Himself totally even in death in order to illuminate the mystery of life and to overcome evil. For He rises to share His eternal life with all believers. He not only shows us who we are but also gives His life to us. He makes us who we are. He can be and is the model and source of all human renewal since God is love in creation and in redemption.

The emphasis on freedom separates John Paul II from both conceptual and transcendental Thomists. They start with the nature of man and employ that nature, whether conceived statically-essentially or dynamically-existentially, as the basis of necessary arguments to discover order in the world and thence to affirm

God's existence. Freedom, whether freedom of indifference or engaged, Augustinian freedom, comes along later and has to find a place among the necessities of natures by making appeal to contingency, whether grounded in matter or in finite existence. But problems inevitably arise from such a starting point in natures with their necessary operations.[27] Wojtyla reverses that order of study.[28] In *The Acting Person* he begins with freedom, which he locates in the person, not in the natural will, even though the person actuates that will and subsumes the will's dynamism into its own free dynamism. For the person acts. Even while functioning as the source of the diversity of the natural faculties, spiritual and material, "person" represents the deepest spiritual unity in man. Person, moreover, is realized only in love. Since love cannot be fully captured in any necessary, abstract, philosophical demonstration, love opens man to a more sapiential approach to reality and relates him existentially to God and to others. Insofar as God's unified, primordial plan of love was disrupted by sin, it had to be renewed in Christ, who alone can shed light on the mysteries of evil, suffering, death, and human freedom, whose depths surpass all human insight and power. He shares men's fate in order that they might share His. The new Adam establishes a new unity of the human race in His own Body, the Church, the mystery of the Bride who is different in freedom, yet of one body and spirit with her eternal Bridegroom. For love, the perfection of freedom (as in heaven, in the blessed Trinity, so on earth) preserves the greatest distinction in the most intimate unity. Admittedly the pope has not worked out all the implications of his personalist vision, and much intellectual work has to be done in order to reconcile the order of natures with the freedom of persons, but he certainly has focused the Church and mankind on the essential problems which call for the growth of understanding that accompanies the infinite love of God revealed in Christ.

NOTES

1.   The following section reproduces in summary form two previous articles: J. McDermott, S.J., "Faith and Critical Intelligence in Theology," in *Excellence in Seminary Education*, eds. S. Minkiel et al. (Erie: Gannon University, 1988), 68-93 (reprinted in *Analecta* 2 [1988]: 9-24), and "The Methodological Shift in Twentieth Century Thomism," *Seminarium* 31 (1991): 245-66. Other references in this section are given in the endnotes when individual theologians are explicitly named or an important point is made.

2.   All the leading transcendental Thomists admit the "paradox": see J. McDermott, S.J., "The Theology of John Paul II: A Response," in *The Thought of Pope John Paul II* (Rome: Pontifical Gregorian Univ., 1993), 63-64, note 36. For Rahner, see J. McDermott, S.J., "Dialectical Analogy: The Oscillating Center of Rahner's Thought," *Gregorianum* 75 (1994): 675-703, and "The Analogy of Knowing in Karl Rahner," *International Philosophical Quarterly* 26 (1996): 201-16.

3.   K. Rahner, S.J., *Hörer des Wortes*, 2nd ed., ed. J. Metz (München: Kösel, 1963), 114.

4. J. Mouroux, *I Believe*, trans. M. Turner (New York: Sheed and Ward, 1959), 15, note 1, notes that in calling God, the First Truth, a Person it is "in the broad sense of a personal Being." Similarly, K. Rahner, S.J., *Grundkurs des Glaubens* (Freiburg: Herder, 1976), 81, 139, calls God a person "in the sense that still has nothing to do with the question of the so-called tripersonality of God" and considers God an "absolute Thou" even before considering the Trinity.

5. P. Rousselot, S.J., "Les Yeux de la Foi," *Recherches de Science Religieuse* 1 (1910): 259, 471. Cf. also Rahner, *Grundkurs*, 85: "As a spiritual person man affirms implicitly in every knowledge and deed absolute Being as his real ground and affirms it as mystery."

6. Rahner, *Grundkurs*, 161f, 177, 246f, 282, 286; "Nachfolge des Gekreuzigten," *Schriften zur Theologie* 13 (Einsiedeln: Benziger, 1978), 197f; "Das christliche Verständnis der Erlösung," *Schriften* 15 (1983), 245; J. Sobrino, S.J., *Christology at the Crossroads*, trans. J. Drury (Maryknoll: Orbis, 1978), 94, 97 (Jesus "could fashion his person as a believer or an unbeliever"), 365f; E. Schillebeeckx, O.P. *Jesus*, trans. H. Hoskins (New York: Seabury, 1979), 94; B. Lonergan, S.J., *Method in Theology* (New York: Herder and Herder, 1972), 118f, and *Philosophy of God and Theology* (London: Darton, Longman and Todd, 1973), 10, 20, 67. For a critique of Rahner's Christology, see J. McDermott, S.J., "The Christologies of Karl Rahner," *Gregorianum* 67 (1986): 87-123, 297-327; for a critique of Lonergan's Christology, see J. McDermott, S.J., "Tensions in Lonergan's Theory of Conversion," *Gregorianum*, 74 (1993): 136-40. On anonymous Christianity, see below.

7. For a brief listing, see J. McDermott, S.J., "Sheehan, Rousselot, and Theological Method," *Gregorianum* 69 (1987): 714-17.

8. In this they do not go beyond Vatican I, which spoke of the divine wisdom and goodness whose "pleasure it was to reveal Himself and the eternal decrees of His will to the human race in another, supernatural way" beyond natural knowledge of God's existence through created realities (*DS*, n. 3004). Though Vatican I emphasized the conceptualist theology, its awareness of God's self-revelation reflected Scripture and the whole Catholic tradition.

9. P. Rousselot, S.J., "Intellectualisme," *Dictionnaire Apologétique de la Foi Catholique*, ed. A. d'Ales (Paris: Beauchesne, 1924), 2: 1075-78, used this argument to refute Modernism. It recurs in the pope's encyclical *Fides et ratio* (hereafter *FR*), n. 84.

10. K. Wojtyla, *Faith According to St. John of the Cross*, trans. J. Aumann (San Francisco: Ignatius, 1981), 94. All the page references in parentheses throughout this section refer to this work.

11. J. Maritain, *The Degrees of Knowledge*, trans. G. Phelan et al. (1959; rpt. Notre Dame: Univ. of Notre Dame Press, 1995), 263-82, 338-408. This work is included in the bibliography of *Faith According to Saint John of the Cross*. For a good overview of Maritain's development in three principal phases see B. Ritzler, *Freiheit in der Umarmung des ewig Liebenden: die historische Entwicklung des Personverständnisses bei Jacques Maritain* (Bern: Lang, 2000).

12. St. John refers to the substance of the soul in *The Ascent of Mount Carmel*, II, 5, 2; 16, 9; 24, 4; 26, 5f; 32, 2f; *The Spiritual Canticle* 14f, 14; 16, 5.

13. Maritain, *Degrees*, 287-90, 295-309; R. Garrigou-Lagrange, O.P., *De Revelatione* (Roma: Ferrari, 1945), 1: 359-76; H. Paissac, O.P., "God Is," in *God and His Creation*, ed. A. Henry, trans. C. Milner (Chicago: Fides, 1955), 85-88; C. Pesch, S.J., *Praelectiones Dogmaticae*, 6th ed. (Freiburg: Herder, 1925), 2: 60-62; 3: 326f, 334f; J. Lange, S.J., *De Gratia*, 2nd ed. (Valkenburg: St. Ignatius, 1926), 148. For a good summary of the various interpretations of Thomas's "natural desire" among the Baroque Scholastics, see W. O'Connor, *The Eternal Quest* (New York: Longmans, Green, 1947), 24-72.

14. A. Grillmeier, S.J., "Dogmatic Constitution on the Church: Chapter II," *Commentary on the Documents of Vatican II*, eds. H. Vorgrimler et al., trans. L. Adolphus et al. (New York: Herder and Herder, 1967), 1:182-84.

15. In "Die neuen Heiden und die Kirche," *Hochland* 51 (1958/59): 1-11, J. Ratzinger postulated a relationship of "representation" (*Stellvertretung*) of Christians for non-believers to account for the possibility of the latter's salvation, but always in relation to the Church. He repeated his view in "Kein Heil ausserhalb der Kirche?" in *Das neue Volk Gottes* (Düsseldorf: Patmos, 1969), 339-61, esp. 357-60. For a good overview of recent theological reflection about the possibility of the

salvation of non-Christians, see G. Rota, "Unicità di Gesù Cristo e pluralità delle religioni: per una teologia cristiana delle religioni," *Teologia* 26 (2001): 256-75.

16. K. Rahner, S.J., "Zur scholastischen Begrifflichkeit der ungeschaffenen Gnade," *Schriften 1* (1954): 352-73; "Gnade," *Sacramentum Mundi*, eds. K. Rahner et al. (Freiburg: Herder, 1968), 2: 457-60.

17. K. Rahner, S.J., *Geist im Welt*, 2nd ed., ed. J. Metz (München: Kösel, 1957), 84., 88f; *Hörer*, 57, 60; *Grundkurs*, 123-30, 132-39, 143f, 146-59.

18. K. Wojtyla, *The Acting Person*, trans. A. Potocki (Dordrecht: D. Reidel, 1979), 38, 150f, 184, 196-99, 202, 212, 255-58, 269-71.

19. John Paul II, *The Whole Truth about Man*, ed. J. Schall (Boston: St. Paul, 1981), 273; *FR*, nn. 17, 24, 28, 32; see McDermott, "Theology of John Paul II," 63f, for further references.

20. H. U. von Balthasar, *Cordula oder der Ernstfall* (Einsiedeln: Johannes, 1966), esp. 85-97; H. de Lubac, S.J., *Geheimnis aus dem Wir Leben*, trans. K. Bergner and H.U. von Balthasar (Einsiedeln: Johannes, 1967), 131-54; L. Elders, S.V.D., "Die Taufe der Weltreligionen," *Theologie und Glaube* 55 (1965): 124-31; H. Kreuse, S.J., "Die 'anonymen Christen' exegetisch gesehen," *Münchner Theologische Zeitschrift* 18 (1967): 2-29; E. Biser, "Ausgegrenzt und eingewiesen," *Münchner Theologische Zeitschrift* 19 (1968): 1-16.

21. K. Rahner, S.J., "Anonymes Christentum und Missionsauftrag der Kirche," *Schriften* 9 (1970), 499-502. He says that in German *Christentum* can signify also "the sum of real Christians." There is, however, a problem with Rahner's explanation of how Christ effected God's universal salvific will; McDermott, "Christologies," 112-17, 303-08, 322-25.

22. *Redemptoris missio*, nn. 5, 9, 18, 20. These truths were forcefully restated in *Dominus Jesus*, issued by the Congregation for the Doctrine of the Faith, Aug. 6, 2000, and confirmed verbally by John Paul II.

23. J. McDermott, S.J., "Storia universale e storia della salvezza," *Dizionario di teologia fondamentale*, eds. R. Latourelle and R. Fisichella (Assisi: Citadella, 1990), 1193-1206. Unfortunately the English version of this work altered the author's original English text for the sake of so-called "inclusive language" without even informing him, much less asking his permission, and thus introduced imprecisions and errors.

24. Freedom recurs as a constant theme in almost all the papal writings: e.g., *Redemptor hominis*, nn. 12, 21. That might be expected since it is the theme of *The Acting Person* and figures heavily in Wojtyla's *Amore et Responsibilità*, 2nd ed., trans. A. Milanoli (Torino: Marietti, 1978). What else is to be awaited from a profound Christian thinker concerned with the essence of Christ's message? "For freedom Christ has set us free" (Gal. 5:1) .

25. For further reflections on freedom in accord with the pope's Catholic vision, see J. McDermott, S.J., "Jesus: Parable or Sacrament of God?," *Gregorianum* 78 (1997): 477-99, 543-64, and esp. "Faith, Reason, and Freedom," *Irish Theological Quarterly* 67 (2002): 307-32.

26. *RH*, n. 21; see D. Stagaman, S.J., "The Implications for Theology of *The Acting Person*," in *The Thought of Pope John Paul II*, 215-19, on the centrality of Christ in and the novelty of the pope's interpretation of freedom.

27. We have indicated some of those problems in "Tensions," 101-40; "Metaphysical Conundrums at the Root of Moral Disagreement," *Gregorianum* 71 (1990): 713-42; "The Neo-Scholastic Analysis of Freedom," *International Philosophical Quarterly* 34 (1994): 149-65; "The Problem of Person and Jean Mouroux," *Sapientia* 52 (1997): 75-97; "De Lubac and Rousselot," *Gregorianum* 78 (1997): 735-59; *Love and Understanding* (Rome: Gregorian Univ., 1983).

28. See McDermott, "Theology of John Paul II," 57-68, for tensions in Wojtyla's relation of person and nature as well as further comparisons with transcendental Thomism in view of G. McCool's fine essay "The Theology of John Paul II," in the same volume.

John Paul II the Countercultural Pope

Martin R. Tripole, S.J.

John Paul II is a countercultural pope. He is a sign of contradiction between Christ and His Church and the spirit of the world.

John Paul has been this sign of contradiction in one form or another since his earliest days. As a young actor in the Polish underground theater and later as a clandestine seminarian during the Nazi and communist eras, he rejected the *Zeitgeist* and trumpeted national identity and freedom. As a young priest, he never reconciled himself to the communist system or its ideology. As Cardinal Karol Wojtyla, he focused on the Gospel of Christ as a countercultural force in history.

That Wojtyla understood Christ and His Church as countercultural is clear as early as 1976 from his Lenten retreat to Paul VI. The retreat was published under the title *Sign of Contradiction*,[1] a phrase taken from Simeon's words to Mary when Jesus was presented in the Temple: "Behold, He is set for the fall and the rising of many in Israel, and as a sign of contradiction" (Lk 2:34). It is noteworthy that Wojtyla understands this sign of contradiction as "a sign of our own times" and has repeatedly used the expression "sign of our times" to address the opposition between Christ and the spirit of the world. For Wojtyla, "sign of contradiction" is the "distinctive definition of Christ and of His Church." It is also "the key to understanding the various symptoms displayed by modern life." Wojtyla notes in his retreat that, while the sign of contradiction refers to Jesus, Simeon links it to "the inner experience of the mother," whose soul a sword will pierce. Wojtyla understands these words to contain the truth about Christ that we are called to love "all the more as the world all the more contradicts it."[2]

This sharp contradiction between Christ and the world takes on cosmological dimensions in an address Wojtyla made before a group of Polish Americans in New York on September 4, 1976:

We are now standing in the face of the greatest historical confrontation humanity has gone through . . . . We are now facing the final confrontation between the Church and the anti-Church, of the Gospel versus the anti-Gospel. This confrontation lies within the plans of divine providence; it is a trial which the whole Church . . . must take up . . . . it is a test of two thousand years of culture and Christian civilization with all its consequences for human dignity, individual rights, human rights and the rights of nations. As the number of people who understand the importance of this confrontation increase . . . we can look with greater trust towards the outcome . . . . The Church has gone through many trials . . . and has emerged victorious even at a cost of great sacrifice.[3]

The contradiction between the Gospel and the anti-Gospel appears in Wojtyla's exegesis of Genesis 3 in *Sign of Contradiction* and elsewhere. For him the passage illustrates the conflict between the God of the covenant and Satan. The covenant represents "God's love for man." It is "built on truth [and] rooted in what is real."[4] The tree of the knowledge of good and evil is a symbol of human nature's limits as a creature: it represents a "frontier which . . . the human person may not cross." The tree stands for "being and value" and is "linked symbolically with the tree of life." It represents a state of "primitive righteousness and happiness"[5] which the human being abandoned by accepting the anti-Gospel of lies. Thus "it becomes clear that the history of mankind, and with it the history of the world with which man is united," will be torn between "rule by the Word and the anti-Word, the Gospel and the anti-Gospel."[6] Life is shown to be a conflict between living by the truth or by lies when Satan, the father of lies, deceives Adam and Eve about their creaturely dependence on God. In Adam and Eve Satan gets humankind to turn against God toward the world, and to "stray progressively" from God's designs. Thus begins the "drama of history," the struggle between living by the truth and God's glory or by lies and human pride.[7]

Here and throughout his writings Wojtyla often identifies this rebellion as a rebellion of the modern world against God expressed in the form of various ideologies. Among those which he attacks repeatedly in his writings for their opposition to the teachings of the Gospel are secularism (which takes the world away from God and gives it to the human being, depriving him of the vision of the "objective order of being"[8]), totalitarianism or communist collectivism (which eradicates the dignity of the individual human person for the sake of tyrannous collective welfare), atheistic or dialectical materialism (which denies the human being the right of religious freedom), unbridled capitalism (with the "exploitation" of the individual by corporations' "economic imperialism"[9]), the individualism associated with Sartrean existentialism (which isolates the human person from God and from the source of life in community), structuralism (which calls into question the value of thought and the meaning of knowledge), consumerism (which reduces the person to a commodity by denying his "transcendental ends"), colonialism, and anthropocentrism (the idolatry of the human). For Wojtyla, all of these are forms of utilitarianism and represent in varying degrees the enslavement of the human person, his reduction to a tool, and a denial of the "objective order of being" and of objective good and evil.[10]

Wojtyla's greatest attacks against utilitarianism are leveled against its two major forms: atheistic or Marxist communism (though rarely mentioned by that name) because of its brutality in its persecution of religion, and exploitative capitalism, which appears to be particularly detestible to him not only because it represents the domination of the powerful and rich over the weak and the poor whom Jesus especially loves, but because it is led by supposed disciples of Christ who pay Him "lip-service" but try to "re-shape" Him to fit their own program of consumerism, not accepting "the full truth of [Christ's] Person, His mission and His Gospel."[11] For Wojtyla, unbridled capitalism and Marxist communism are of a kind. Both are exploitative. They "dehumanize man," he argues. As George Huntston Williams, a noted authority on John Paul's thought, says, for Wojtyla, "capitalistic exploitation" and Marxist communism "subordinate man to his own products and inhibit personal initiative or any action independent of big corporations or state economic planning."[12]

The dignity of the human being is preserved, according to Wojtyla, "only if human freedom is exercised justly and responsibly." What our history shows today, he says, is "that we are in the front line in a lively battle for the dignity of man."[13]

JOHN PAUL II'S PHILOSOPHY

There are many different ways in which John Paul sees Christ and His Church as a sign of contradiction to the world, but I will focus on what I consider to be three of the most outstanding.

The first is found prominently in the first phase of Wojtyla's scholarly career (but also present throughout the course of his writings), for example, in his dissertation in theology in 1948 on faith in the thought of St. John of the Cross, as well as in the large corpus of his philosophical writings before becoming pope in 1978. These writings show that the outlook and basic concepts which permeate his writings as pope were already in place from his earliest days. In many ways the later encyclicals are an application or implementation of the insights already in place in his early career.

It was through John of the Cross that Wojtyla was introduced into what Rocco Buttiglione calls "a kind of phenomenology of mystical experience." According to Buttiglione's brilliant work on Wojtyla (recently translated into English), Wojtyla "strongly emphasized the personal character of the encounter between God and man" in John of the Cross. "Mystical experience is a God-given experience in which creaturely boundaries transcend themselves toward God." In the "theological transcendence" of faith, "God does not come to be known as an object is known, but as a person is . . . in a reciprocal relation of self-giving . . . . [F]aith is subjectivized by becoming experience," but this subjectivization is also "absolutely objective." Thus a relation with the truth of God as "Absolute value" is constituted in the subjective experience of faith.[14] This understanding of God as person and objective truth known through subjective experience coming through the phenomenological process and yet transcending it was to remain with Wojtyla throughout his career.

A philosophical anthropology that understands the human person as created and self-determined by his moral decisions regarding objective truth and the objective good which refract their light back upon the subject pervades all of his writings. It is an anthropology that is easily converted into the theological and moral positions of his encyclicals and letters as pope because it was already set in a Christian context, due to the many Christian influences upon his thought from his earliest days.

What is so distinctive about Wojtyla's philosophy in his early period is what remains so distinctive about his theological views as pope in the final period of his thought: his unstinting emphasis upon the dignity of the individual human person and his determination to preserve that dignity, no matter the cost to philosophical, political, or moral causes. And while his campaign for human dignity may have put him in a contentious position toward the prevailing socialist culture in his native Poland in his earliest years, it has also made him critical of the widespread secularism and materialism today in Western culture. It is the chief reason why as pope he has become the sign of contradiction to both Eastern and Western cultures.

This emphasis upon the dignity of the human person is already present in the "existential personalism" of his earliest writings.[15] We know, however, that that emphasis is also found in the teachings of Vatican II, especially in *Gaudium et spes* (Pastoral Constitution on the Church in the Modern World). Since Wojtyla was a force in the commission that composed that document, it is difficult to determine the exact dependency between his thinking and the teaching in that document. It is safe to say that there was a mutual interaction. Since he also made interventions at Vatican II during discussion on the composition of *Dignitatis humanae* (Declaration on Religious Freedom), we know that he had some impact on that document too, especially when he stressed the freedom of the individual to live by his/her own vision of the truth.

In his philosophical anthropology Wojtyla borrows heavily from the phenomenological methodology of Max Scheler (1874-1928), a convert to Catholicism. In this respect Wojtyla makes the starting point of his anthropology a phenomenological "inspection" of what is manifest in experience. It is in an analysis of that experience that Wojtyla discovers the existence of the human being as subject who acts, or "man-acts," as he says in *The Acting Person*, his major philosophical publication.[16] The point is then that the essence of the human being consists not simply in a static nature as rational animal, as might be understood from Aristotelian-Thomistic philosophy, but as a subject whose actions are dynamically related to the existing subject in a totality of person-in-act that begins with the act of existence itself and continues to express thereafter the subject's uniqueness as well as dignity. For Wojtyla, it is in the dynamism of the act understood as an inner dimension of the person as subject that the human being constitutes and realizes himself as a person. While the actions may be of many kinds, the most distinctive feature of all actions is their moral quality: "Morality constitutes their intrinsic feature and what may be viewed as their specific profile."[17]

Like Scheler, Wojtyla sought "to establish the objective status of value and moral obligation."[18] But for Wojtyla, unlike for Scheler, moral decisions are made not simply on the basis of feeling of some essential value, but on the basis of a real experience of the good and the truth or truthfulness that is found in that good. That decision that puts the individual in contact with truth in goodness makes the intrinsic value of the truth in the good recoil upon the individual himself in a reflexive action that makes the decision for the true and the good creative. When the individual reflects upon the moral choice that is known in consciousness, that intransitive reflexion becomes integrated into a self-consciousness and a self-cognition that is self-determinative: it constitutes the person as who the person is. The self is then not simply consciousness for Wojtyla, as he perhaps incorrectly understands it to be for Scheler, but a unique ego acting in the world through his integral actions, those of both soul and body. In other words, the acts or actions are existential or real: they constitute the self not simply as a subject of conscious decision, but as one who really creates oneself in and through the concrete actions of being-in-the-world: "the concrete human self is slowly revealed and at the same time constituted: it reveals itself by constituting itself." [19]

The subject objectifies itself in its actions. The actions, therefore, not only constitute the person as unique but also give quality and fulfilment to the life of the person, provided the person makes transcendent choices—that is, choices oriented toward what is true and good. For Wojtyla, "there is a close connection between self-fulfillment and transcendence" toward the true and the good. It is with transcendence that Wojtyla seems to identify most closely the person. He sees it as the manifestation of one's spirituality. For in the consciousness of the human act in experience, there is also an experience of conscience. Wojtyla states: "in the conscience truth makes itself heard as the source of moral duty, . . . as the condition which constitutes the liberty proper to act."[20] In other words, it is in such transcendent choices toward the true and the good that the person realizes his freedom. Indeed, for Wojtyla, "The very existence of the person," the person's spiritual becoming, "is identified with this freedom."[21] If the person chooses evil, the individual becomes inauthentic, enslaved, and loses transcendence. The moral value contained in decision, therefore, reaches not only to the psychological or conscious level, but also to the "metaphysical structure of the human subject."[22] Thus moral choices make the person the kind of person that one is, and it is by the real orientation of one's life toward the objective existence of truth in goodness that the self determines the self's own objective state.

Human action is not only individual action. It is action "together with many people" where each person is able to be and to fulfill the self. Community is present not simply when the participation is a plurality of subjects acting but where there is a "unity of that plurality." Nor is community for Wojtyla simply an accidental construct desirable for human fulfilment; it is "a reality essential to human coexistence and cooperation," in other words, a reality essential to the self-determination and survival of the person. Wojtyla sees community essentially contained in the primary interpersonal pattern "I-you," where there is "participation in the very humanity of another," where "'you' help me to more amply ascertain and affirm my own 'I.'"[23] But Wojtyla argues that the "full specificity of the community," the "authentic interpersonal community," is present only when there is the "mutual confirmation of the transcendent value of the person."[24] That transcendence is realized in the decision to act responsibly toward the objective moral value, in a participation in a community of persons "co-existing and co-acting with others for reciprocity in self-fulfillment."[25] Such community often takes the shape of "friendship and love," as between married couples, parents and children.[26]

Wojtyla distinguishes community from society (as does Scheler). In society, it is not an "I-you" but a "we" relationship that prevails. Society is realized, as is community, "in the relation to truth and to good,"[27] to "objective reality," but in this case, the unity is a reality with a "complex of relations"[28] of persons existing for the "common good," "the good of many" or the "good of all" humanity.[29] Society's common good has a character superior to the good of each separate individual "I," inasmuch as the common good represents the "more complete expression and realization of the good of each of the subjects."[30] At the same time, Wojtyla affirms the "priority of the personal subject in regard to the community"[31] or society since the goal of society is always the fulfilment of the human "I." The priority of the person is necessary to avoid utilitarianism and totalitarianism.[32]

There is for Wojtyla a still deeper form of participation that is "far more absolute" than simply membership in a community or society. It is found in my relationship to my "neighbor," and this is one of the most distinctive bridges between his philosophy and his theology. For Wojtyla, neighbor speaks to "the most fundamental principle of any real community."[33] It speaks to the value of the person as such, independently of membership in any specific community:

> The notion [of neighbor] takes into account man's humanness alone, . . . concretized in every man just as much as it is in myself. It thus provides the broadest base for the community . . . . It unites human beings, all human beings who are even members in different human communities . . . . [It stresses] the most fundamental interrelationships of all men in their humanness. The notion of "neighbor" refers then to the broadest, commonly shared reality of the human being and also to the broadest foundations of interhuman community. Indeed, it is the community of men, of all men, the community formed by their very humanness that is the basis of all other communities."[34]

According to Wojtyla, it is in our ability to participate "in the very *humanness of others*" that the personal dimension of our human relationships is rooted.[35] It is only because we share in humanness itself, which is what is at stake in the notion of "neighbor," that our participation in community "attain[s] its personal depth" and universal significance. "Only then [when we participate in humanness itself] can we claim that participation serves not just the fulfillment of some individual being," but that of everyone in the community. The "ability to share in the *humanness itself of every man is the very core of all participation and the condition of the personalistic value of all acting and existing 'together with others.'*"[36]

In the light of these principles, the scriptural commandment "love thy neighbor as thyself" takes on special meaning for Wojtyla. He notes that the commandment juxtaposes my neighbor and "my own ego." Since neighbor refers to all human beings in their humanness, it sets up a fundamental reference[37] which is second to no other relationship. The commandment of love establishes what is absolutely necessary for "*a community to be truly human.*"[38] Thus, any civilization that undermines the principle of love of neighbor or refuses to support "that fundamental subordination of my own good to that of my fellowman" dehumanizes the community and leads to its disintegration.[39] The commandment of love "imparts the specifically human quality to any community"[40] and must be the "measure" of all the operations of a community if that community is to endure.[41]

These principles regarding the objectivity of truth and morality, the dignity and freedom of the human person who lives in conformity with objective values, and the fulfilment of life that comes only from mutual self-donation in community and society continue to provide the metaphysical and social structures for all of John Paul's subsequent thought.

IMPACT OF PHILOSOPHY ON ENCYCLICAL TEACHING

The enormous importance of Wojtyla's metaphysical phenomenology to his theology as pope becomes obvious when one examines the encyclical teachings. We see its influence, for example, in *Redemptor hominis*, where the role of the Church includes "the duty to act for the common good" based on the "objective ethical order" and the "objective and inviolable rights of man."[42] But the strongest recent statement reaffirming a metaphysics of objective truth and morality is probably to be found in *Veritatis splendor*, the encyclical designed to be a reaffirmation of the basic moral teachings of the Church.[43] There John Paul identifies the splendor of truth with the reflection of God's glory that shines in the face of Jesus Christ.[44] The truths of faith and moral obligation are found in the Gospel.[45] John Paul rejects relativism, subjectivism, individualism, empiricism, liberalism, situationalism, consequentialism, proportionalism, secularism, totalitarianism, and utilitarianism—all trends in current moral theology that are incompatible with revealed truth[46] because they reduce the norms of morality to those produced by the rational autonomous self[47] or take "concrete human behavior patterns" as the standard for morality.[48] John Paul recognizes that freedom is intrinsic to the dignity of the human person, but it must be a freedom that is found in the decision for the good and the avoidance of evil.[49] Fighting off the notion that "individual conscience" decides what is good and evil for itself, he reaffirms the notion of "a universal truth about the good" that is "knowable by human reason" though "*enlightened by Divine Revelation.*"[50] Conscience is called to be guided by "objective truth."[51] The morality of human actions is primarily determined not by subjective intention, but by whether the object chosen by the will of the acting person[52] is rooted in "the transcendent value of the person" and the objective moral order.[53]

COUNTERCULTURAL DIMENSION OF THE POPE'S TEACHING

How much John Paul's views on the existence of objective truth, morality, and the primacy of the commandment of love of neighbor are countercultural is evident when we see how these principles are questioned today. Arguments in favor of the legitimacy of infanticide were proposed long ago by the well-known situation ethicist, Joseph Fletcher. Fletcher had abandoned any notion of objective truth or goodness, and he proposed a principle of proportionality regarding abortion and infanticide when he stated: "I would support the . . . position, i.e., that both abortion and infanticide can be justified if and when the good to be gained outweighs the evil—that neither abortion nor infanticide is as such immoral."[54] Fletcher's point was that one should not be enslaved by a concept of objective moral rule but should let autonomous rational choice be the basis for morality. We have lived to see the day when such autonomous rational choice has become the basis for the legitimacy of late-term abortions by our President and many congressmen, many of whom were born Catholics.

Richard John Neuhaus noted in *The Wall Street Journal* in October 1994 that a panel of experts put together by the National Institutes of Health had recommended experimentation on human embryos for scientific purposes and had justified such action on the basis of the fact that they were not persons. Neuhaus notes that the position of the panel is that "there are no 'qualities existing out there' in any human being that require us to respect him or her as a person"–in other words, there are no objective norms of truth and goodness. Personhood, according to Neuhaus, is considered by much of academia as a "social construct" based on the compelling presence of certain qualities that we determine to be necessary for the presence of a person: "Whether someone is too young or too old, too retarded or too sick, too useless or too troublesome to be entitled to personhood is determined [according to social relativists] by a 'decision on our part.' Thus we move from embryos in the laboratory to a 'Copernican Revolution' in our understanding of human dignity and human rights."[55]

This same view is presented in an article by Steven Pinker, a professor of psychology at MIT. He reflects on the recent and well-known case of two teenagers in New Jersey who killed their newborn child and left him in a dumpster. Pinker sympathizes with them, saying "Several moral philosophers have concluded that neonates are not persons, and thus neonaticide should not be classified as murder." According to Pinker, the right to life would come from the presence of "morally significant traits that we humans happen to possess," such as having "an ability to reflect upon ourselves as a continuous locus of consciousness, to form and savor plans for the future, to dread death and to express the choice not to die. And there's the rub: our immature neonates don't possess these traits any more than mice do."[56]

The acceptance of objective truth and the intrinsic value of human life is in serious jeopardy in our culture today. Perhaps no greater setback occurred than the five-to-four ruling of the U.S. Supreme Court, which asserted, in defending *Roe vs. Wade*: "At the heart of liberty is the right to define one's own concept of existence, of meaning, of the universe and of the mystery of human life. Beliefs about these matters could not define the attributes of personhood were they formed under compulsion of the state."[57] Many scholars of jurisprudence, such as Gerard Bradley, professor of law at the University of Notre Dame, argue that this new "megaright" is based on "the worst kind of moral subjectivism—that people can and should make up their own minds about what is good and what is evil. If people think life is not a good, then they can just extinguish life."[58]

There are some signs of hope. Americans are becoming genuinely concerned about the erosion of the level of morality in our society. A number of councils or commissions have been formed in recent months to assess the state of American society, and their statements have been promising. In May 1998 the Council on Civil Society, a group of twenty-four civic-minded persons in education, religion, and government, released a report entitled *A Call to Civil Society: Why Democracy Needs Moral Truths*. The report cites a Daniel Yankelovich survey of 1996 indicating that 87% of Americans fear "that something is fundamentally wrong with America's moral condition." Yankelovich stated: "In general, a widespread feeling of moral decline has sharply expanded within the public over the last two years, regardless of gender, age, race or geographical area." Reading the Council's report is like reading from the writings of John Paul. The Council in its report accepted that we live in a period of "declining morality," and affirmed that "reverent regard for a public moral philosophy—an ensemble of knowable, objective truths—is our democracy's most indispensable foundation . . . . For many of us, the answer is that all people, as persons created in the image of God, possess transcendent human dignity, and that consequently each person must always be treated as an end, never as a means" (the latter a principle from Immanuel Kant repeatedly cited by Wojtyla).[59]

John Paul emphatically affirmed in *Evangelium vitae*, in declarations that ring with infallible teaching, the intrinsic, objective value of human life at every stage of its existence, from womb to natural death.[60] In *Centesimus annus*,[61] he speaks of the evils of totalitarianism and how that system collapsed in 1989 because it violated human rights.[62] He warns the West in that same encyclical about its own violations of human rights and the need to be guided by a "correct understanding of the dignity and the rights of the person," a vision of objective truth and a social order that promotes "the common good" if it wishes to avoid succumbing to its own form of totalitarianism.[63] Let me more briefly indicate two other counter-cultural elements in John Paul's teaching.

JOHN PAUL'S INCARNATIONAL UNIVERSALISM

We have in John Paul's teaching what has been called incarnational universalism.[64] This thinking seems to represent the influence of Scheler, but even more, that of the "New Theology." This influence probably comes from Wojtyla's two years of living at the Belgian College and studying at the Angelicum in Rome from November 1946 to June 1948, but its influence would also be felt from Vatican II, where the New Theology emerged "as a dominant current,"[65] especially in the composition of the documents with which Wojtyla was involved. According to Williams, common to the thinkers of the New Theology school is a "restatement of Christian salvation in terms of the whole created order and its redemption by Christ as the head of mankind."[66]

45

Evidence for The New Theology is found especially in *Gaudium et spes,* n. 22, the section on "Christ as the New Man," a passage which John Paul cites repeatedly in his encyclicals. The passage states as "truth" that the "mystery of man" is illuminated only in the "incarnate Word." Christ, the second Adam, "fully reveals man to man himself." Christ, the "perfect man," "restores the divine likeness" to "the sons of Adam." By His incarnation, "the Son of God has united Himself in some fashion with every man." He has achieved reconciliation between us and God and among ourselves. Since Christ "died for all men," His grace is understood to be at work not only among Christians, but among "all men of good will . . . in an unseen way." *Gaudium et spes,* n.10 affirms that in Christ "can be found the key, the focal point, and the goal of all human history." In n..29, the extraordinary affirmation is made that "all men . . . are created in God's likeness, . . . have been redeemed by Christ, and enjoy the same divine calling and destiny."[67]

Wojtyla's most complete expression of this incarnational universalism is probably found in his first encyclical, *Redemptor hominis*. Here John Paul seems to go even beyond the incarnational universalism of *Gaudium et spes*. The Pope speaks of a "new advent of the Church connected with the approaching end of the second millennium"[68] (a theme which continues throughout his writings). The Church is also "the Church that is continually preparing for the new coming of the Lord."[69] Williams tells us the pope is referring here to a second advent Christ will make "to each person in the impending third millennium of His salvific work," to the effect that "all of humanity should be potentially touched and permanently affected for the good by the Incarnation."[70]

The meaning of this new coming of the Lord is connected with the first coming. The Church is to make available to every person, according to *Redemptor hominis,* "the truth about man and the world that is contained in the mystery of the Incarnation and the Redemption" and to reveal "the power of the love that is radiated by that truth."[71] The pope insists upon the truth regarding the unity of Christ with the human being—not with humanity in general or in the abstract, but with each individual concretely: "We are not dealing with the 'abstract' man, but the real, 'concrete,' 'historical' man. We are dealing with 'each' man, for each one is included in the mystery of the Redemption and with each one Christ has united Himself for ever through this mystery." Later, in the same section, the pope insists again that the "Man" who is "'willed' by God" and "'chosen' by him from eternity," the human being who is "destined for grace and glory" is "'each' man, 'the most concrete' man, 'the most real'; this is man in all the fullness of the mystery in which he has become a sharer in Jesus Christ, the mystery in which each one of the four thousand million human beings living on our planet has become a sharer [in Jesus Christ] from the moment He is conceived beneath the heart of His mother."[72]

In *Dominum et vivificantem*, John Paul dwells on the "cosmic dimension" of the Incarnation.[73] "'By the power of the Holy Spirit,'" he says, "the mystery of the 'hypostatic union' is brought about—that is, the union of the divine nature and the human nature." But this is not simply a hypostatic union in Jesus for John Paul. The Incarnation represents to him the "taking up into unity with God . . . everything that is 'flesh': the whole of humanity, the entire visible and material world . . . . in some way [a unity] with the entire reality of man, . . . and in this reality with all 'flesh,' with the whole of creation."[74] What the Great Jubilee of 2000 is to celebrate is the fact that God, who at creation gave "life to man and the cosmos" through the work of the Holy Spirit, renewed this life through the mystery of the Incarnation, "the greatest work accomplished by the Holy Spirit in the history of creation," so that "there [began] in the heart of all human beings" the gift by which they "'become partakers of the divine nature' (cf. 2 Pet 1:4)." The Incarnation "opens in a new way" divine life into the history of the human race, especially by reason of the fact that Christ "becomes the head of the body, which is the church, . . . and in the church He becomes the head of humanity."[75] According to John Paul, creation itself is "completed by the incarnation and since that moment is permeated by the powers of the redemption, powers which fill humanity and all creation." Human life "becomes permeated through participation by the divine life, and itself acquires a divine, supernatural dimension."[76]

With the year 2000, a "new phase of man's history on earth" begins,[77] says John Paul. But what is this new phase? It seems to include a deeper understanding of the mystery of the Incarnation.[78] It includes a deeper awareness of the continuing penetration over the past two thousand years of the life of the Holy Spirit into the life of the world, as well as a hope for a "new Advent"[79] of Christ in the power of His Spirit in the event of the jubilee. John Paul speaks of a "pneumatological dimension" to the jubilee, "seeing with the eyes of faith the two thousand years of the action of the Spirit of truth."[80] "As the year 2000 since the birth of Christ draws near," he asserts, "God comes close to man and permeates more and more completely the whole human world."[81] Through the power of the Holy Spirit, Christ comes "now and forever in a new way" in "His constant presence and action in the spiritual life" and in the sacramental life of the Church.[82] The world has also been invaded for the past two thousand years with the presence of the triune God "giving it life from within."[83] God works to make His kingdom present where God will be all in all "as gift and love." The goal in the year 2000, which John Paul speaks of as "a possibility and a hope,"[84] is that there may "be accomplished in our world a process of true growth in humanity, in both individual and community life," that "an ever greater number of people 'may fully find themselves . . . through a sincere gift of self,'" where "the full discovery of the meaning of humanity" occurs,[85] inasmuch as people grow more and more into making life a gift of themselves "through communion with God and with others, [their] brothers and sisters."[86] This discovery will include a greater awareness of the presence of the transcendent reality of the triune God, who is "penetrating [the world] and giving it life from within,"[87] transforming "the human world from within, from inside hearts and minds."[88]

According to *Redemptor hominis*, the goal is that the human being attain the "full truth of his existence." This includes for the pope the realization of the human being's uniqueness as a "personal being," and his fulfilment in the various interpersonal areas of life in the world: existence "in the sphere of his own family, in the sphere of social society and very diverse contexts, in the sphere of his own nation or people," and "in the sphere of the whole of mankind," as one aspires for "the truth, the good, the beautiful, justice and love." It is to the fulfilment of this human being that the Church must find her way "because man—every man without any exception whatever—has been redeemed by Christ" and is united with Him.[89]

For John Paul, the pinnacle of this growth in human existence is found in self-donation in love. This donation has been essential to human existence since the time of the Incarnation and Redemption. Participation in love is for John Paul "the human dimension of the mystery of the Redemption." But if the human being becomes understandable only insofar as there is an experience of love, then it is only Christ who "fully reveals man to himself."[90] In the Redemption man is "newly created!" If he wishes to understand himself fully, then, he must "draw near to Christ" and "'appropriate' and assimilate the whole of the reality of the Incarnation and Redemption." In that mysterious event, the "worth and dignity" of human life has definitively been restored, so that now we are all one in Christ Jesus (Gal 3:28). The reality of that worth and dignity is named the "Gospel," the "Good News" that is Christianity, that is, that God gave His Son for humanity[91] to know the truth which will make the human being free (Jn 8:32)[92] and to become "transformed inwardly" by the power of the new life that makes the human being a sharer in the life of God himself (2 Pt 1:4) and a child of God (Jn 1:12).[93]

Williams sums up Wojtyla's incarnational universalism this way: "In a word, [Wojtyla] has been saying that Christ is not only a revelation *of God* and His salvific will for all mankind through the Church but also a revelation of *man*, of what man was intended to be at creation and is by reason of the Incarnation of the Son of God and by reason of the Crucifixion, Resurrection, and Ascension of the God-Man Jesus Christ."[94] John Paul's incarnational universalism understands the Incarnation to have essentially altered the nature of the human being by incorporating divine presence into human existence, and yet this divine presence achieves its existential completeness only in the redemptive event of Jesus's Crucifixion and Resurrection, to which all are called to respond by a decision for the Truth.

What is the sign of contradiction here? It resides in the fact that, as a result of the Incarnation, a secular conception of human life is no longer adequate, and yet our society continues to foster a secular social and political agenda as if it were the only one acceptable. This may be understandable among non-Christians, but would Christians do this too? If the nature of the human being has been divinized, as John Paul affirms, and yet the presence of that divinization is not incorporated into our discussion of the human situation, that discussion is based on principles that are flawed, inaccurate, unrealistic, and unworkable. Unfortunately, most Americans, including Christians, see the re-creation of human nature by the divine presence as merely the product of a relativistic subjective faith. We do not understand our faith as giving us knowledge of what really is so. Thus the pope's thinking is countercultural to the popular American conception that faith perceptions are culturally conditioned, biased, and of marginal importance to the operations of the public order. In addition, we have in America falsely understood the First Amendment to the Constitution of the United States in 1791 to provide a "wall of separation" (the words of Thomas Jefferson used in a letter he wrote in 1802) between faith experiences and the social and political orders, an understanding that has only fostered erroneous perceptions of what it means to be a human being in the world since the event of the Incarnation.

ON THE VALUE OF SUFFERING

One final area where John Paul is a sign of contradiction pertains to the meaning and value of human suffering. In a society that links the pleasure principle with a "culture of death," suffering seems to serve no useful purpose. As John Paul says in *Evangelium vitae:* When "pleasure and well-being" are considered to be life's only value and "suffering seems like an unbearable setback," death is understood as a "rightful liberation."[95] Eliminating suffering is more important to our society today than preserving life—thus the value of abortion and euthanasia. Naomi Wolf, a feminist writer, tells us that she had an abortion because it interfered with her pursuit of her graduate studies. While she feels it was selfish of her to have done that and that the action may be sinful, she wants it to remain legal for women to be equally selfish and sinful.[96] The right to choose to pursue one's life at the cost of another's unborn life has now been extended by some courts to the right to choose to end one's own life to terminate suffering.[97] The presumption now is that life has no meaning apart from the meaning that one gives it—so the Supreme Court has declared—and suffering has no meaning at all.

John Paul argues otherwise, especially in his apostolic letter *Salvifici doloris*, one of the most profound Church statements delineating the significance of human suffering, and one of the major applications of John Paul's understanding of love of neighbor to his later thought.[98] According to John Paul, suffering is really our sharing in the redemptive suffering of Christ out of love for sinners. Although suffering remains an evil, it is transformed by the Father's love expressed in the love of His Son into a saving power that invades the "cosmic" struggle between the forces of good and evil present since the sin of Adam and Eve, and opens the way to the victory of the saving power of the good. By our suffering we complete the saving work of Christ's suffering in His body, the Church. Says John Paul:

> [the suffering person] is serving, like Christ, the salvation of his brothers and sisters. Therefore he is carrying out an irreplaceable service. In the body of Christ, which is ceaselessly born of the cross of the Redeemer, it is precisely suffering permeated by the spirit of Christ's sacrifice that is the irreplaceable mediator and author of the good things which are indispensable for the world's salvation. It is suffering, more than anything else, which clears the way for the grace which transforms human souls. Suffering, more than anything else, makes present in the history of humanity the powers of the redemption.[99]

Thus the "strange paradox": the "springs of divine power gush forth precisely in the midst of human weakness." Those who suffer share "the infinite treasure of the world's redemption" in Christ's sufferings with others.[100] In this way they live out the parable of the Good Samaritan: treating another who suffers as a "neighbor" and being a neighbor to the sufferer. In the "unselfish gift of one's 'I' on behalf of other people, especially those who suffer," the "world of human suffering unceasingly calls for . . . the world of human love."[101]

Since it is the suffering Christ's love that is the saving power in the world, it is that saving love that is brought to completion in the parable of the good neighbor, who draws on those "infinite resources" of redemption in Christ's love at Golgotha and unleashes them toward others throughout history.[102] Wojtyla's earlier philosophy of love of neighbor which was rooted in our common sharing in humanity and which affirmed the personal donation of self as necessary for the vitality of the community, continues in John Paul's theology of suffering to be a principle of vitality, but now because it shares in the redemptive power of the suffering Christ.

At the same time, through the power that a person experiences in suffering, the person is drawn more closely to Christ and "becomes a completely new person."[103] The human sufferer shares in the "gospel paradox of weakness and strength": by sharing in Christ's emptying of self in love, the human being is able to share in Christ's lifting up in the glory of the resurrection.[104] The redemption Christ "accomplished through satisfactory love . . . is in a certain sense constantly being accomplished" and completed through the loving union of our suffering with Christ's.[105]

Conclusion

We may, by way of conclusion, bring together in some unity these three signs of contradiction in John Paul Wojtyla's thinking: first, the affirmation of the objectivity of truth and the moral order as the only foundation for maintaining the dignity of the human person and as a necessary principle for combating the many utilitarian ideologies that repeatedly seek to destroy the dignity of the person by reducing the person to an instrument in the service of personal and political gain; secondly, the foundation for that dignity that is now to be found in the divinizing universalism of Christ's Incarnation and Redemption, an event which makes necessarily incomplete and outdated all purely secular conceptions of human life that neutralize the objectively divine dimension of historical existence by reducing it to a relativistic personal feeling; and, finally, our participation in that mystical saving grace present in Christ's Redemption that is extended to all the world more than in any other way through our completion of the suffering of Christ in our suffering as a continuing expression of the redemptive love of Christ for the neighbor. Thus three points: the dignity of the human person vs. utilitarianism; a dignity that is based on a sharing in divine life through the Incarnation and Redemption of Jesus Christ; a dignity that is especially present in sharing in Christ's redemptive suffering for others as our neighbor, in a self-donation in love.

These, I would contend, are three of the major countercultural principles operating in the theology of John Paul II, which, if implemented, could have major impact on the life of the Church and the world. And yet, the question may be raised: Is anyone listening? There is probably no living figure more well-loved in the world than John Paul II, if we may draw the logical conclusion from the popular success of this figure as he circles the world. But in what nation of the world are his views accepted or adopted? If we may trust the polls in our own society—and there seems little reason to doubt them—the majority of those supposedly sharing in John Paul's faith in Christ do not accept his moral teachings. People seem to applaud his imposing figure, but not the principles he stands for, in spite of the fact that no one has been able to find better ones.

John Paul today is the head of a faith community that stands divided between those who are willing to adjust their thinking to the ways of the world and those who are not. So far, he has not been able to bring these two groups together. What John Paul represents more and more is that smaller group of Christians who have not been willing to accommodate to the ways of the world, a Christian faith experience that has more than ever become countercultural in response to a culture that is increasingly counter-Christian. But it is important for all Christians to recognize that the pope has made himself the sign and symbol of the countercultural Christ, to whom he has dedicated his life from his earliest days, a countercultural Christ who, I think, needs to become more and more embodied in our world today in a countercultural Church.

NOTES

1. Karol Wojtyla, *Sign of Contradiction* (hereafter *SC*), trans. St. Paul Publications (New York: Seabury, 1979 [1977]).
2. *SC*, 7-8.

3. George Huntston Williams, "The Ecumenical Intentions of Pope John Paul II," *Harvard Theological Review* 75 (1982): 141-76, at 147.

4. *SC,* 23.

5. Ibid.

6. Ibid., 28-29.

7. Ibid., 29-32.

8. Ibid., 34.

9. George Huntston Williams, *The Mind of John Paul II: Origins of His Thought and Action* (New York: Seabury, 1981), 251.

10. *SC,* 32-34, 199, 11.

11. Ibid., 199.

12. Williams, *The Mind of John Paul II,* 251.

13. *SC,* 124.

14. Rocco Buttiglione, *Karol Wojtyla: The Thought of the Man Who Became Pope John Paul II,* trans. Paolo Guietti and Francesca Murphy (Grand Rapids: Eerdmans, 1997 [1982]), 45-48.

15. The term is first used by Andrew Woznicki to identify Wojtyla's thought: see Andrew N. Woznicki, *A Christian Humanism: Karol Wojtyla's Existential Personalism* (New Britain, CT: Mariel, 1980), 9.

16. Karol Cardinal Wojtyla, *The Acting Person* (hereafter AP), trans. Andrzej Potocki, revised and with the collaboration of Anna-Teresa Tymieniecka, Analecta Husserliana X (Dordrecht: Reidel, 1979 [1969]), 9.

17. *AP,* 11.

18. George Huntston Williams, "Karol Wojtyla and Marxism: His Thought and Action as Professor, Prelate and Supreme Pontiff," in *Pope John Paul II Lecture Series* (St. Paul: College of St. Thomas, 1985), 24-32, at 25.

19. Karol Wojtyla, "The Person: Subject and Community," *Review of Metaphysics* 33 (December 1979): 273-308, at 277.

20. Ibid., 285.

21. Ralph J. Masiello, "A Note on Transcendence in *The Acting Person,*" *Doctor Communis* 35 (1982): 327-35, at 332.

22. Wojtyla, "The Person," 287.

23. Ibid., 294.

24. Ibid., 294, 297.

25. Masiello, "A Note on Transcendence," 334.

26. Wojtyla, "The Person," 295.

27. Ibid., 300.

28. Ibid., 289.

29. Ibid., 300.

30. Ibid., 301.

31. Ibid., 289.

32. Ibid., 301.

33. Ibid., 297.

34. *AP,* 293.

35. Ibid., 294.

36. Ibid., 295.

37. Ibid.

38. Ibid., 296.

39. Ibid., 297-98.

40. Ibid., 297.

41. Ibid., 299.

42. *Redemptor hominis* (Redeemer of Mankind), March 4, 1979, n. 17 (hereafter *RH*).

43. *Veritatis splendor* (The Splendor of Truth), August 6, 1993.

44. Ibid., n. 2.

45. Ibid., n. 26.

46. Ibid., nn. 1, 29, 34, 46, 56, 75, 88, 99, 106.
47. Ibid., nn. 35, 75.
48. Ibid., n. 46.
49. Ibid., n. 35.
50. Ibid., n. 44.
51. Ibid., n. 61.
52. Ibid., n. 78.
53. Ibid., n. 101.
54. Joseph Fletcher, *Humanhood: Essays in Biomedical Ethics* (Buffalo: Prometheus, 1979), 144.
55. Richard John Neuhaus, "Don't Cross This Threshold," *The Wall Street Journal*, October 27, 1994, A20; Neuhaus's first two citations are taken from a writing of a panel member.
56. Steven Pinker, "Why They Kill Their Newborns," *The New York Times Magazine*, November 2, 1997, 52-54, at 54.
57. U.S. Supreme Court, *Planned Parenthood of Southeastern Pennsylvania vs. Casey*, June 29, 1992, in "Supreme Court Rules on Pennsylvania Abortion Control Act," *Origins* 22 (July 9, 1992): 113, 115-32, at 117.
58. Ann Carey, "Saith the High Court: The I's have it," *Our Sunday Visitor*, May 17, 1997, 6-7, at 6.
59. The Council on Civil Society, *A Call to Civil Society: Why Democracy Needs Moral Truths* (New York: Institute for American Values, 1998), 4-5, 13.
60. *Evangelium vitae* (The Gospel of Life), March 25, 1995, esp. nn. 57, 62, 65 (hereafter *EV*).
61. *Centesimus annus* (The Hundredth Year: "New Things" One Hundred Years Later), May 1, 1991, nn. 1, 3, 24 (hereafter *CA*).
62. CA, n. 23.
63. CA, nn. 41, 47, 44, 46.
64. Williams, "Wojtyla and Marxism," 27-32.
65. Williams, *The Mind of John Paul II,* 93, 96.
66. Ibid., 96.
67. Walter M. Abbott, S.J., ed., *The Documents of Vatican II* (New York: Guild, 1966).
68. *RH*, n. 7.
69. *RH*, n. 20.
70. Williams, *The Mind of John Paul II,* 309-10.
71. *RH*, n. 13.
72. Ibid.
73. *Dominum et Vivificantem* (Lord and Giver of Life), May 18, 1986, nn. 77, 79-102 (hereafter *DV*).
74. Ibid., n. 50.
75. Ibid., nn. 50-53.
76. Ibid., n. 52.
77. Ibid., n. 51.
78. *RH*, n. 1.
79. Ibid.
80. *DV*, n. 53.
81. Ibid., n. 59.
82. Ibid., n. 61.
83. Ibid., n. 54.
84. Ibid., n. 56.
85. Ibid., n. 59, citing *Gaudium et spes*, n. 24.
86. Ibid., n. 62.
87. Ibid., n. 54.
88. Ibid., n. 59.
89. *RH,* n. 14.
90. Ibid., n. 10.
91. Ibid., n. 10.
92. Ibid., n. 12.
93. Ibid., n. 18.

94.   Williams, *The Mind of John Paul II*, 265.

95.   *EV*, n. 64.

96.   Naomi Wolf, "Our Bodies, Our Souls," *The New Republic* 213 (October 16, 1995): 26, 28-29, 32-35.

97.   We are referring to the 8-3 decision of the Ninth U.S. Circuit Court of Appeals in San Francisco, March 6, 1996, striking down the state of Washington's ban on physician-assisted suicide (cf. "What the Appeals Court Ruled," *Origins* 25 [April 11, 1996]: 723-25); and the April 2, 1996 unanimous decision of the Second Circuit Court of Appeals in Manhattan overturning two New York laws banning physician-assisted suicide (cf. "The Court's Misguided Judicial Activism," *Origins* 25 [April 18, 1996]: 752).

98.   *Salvifici doloris* (On the Christian Meaning of Human Suffering), February 11, 1984.

99.   Ibid., n. 27.

100. Ibid.

101. Ibid., n. 28.

102. Ibid., n. 24.

103. Ibid., n. 26.

104. Ibid., nn. 22-23.

105. Ibid., n. 24.

A Response to Martin R. Tripole, S.J.

William S. Kurz, S.J.

I appreciated and enjoyed Martin Tripole's treatment of Pope John Paul II as a truly countercultural pope and thinker and writer. In my judgment, he made his case on the basis of John Paul II's personal history since his youth, of his constant confrontations against the many current anti-Gospel ideologies, and of three key aspects of his thought and writings: (a) John Paul II's philosophical defense of objective truth and a moral order; (b) the divinizing universalism resulting from Christ's Incarnation; and (c) completing the suffering of Christ through loving our neighbor.

I appreciated his especially helpful overview of John Paul II's philosophy and theology. I had been somewhat aware how John Paul II's encyclicals and apostolic exhortations have flowed from his more basic philosophical thought, but it was helpful to have it laid out so clearly.

Regarding John Paul II's divinizing universalism and optimism about the coming of the new millennium, I confess that I do not understand and appreciate as well this aspect of his thought and writings. I understand how the Incarnation makes a purely secular view of the human being impossible. But it is not clear to me, especially as a Scripture scholar, on what John Paul is basing his profound aspirations and hopes for the years after 2000. He does not seem to be envisaging the biblical apocalyptic second coming as such. On what is his fascination with the year 2000 based?

Martin's emphasis on John Paul II's affirmation of the importance and value of suffering as a main counterthrust to the "culture of death" is very helpful. This defense of the value of suffering is perhaps one of John Paul II's strongest countercultural stances. Martin ends on a wistful note. Though these three aspects of John Paul II's thought could have a major impact on the life of the Church and world, he asks, "Is anyone listening?" Martin rightly observes that the pope has been

57

unable to unite those Catholics willing to adjust their thinking to the ways of the world and those countercultural Catholics like himself who are not.

Personally, I am finally beginning to have some hope on the human level about the countercultural future of the Church, especially in America. Since 1994 I have been teaching as our Marquette introduction to theology the *Catechism of the Catholic Church*. I have been surprised how positively the Marquette freshmen and sophomores have received this catechism. They truly find it a refreshing new and clear presentation of what Catholicism has taught for some 2000 years. Even Protestants and a Buddhist student went out of their way to say how much they liked the catechism.

However, the honeymoon ended when we reached the sixth commandment, when the students looked on me as if I was from some other planet. No matter what I said to explain the church's teaching on sex, the students were too brainwashed since their grade school sex education to even comprehend what I was saying.

Finally, I gave them an outline of a talk by Marquette University journalism teacher Dr. William Thorn on "Boomers and Generation X," which cleverly contrasted what it was like for the students' Boomer parents growing up, and what it was like for their Generation X growing up. They responded enthusiastically to the handout, and were clearly touched by the contrast between their parents growing up in relatively stable two-parent families, with no day care or latch key kids, virtually no teenage suicide, much less sexual abuse, violence, etc. I pointed out that one of the most telling differences between the raising of the two generations was the sexual revolution.

I challenged them, "If you like the suffering you've gone through, so much of which is caused by family breakdown and the sexual revolution, then 'Hooray for the Sexual Revolution.' But if you don't like what has happened to you and/or your age group, then maybe the Church has something worth learning to teach you about the meaning of sex and marriage and family." Finally, they showed more willingness to listen to the catechism's teachings on sex. And many of them tried to adjust their own ways of living as a consequence.

One other hopeful sign for me of a countercultural phase for the Church in America are the new kinds and numbers of vocations that we are getting to the priesthood and religious life. I refer especially to the Feb. 28, 1998, *America* article, "A View of Religious Vocations," by Albert DiIanni, and the April letter by Richard Hermes, S.J., in response to it. The main point of the article was: those religious orders that are recovering their classic purposes and spiritualities are starting to get many strong vocations. Those that continue in their progressive ways so that they are not very distinguishable from the culture around them are dying out for lack of vocations. This confirms my personal experience as a university teacher: I know personally some eight to a dozen young seminarians and priests from Marquette or Milwaukee who are studying or functioning as priests, but all for other dioceses or orders because they did not want to be subjected to a "progressive" seminary. There was an initial flood of angry hate mail against this article, but then came an April response to these negative letters from then seminarian Richard Hermes, S.J., "From the 'Younger' Generation." He observed that it is true that most seminarians and young religious of the past fifteen years are more "conservative" than the previous generation, and he noted four manifestations of the "new" conservativism:

1. *Prayer.* It is true that many new seminarians do value the rosary and adoration of the Blessed Sacrament (a point of criticism in the negative mail), but do not these have sanctifying effects?

2. *Liturgy.* Many seminarians dispute the informality and frequent abuses of liturgy to which they are subjected (improper liturgical garments, unauthorized changes, etc.). They want to retrieve the authentic aims of the liturgical movement, along with a healthy fidelity to authoritative liturgical directives of the last forty years.

3. *Garb.* The new seminarians' increased willingness to wear clerical garb or religious habit is not only from obedience to universal church law and the clear will of the pope, but from their personal desire to give tangible witness "to who we are" and to refuse to further the disappearance of our states of life by our individual disappearance into the anonymity of secular society.

4. *Theology.* Consider the controversial teachings which are much more likely to be embraced by a 30-year-old priest than a 60-year-old: that women are not called to orders, that marriage is permanent, that intentional sterilization of the marriage act is not God's will, that celibacy is an indispensable element of Catholic understanding of priesthood, that homosexual activity is not part of a virtuous life, and that it is a grave moral offense to destroy a human being in its mother's womb. Belief in these teachings is hardly reducible to the tired charges of "fundamentalism" and "traditionalism." At the very least they are the common faith and practice of the Church across many centuries; even now they continue to have wide theological support, and they have been reiterated against the academic established guild of dissent by Church authorities who have God's mandate to interpret Christ's will and to bind consciences.

The seminarian notes that even if there have been excesses in this desire of young seminarians and religious to recover lost riches of Catholic faith, many of these efforts were undertaken in good faith, with little local guidance and sometimes in the face of hostile opposition from those training the seminarians and religious.

In an April 1998 conference to the priests (and Archbishop Chaput) of Denver, I passed out three handouts to describe human aspirations that we face as we enter the third millennium: "The Wounded Generation," by Vicky Thorn, founder of Project Rachel for women who have had abortions; "Boomers and Generation X," by William Thorn, her husband, chair of Journalism at Marquette University; and the *America* article: "A View of Religious Vocations" by Albert DiIanni, former superior general and current vocation director of the Boston Province of the Marists. After two generations who did not receive solid catechesis, there is a growing hunger in the young (and the dissatisfied of all ages) for solid and clear Catholic teachings, for straightforward direction in how to live one's life, for unambiguous distinctions between right and wrong behaviors, for an end to the relativistic confusion rampant in so many parishes. At Marquette University we've gathered some 100-350 students from groups like Marquette Students for Life, Knights of Columbus, Catholic Outreach, and the Cardinal Bellarmine Society who want Marquette to become more classically Catholic. They are forming a new group, a kind of unofficial chapter of the Newman Society, dedicated to fostering the implementation of *Ex corde ecclesiae* on Marquette's campus.

Therefore, in response to Martin's question, "Is anyone listening?" I find reasons for hope that the future generations will be more open than the Boomers were to the counter-cultural message of Pope John Paul II. I do believe that the future lies with these new desires and hopes for restored and renewed Catholicism, and not with the tired mantras of political correctness from the dissenting and greying Boomers.

The Distant Country of John Paul II

Raymond Gawronski, S.J.

In 1968 I made my first trip to Poland. At the Czech border, a red-nosed grandmother, in trenchcoat, came and asked: "Are you from America?" "Yes." And, suddenly, she began weeping: "God bless your ancestors who went there. This land is soaked in blood. Welcome."

In 1977, the summer I entered the Society of Jesus, before anyone dreamed of a Polish pope, my mother and I went into Manhattan for a talk at a café. A survivor of World War II in Poland, she said: "I survived the Soviets and the Nazis. Growing up in the Sixties in America, you had a harder time than I had in Europe. Because in this country you forgot the difference between good and bad, and we always remembered that."

At one of the Thornfield Conferences in my grad school days at Syracuse University, the faculty and graduate students did an exercise: Imagine you are in heaven. What is it like? Angels, lights, music. Mercifully, Michael Novak was the guest directing the session. He understood my vision of Heaven, for after all the visions that seemed so sterile to me, my vision was bathed in blood. He said, "You said that because you're Polish." He knew some history.

"The Polands of the Pope," a phrase created by George Hunston Williams in his intellectual biography of the pope, suggests the very fluid nature of this nation and culture, and of the states in which Karol Wojtyla was formed. Looking at Polish history, at least, one sees, if not a circle, at least a gyre, a turning back on themes which have been present from the start of the nation's experience and which keep coming back in one form or another.

Eighty years of history have transpired in this lifetime; Poland's frontiers have been drawn and redrawn, the whole country has shifted 150 miles west of what it was when Karol was born. Born at the same time the Polish state was reborn, he was raised in the Second Republic, saw the fourth partition of Poland between Nazis and Soviets, came to manhood in Nazi German occupied Poland, served most of his priestly life in that western remnant of historical Poland which emerged from the War as a Soviet colony, and has since become the key player in bringing down the Soviet Empire. Now he has been facing a new Polish republic, with a new cultural invasion, this time from the secularized, wealthy West.

What is this nation from which Karol was called? Before we can understand what the twentieth century meant, we must spend some time looking at the millennium of history which led up to it.

One often hears the pope referred to as a man "from the East." Of course, this is true in a way—Poland is east of Germany, to be sure. But so is much of Sweden. Poland has been a country at the borders for all its existence: it is located at a crossroads. Situated in the middle of the North European plain, with no natural boundaries on the east or west, geography has been unusually determinative in the Polish experience. West are the Germans; East, the Russians, and through their lands, the Mongols. South are the Czechs, Slovaks and Austrians and Hungarians. Southeast are the Ukrainians and, beyond them historically, the Turks and Armenians. North, Denmark and Sweden. Northeast, the Baltic peoples of today and those who in some part became the Prussians.

Culturally, the Poles had most exposure to western Christianity, though the eastern borderlands are precisely the border with the cultural sphere of Byzantium. All along the eastern borders, Poles (and Lithuanians) represent Roman Catholicism; their neighbors, the Ukrainians and White Russians, Greek Christianity, Catholic and Orthodox. There might have been some question at the very start as to whether Latin or Greek Christianity would be dominant in Poland, but the question was settled by the baptism of the country into Roman Catholicism in 966.

Culturally the Poles are passionate defenders of all things Western, though history—Yalta and other betrayals—has left a residue of suspicion among many, and a sense of being somehow excluded from the European community as well. I have heard them call themselves the "French who live on the Vistula." They have been styled the "bulwark of Christendom"—the "antemurale"—against the Turk, the Russian. Curiously enough, perhaps the single greatest cultural influence on Poland was Renaissance Italy.

To develop their own culture, on a plain with stronger neighbors, the Poles have had to develop keen orneriness. They are notoriously stubborn—witness Jesuit Walter Ciszek. First, to keep out German hegemony, political and economic. Second, to keep out Russian "soul" penetration. The Germans were different:

radically different from all the Slavs. The Russians were in fact fellow Slavs, however much each was influenced by other groups historically. The languages could be close, the ways of thinking related—but the adoption of different cultural paths from the very start ensured that all the differences between Rome and Greece would be continued and, in fact, highlighted in the northern forests.

Although the borders of Poland have varied wildly over the millennium since the baptism of Duke Mieszko in 966, the borders as they are today roughly approximate the territory of the Polanie at the end of the first millennium.

The Czech lands were really the first Christianized of the western Slavs, through the missionary efforts of Cyril and Methodius, in the ninth century. There was a considerable Moravian kingdom, including southern Poland (=Krakow). The form of Christianity at very first, thus, was Byzantine. The mission there, however, lasted less than a century before the more powerful German bishops to the west managed to squelch the Byzantine mission and proceed to incorporate the Czech lands into the Roman Church. The Czech struggle with German domination continued into the twentieth century, finding Polish ecclesial support for Jan Hus at the Council of Constance. Brother peoples at the dawn of their Christianization, the Czechs and the Poles had very different experiences of Germanization. The Czechs were eventually overwhelmed by the Germans and were integrated into their empire. Prague would become a masterpiece of German urban culture in a Slavic neighborhood, Czechs living in uneasy relation with the Germans, yet being profoundly influenced by them.

The Poles early saw the threat to their identity which the expanding German Empire—"Drang nach Osten"—presented. Their Slavic neighbors to the West—everything east of the Elbe was Slavic at one time, Berlin itself a Slavic place name—were being incorporated/destroyed by the German advance. So though entering into relations with the German emperor, religiously, the Poles placed their nation directly under the pope, under Rome.

To the east, Kiev at the end of the first millennium was emerging as a tremendous cultural center, a Byzantium of the Slavic lands. It would grow and expand for 250 years, its cultural reach extending as far north as Vilno in Lithuania, one of its princesses marrying into the French royal house—until the Mongol invasions of the early thirteenth century, when all that moved was killed by the Mongol Horde. Decades after the Mongol Horde had come through Ukraine in its way to raid Poland and Central Europe, a Franciscan traveler on his way to the Khan observed that all that was left around Kiev were heaps of bones. So, to the east, the lands of Rus, the eastern Slavs, first experienced a great development, and then a cataclysmic destruction from which they never really recovered. They became depopulated, most of the lands being suzerain to the Mongol Khan. Gradually, a new center for the eastern Slavs would emerge, far to the north of the steppes and it would become Moscow. But that would take some 300 years, during which time Poland herself expanded into the lands of Rus and was the great power in the region. Ukraine was under Polish rule for centuries.

Poland herself was attacked and badly devastated by the Mongols. But unlike the Russian lands, the Mongols drew back—in fact, they never occupied Poland, but rather had devastating raids which left the countryside depopulated. The famous trumpeter of Krakow, a tradition of eight centuries, recalls those times. Into these depopulated lands, the kings invited settlers from the West, that is, German settlers, who were allowed to have their own law. The city of Krakow and other cities developed as centers of German burghers (who gradually became polonized). A pattern began here, however, that hardened and that the Poles would never fully overcome: the indigenous people were landowners and rulers, peasants and clergy; the craftsmen, guildsmen, townspeople in general, were a foreign element, immigrating from the West. At first German, eventually largely Jewish. There emerged five main estates which became virtual castes which exist to some extent even to this day in Polish society: nobility—magnates and gentry/*szlachta*—clergy, burghers, peasants, Jews.

With the destruction of Kiev and the stabilization of a monarchy in Poland, and also under ongoing pressure from the German west, the Polish state began to develop rapidly toward the east. Whole families moved from traditional southern and western Poland to the north and east. St. Andrew Bobola's family were of these transplants. So it was with many Poles throughout their history. To the east, lie two main groups of people. The largest by far were the "Ruthenians," or "little Russians," the ancestors of today's Ukrainians and White Russians (Byelorussians). To their north were the Baltic peoples, viz., the Lithuanians who, after the downfall of Kiev, had filled the vacuum and taken over leadership of those Slavic regions, until it was all called "Lithuania," stretching from "sea to sea," that is, the Baltic to the Black. But whereas the eastern Slavs were Christian, the Lithuanians remained pagan for centuries, along with their neighbors to their west, the Prussians.

A tribe of Baltic peoples, the Prussians were warlike and troublesome to the Poles to the south. So the Polish Duke of Mazovia in the thirteenth century had invited a military monastic order in to watch their northern borders. This order, which had fought in the Crusades and then served in Hungary, became the ancestors of the Teutonic Knights, which, secularized, became the foundation of the Prussian state. They and others received a mandate from the pope for the so-called "Northern Crusade"—to baptize or exterminate these pagan tribes along the Baltic Coast. Brought in by the Polish Crown, they gradually became so powerful as to threaten the Polish state itself—and they were making forays into Lithuania to the east. In 1410, the Lithuanians allied themselves with the Poles and, along with units from all the east, Russian as well as Mongol, they fought the Teutonic Knights representing all the Germanic west at Grünwald (Tannenberg). The Westerners were shocked to find pagan Lithuanians and Muslim Tartars fighting alongside the Catholic Poles and ever since saw Poland as a pagan country. Hitler would make much of this in his propaganda, and not long ago it showed up in the pages of *The Wanderer*. Seemingly invincible, the Teutonic Knights lost on the field that day, a stunning defeat. For the next two hundred years, the Polish-Lithuanian Commonwealth went from glory to glory. Jagiello, head of the Lithuanian nation, became a Roman Catholic and was crowned king of Poland. Poland and Lithuania became a commonwealth, like England and Scotland, united at first by a personal dynastic union which subsequently became constitutional.

The fifteenth and sixteenth centuries were centuries of glory. The Polish Lithuanian Commonwealth was the largest country in Europe. The granary of the Ukraine was part of this country. Polish lords owned vast estates in Ukraine and wrote notable works of things like Latin poetry. The poet Sarbiewski was studied throughout the world as a "Polish Horace," while the Jesuit Lencicius Leczyski wrote noted theological tracts. The dark side of this was the lot of the Ukrainian peasantry. Not Roman Catholic like the recently converted Lithuanians, they were Greek in religion, and so could not be readily integrated into the western Polish state. They were treated ever more poorly from the start; their bishops—if Orthodox—refused membership in the Polish senate.

One other note at this time. At the time of King Kazimierz the Great (who favored a famous Jewish mistress, Esther) the Jews were given official status and invited into Poland, fleeing savage persecution in many of the countries of Western Europe. Poland became for centuries a haven for the Jews. The Krakow rabbi Moses Isserles "Remuh" wrote in the sixteenth century: "It is better to live on dry bread, but in peace, in Poland,"[1] a comment both on Polish toleration as well as on the notorious "polnische Wirtschaft." With legal protection, in the service of the king and the magnates, the Jews became the financiers of the Polish aristocracy, especially in the eastern lands, the Ukrainian wheat lands. The Jewish population would continue to grow rapidly, until by end of the nineteenth century and the great exodus to the United States, 80% of the Jews of the world lived in Poland. Poland became the second Jewish homeland, with more Jews living longer in that country than anywhere else on earth except Palestine. By 1939 there were 3.35 million Jews in Poland. They made up 40% of the populations of Warsaw and Vilno, and large majorities especially in eastern provincial capitals.

At the time of the Reformation, the Lithuanian nobility especially went over to Calvinism. Lutheranism, associated with the Germans, never made serious inroads among ethnic Poles. But Protestantism in its Calvinist (and Unitarian forms) made such inroads into Poland that for awhile it seemed the whole nation might become Protestant—that is, the gentry, for the common people remained faithful Catholics. Then came the Society of Jesus. There is probably no country in Europe in which the Jesuits had greater influence than in Poland (with the possible exception of Spain). Famous court preacher Piotr Skarga—a Polish Canisius— preached up a storm to an aristocracy whose greed and selfishness were plunging the country into ruin. The Jesuits, with their many colleges, especially in the east, most notable of which was the Vilno Academy (1564), which became the University of Vilno, brought the country about, and she returned firmly to the Catholic fold. But along with this, critics maintain, there was no development of a "Protestant ethic," a rising Polish burgher class didn't develop. Poland remained exceptionally tolerant religiously. Religious persecution was virtually unknown, the absence of burnings of heretics and of witches prompting one author to call it "the State without stakes." Something of the multi-religious character of the traditional Polish commonwealth is shown by the following figures: in 1791, Roman Catholics were only 54% of the state. In the Second Republic, in 1931, Roman Catholics made up 65%. In 1946, they were 97.6%. Each group followed its own laws and ways, German Lutheran, Jewish, Armenian. Emerging from the Counter-Reformation, the Church became an ever stronger force: the cardinal primate served as "interrex," heading both church and state while a new king was being elected.

As the German nation in large part left the world of Latin culture, Poland thus became an island of that culture in between a Teutonic Christianity cut off from the Mediterranean "catholica" and the Russian Orthodox east. The centuries after the Renaissance were a Golden Age for Poland, a time when Western European culture poured into Poland, while Polish students continued to study abroad. Krakow itself became a noted seat of learning: its Jagiellonian University, founded in 1364 where Pope John Paul II studied, is the school where the original Faust studied as well. While Western Europe was having savage wars of religion, Poland was noted as a place of tremendous tolerance. The Jesuit Jakub Wojek translated the entire Bible into Polish in the sixteenth century.

At the beginning of the seventeenth century, Poland was at its peak. In 1648, the king crowned the Virgin Mary as Queen of Poland, in the city of Lvov, a Polish city in the Ukrainian countryside. The Jesuits had established dozens of colleges throughout the country, most notably in the east as outposts of Latin civilization. One note: perhaps because of the Society the Polish crown had an extremely idealistic vision of peace, concord and freedom in government—and this at a time when Ivan the Terrible was helping articulate the Russian way of governing. Subsequent historians have at times blamed the Society for many, if not all, of Poland's troubles in the world of Realpolitik.

Then disaster struck, a disaster from which Poland never recovered. One might call it a "slave rebellion" combined with a devastating invasion. Ukrainian peasants in the east rose under the leadership of Bohdan Chmielnicki. Their banner read: "Death to all Poles, Jews and Jesuits." It was an extremely bloody uprising: it is said that this was the worst massacre in Jewish history before the Holocaust. Poles suffered as well and never fully recovered their hegemony in the East. Gradually, Kiev became the center of a new Ukraine, but this time, not under Poland but under Moscow. Russia, the emerging champion of Orthodoxy, gained a "breadbasket" even as Poland lost hers, and the Ukrainian dream of independence would be buried again for centuries.

All this while, it should be added, in the southern Ukraine, the Poles had been fighting a long history of border wars with the Turks. This reached its peak when in 1683 King John Sobieski with a Polish army came to the rescue of Vienna as that city was threatened with Turkish takeover.

At the time of the Ukrainian troubles, there came a new disaster from the north—an avalanche in the form of the Swedes who were involved in various wars in Europe. This mid-seventeenth century period is called "the Deluge" in Polish literature. Poland had been becoming a Baltic power: the grain from Ukraine and the timber from the forests all passed through the Hanseatic city of Danzig, which was under the Polish crown. Now, Poland, depleted by the wars in Ukraine and with the Turks, collapsed before the Swedish invader. Something of the Viking must have remained in the Swedes, for I have read that no invasion, including that of Hitler, did as much damage as the Swedes. It was only at a town called Czestochowa where the invading Swedes were repulsed, after the miraculous image of Our Lady was brought out and rallied the people. The Poles recovered their strength and expelled the invader. This would not be the last miracle in Polish history.

In the eighteenth century, after these wars and invasions, Poland fell into a long decline under a Saxon dynasty. There were three neighbors whose stars were rising: Moscow, Prussia and Austria. Internally, the Poles during their golden age had also enjoyed a "golden freedom." Their gentry, a significant proportion of the population, had veto power at the meetings of the Parliament, the Sejm, the famous "liberum veto." That is, consensus was required for all decisions, something echoed in the Slavophiles' concept of "sobornost" and something strongly present, one suspects, in John Paul's cultural background. In an ideal world, that could work; but Poland did not live in an ideal world. First of all, as the Jesuit preacher Piotr Skarga never ceased haranguing his congregations, rule demands great discipline, a real asceticism, and the aristocracy was soft and not at all prepared to think of the common good. Perhaps more importantly, however, was the rise of those powerful neighbors, with strong centralized governments and absolutism. The Muscovites had learned some pretty strong lessons from their centuries under the Mongols. The Prussians were developing an explicitly spartan state.

So while the Poles wrote Latin verses on their eastern estates and developed an ever more refined culture, proud and jealous of their freedoms, powerful and aggressive forces with no interest in and less sympathy for Catholic and humanistic culture were rising to east and west. And Catholic Austria would aid and abet these powerful neighbors when the time finally came to dismember Poland.

It has been observed that this was the first time in history that Christian states dismembered another Christian state. In three successive partitions beginning in the late eighteenth century and completed by 1795, Poland disappeared from the map of Europe. The lion's share went to Russia who took all the eastern lands culturally "colonized" by the Poles over the preceding 500 years. Most of the original Poland was incorporated into Prussia, while the southern slice became the provinces of Galicia and Silesia in Austria.

By 1800 Poland had ceased to exist as a state—a combination of poor administration and government along with aggressive neighbors—a hard school, providing lessons for over a century of self-reflection. Anglo-Saxons often smile at the Italians who have tended frequently to change governments and at times to live entirely without one: the Poles also learned to be a nation independent of a state. Literature, especially poetry, played a leading role in arousing and keeping the sense of nationhood alive, as it did in Ireland as well.

It was in the Austrian part of divided Poland that John Paul II was born. The administration there was relatively mild, and Polish culture flourished in Krakow. Indeed, to this day Austria is affectionately referred to as "Babcia Austria"— "Grandma Austria." Galicia was an extremely poor province even on global terms: but it was rich intellectually. Krakow became a Hapsburg city, an overnight train ride from Vienna.

The administration of this part of Poland was more benign than that of either Prussia or Russia. In the Russian part, there were serious and bloody uprisings throughout the nineteenth century. Poles became known as great freedom fighters in that century. No less a prophet of freedom than Friedrich Nietzsche sought to disassociate himself from the German nation, which he saw as docile followers, and he created an image for himself of Polish ancestors, a noble, freedom-loving people. The Polish opposition to absolute monarchy drew the fire of the nineteenth-century papacy. In light of this and other factors, though loyal to Rome, the Polish Church experience has hardly been unambiguously pro-Roman.

In Galicia, the Austrian part, the Poles were given far greater freedom than in either of the other partitioned parts of Poland. The Russians eventually closed the universities of Warsaw and Vilna, and both Prussians and Russians attempted to destroy Polish language and culture. This did not happen in the Austrian part, in which Poles were part of a Central European Empire. One thinks of Dr. Krakowski in Mann's *Magic Mountain*. And the Austrian Poles had a much more easy-going temperament and style from the fiery, vodka-drinking Poles of Russian Poland— their music influenced waltzes, and the "oompah" tempers the ferocity of the more northern parts of the country. It is largely from this Austrian part of Poland that the ancestors of most American Poles came, hence the identification with a sort of oompah, polka band Central European culture.

The aristocratic Polish culture had survived the political transitions. In the capitals of the occupying powers, the most elegant dances of the courts were long the polonaise and the mazurka. This period saw some Poles gain great fame, mostly abroad. Marie Sklodowska Curie won the Nobel Prize, as did Henryk Sienkiewicz. Joseph Korzeniowski Conrad made his contribution abroad, and in another language.

The trenches of World War I dug deeply into Galicia, the Austrian part of Poland. In general, the Poles did not mourn the passing of the monarchies. The Polish state was recreated—"A Nation Once Again," or rather, the nation had a state once again. It was in this world of reborn Poland that the Holy Father was born and raised, his father having been an officer in the Austrian army. It was a world at once poor materially but very rich in hope.

The pope belongs to a generation of Poles more unusual than most. For the 120 years in which the Polish state disappeared from the map of Europe, the Polish nation passed through a crucible in which their identity was forged. For that century, Poland was an idea rather than a reality.

The nineteenth century, the nadir of her historical existence at least as a state, was likely the most glorious time of her specifically national culture. It is as if the entire nation were preparing itself for its rebirth as a state. That is, the Church, the intelligentsia, and, perhaps most importantly, the mothers of the nation were forming a leadership to be ready to learn from the experiences of the past in the day when the purified sense of nationhood could be reunited with the existence of an independent state. This time saw the emergence of Poland's answer to Russian Slavophilism—her Messianism: the notion that Poland was the "Christ of the nations." This tendency, which came to dominate Polish literature in the nineteenth century, had a rather anti-Catholic flavor, and was opposed by the poet Cyprian Norwid, a favorite of the pope's. However, the phrase the "Slavic Pope," the brother of the common people, which comes from this time and this movement, has been embraced by the pope and claimed as his own.

The interwar generation of Poles was unique, both in their confident and energetic hope for their nation, and in the tremendous tragedies which awaited them. When the war broke out, it was a firestorm of racial hatred unleashed against the peoples of Eastern Europe. Jews first and foremost, of course, but Slavs, and especially Poles were slated for ultimate destruction. Hitler said that "all Poles will disappear from the world": one week before the invasion he gave the Wehrmacht the instructions to "Kill without pity or mercy all men, women and children of Polish descent or language. . . . Be merciless. Be brutal. It is necessary to proceed with maximum severity. The war is to be a war of annihilation."

Two months after the Nazi occupation, the professors of the Jagiellonian University were sent to the concentration camp at Sachsenhausen. Auschwitz was first used as a concentration camp for Polish intelligentsia, before the Final Solution was enforced on the Jews. Polish intellectuals and clergy were to be exterminated as potential leaders in a race slated for slavery and eventual extermination by the master race to the West. The pope survived these years, working as a laborer to avoid deportation, studying in an underground seminary.

The wartime occupation of Poland was a two-pronged affair. Poland was invaded by Germany on September 1, 1939, and by the Soviet Union on September 17. Poland suffered a new partition between these two. The Soviets annexed all of eastern Poland outright, and to this day, what had been eastern Poland is distributed among three former Soviet republics. What became the Poland of today was divided in two ways by the Germans. Much of it was simply annexed to the German Reich, where the inhabitants either were "Germanized" or killed or expelled in massive ethnic cleansing. Racial laws applied even in church, where Poles had to receive communion after Germans.

There remained a rump Poland, called the "Generalgouvernmenet." This was headed by the notorious Hans Frank, headquartered in Krakow. It was in this part that the pope lived. The Poles in the German lands were slated for destruction as a nation, to make "living space" for the German race. They were to be slave laborers for one generation, until they died. Terror was applied to the population on a massive scale. Wholesale roundups of people coming out of church or out of theaters were common—roundups in which those unable to show proof of gainful employment in the German war effort were sent to Germany for forced labor. In fact, the plan was to destroy all the leadership of the nation, and to leave a herd of slaves. At war's end, four bishops and 2,000 priests had died in German camps, while a total of 3,600 priests and 1,100 sisters were imprisoned in these camps.

The Russians engaged in this destruction of the leadership as well, slaughtering the entire captured Polish officer corps at a place called Katyn, deporting millions of Poles from Eastern Poland to slave labor and death in the Gulag. Meanwhile, in the German sector, Poland was the one state in Europe in which no colloborating government could be found, the only state in which the simplest sympathetic contact with a Jew meant the death penalty for a Polish Gentile and his family.

There were two parallel holocausts in Poland during the Second World War. The Holocaust of the Jews in Nazi-occupied Poland is well documented. What is less known is that three million Polish Gentiles also died during the same war. Tensions had been growing between the Polish and Jewish communities since they took increasingly divergent attitudes towards the partitioning authorities in the nineteenth century. With the creation of a Polish state after World War I, communal tensions increased, especially as most Jews in Poland were not assimilated into Polish culture and as Poles attempted to find a place in modern urban life. These tensions were exacerbated by the heavy involvement of Jews in the Polish Communist Party and its organs both before and after the War, especially during the Stalinist period. In eastern and postwar Poland, Polish Jews came to be largely identified with the occupying Soviet Union. This tragic struggle which increasingly divided two stateless peoples who for long had lived side by side was perhaps best summarized by the historian who observed that the experience of World War II demonstrated that it is impossible for two "chosen peoples" to walk through the same desert at the same time. Yet underneath the mutual bitterness of recent times lay an interwoven history of many centuries.

Many of the pope's Polish countrymen fought along with the Allies—"for our freedom and yours" was their motto. Yet when the war ended, those Allies signed Poland over to yet another occupation, this time at the hands of Stalin, an occupation which has only recently ended. It has been calculated that the Nazis had destroyed everything created in Poland since the late eighteenth century, 38 percent of the nation's wealth. With no Marshall Plan, Poland became a Soviet colony. Playing on the recent experience of genocide, the rulers in Moscow found sympathetic hearers in Poland, where much of the post-war country consisted of formerly German lands, and where fear of the Germans returning could be played upon to keep people in Moscow's embrace. The Polish hierarchy infuriated the Communist authorities, when, Wojtyla taking the lead, they celebrated a public ceremony of reconciliation with the German hierarchy in the mid-sixties. This included a statement of mutual forgiveness, the Polish Church repenting for atrocities committed against Germans during the expulsion and resettlements at war's end. It would seem that his contacts with the German-speaking world would largely pave the way for his eventual accesion to the papal throne.

Having learned how to survive throughout the nineteenth century, Polish culture did not cease, but went underground, its survival centering on the home and on the church. I remember my father—himself born in Massachusetts—insisting we speak Polish at home, using the hallowed phrase "to jest polski dom," this is a Polish home. The only Catholic University from the Elbe to the Pacific was founded in Lublin, where the pope would become a professor of philosophy. Polish intellectuals were able to maintain contacts with their peers in the West, continuing the intellectual tradition of centuries. Philosophy especially became a Polish specialty.

And, in the first massive move of public defiance of the Marxist overlords, Cardinal Wyszynski, heir of the tradition of the cardinal as "interrex" created a pilgrimage of the image of Our Lady of Czestochowa which was carried in procession throughout Poland. This reached its peak in the celebration of the millennium of Christianity in 1966. The Poles had learned defiance to Prussian and Russian autocracy and militarism throughout the nineteenth century: this was only reinforced in the twentieth, when ideology was added to the armament of these crushingly depersonalizing systems. Now, tempered by the bloody uprisings of the nineteenth century, a new form of resistance emerged, culminating in Solidarity. Freedom, responsibility, solidarity—all key notions for the pope.

Polish culture was not just high culture, of course—Renaissance Italy, French manners. More than the West, Poland remained an agricultural country for a long time. People's ties with nature were strong. Slavs are noted for their rich emotional lives. Listen to the music of Chopin. No coincidence, then, that the pope is a published poet and playwright as well as scholar. Close families were very warm: westerners have remarked to me how much Poles hold their babies. And a closeness to the earth, especially to wilderness, pervaded Polish life. On holidays, everyone would go mushroom or berry picking in the forest. Nobel prize winning poet Czeslaw Milosz sees this closeness to nature as something that distinguishes eastern from western European: stranded as a young student in Switzerland, he sought refuge in a forest, rather than wiring home for money as a westerner might have done. And so we see pictures of the Holy Father skiing or hiking through forests.

I think the Polish pope has brought a unique perspective to the Church, one clearly chosen by the Holy Spirit. If Auschwitz has become a main symbol of the twentieth century, it surely means something that Auschwitz was located in what would become the archdiocese of Cardinal Wojtyla. The Poles were the one large Catholic people of Europe whose country was untouched by the Roman Empire, and yet, Poles adored Latin culture—Polish gentlemen were writing Latin poetry on their estates on the steppes well into the modern era. For all that, the Poles had to fight long and hard for their own language and culture, and liturgically they were delighted to use the vernacular. As the Polish pope, then, as the Slavic pope, he is the first since Peter to point the way to other centers of culture than that of the western edges of Europe. Though oh-so-close to Vienna, Krakow speaks a language sister to that of Moscow, closer cousin to that of Delhi or Teheran than that of Vienna. Trained in suffering as a defeated minority people, having seen two colossal imperial systems rise, slaughter, and collapse, the pope has the unique perspective of an eternal outsider who yet belongs, not unlike a black person in the U.S. His strength comes from his faith in God, a God who has preserved His People through the fires, and has created saints before the pope's very eyes; his strength comes from the Mother of God, mother, and so warm and tender, Virgin, and Queen. He is an intellectual of international repute on his own merits, yet a man who has known the villages of Poland, and so is at home with the village people of Africa or Mexico or Pacific islands.

The Polish Church, though disciplined and demanding, has lived in a pluralistic context for centuries. If its history has been less than perfect, it is still radically different from the history of other Catholic countries like Spain because of this pluralism and relatively great tolerance. One instance of this pluralism is striking. There developed in Poland, at the turn of the century, a breakaway movement from the Church called the Mariavites. Numbering 200,000 by 1909, this group began ordaining nuns in 1929—imagine any Western Catholic country at that period experiencing anything of the sort and you will have some sense of the surprising richness of the pope's Polish experience.

As a new millennium begins, Poland finds herself at the heart of Europe, and her chief son speaks from that heart to the world, breaking through that European racism from which his people had suffered in his own lifetime, yet taking the best of that European tradition along, into a Church which is breaking beyond the confines of the Roman Empire. He knows the West, then, very well: but he clearly knows the dark as well as the light sides. In his youth, the men who proclaimed themselves the most advanced in the West, and whose claim was backed up by technical superiority, proceeded to incinerate millions of Jewish human beings, and declared his own people "subhuman": he is not going to stand aside for those most technically advanced who now claim that the baby in its mother's womb is not a human being.

The post-Vatican II Church is moving on from its First World, West European ghetto. And now the flower of the nation that links Europe's proud western Christians with her oft humiliated eastern children has become visible head of the Church. The pope himself has used the image of a Russian writer, who describes the Church as having two lungs, the East and the West: one of his great strengths as Polish pope is to be the first pope in a millennium to be able to breathe with those two lungs.

During my studies in Rome in the late 1980s and early 90s, poor emigrants from the pope's beloved homeland washed car windows at stop lights outside the papal apartments. Given God's preferential option for the poor, what better choice for pope than a Pole, than this brother to windshield-washing refugees, to world-shaking trade unionists, professor, poet and priest.

NOTES

1. Quoted in Norman Davies, *God's Playground*, vol. 2, p. 240.

A Critical Reading of Pope John Paul II on Culture

John C. Haughey, S.J.

I. THE PHILOSOPHER

Karol Wojtyla was a philosopher before he became pope. He had already fine-tuned his ideas about the central category and starting point of philosophy: for him, personal subjectivity. He thinks from the categories of philosophical anthropology. By starting with personal subjectivity, he refuses to get mired in the epistemological mazeways of what is objective and what is subjective or rather the extreme "isms" of each of these two positions. Although deeply indebted to Thomas Aquinas, he expressed dislike for an anthropology based on Aristotelian Thomism, that is, seeing man primarily as rational animal and focusing analysis of the human on human nature. Nor does he choose consciousness as central to his anthropology. All three of these approaches—an animal which is rational, a nature that is human, and a capacity for consciousness—use a part to analyze the whole which is the personal subject fully grasped in acting.

His is an "I-act" anthropology. In his or her acts the person comes to self-possession through self-determination. Self-consciousness and self-transcendence happen in our acts. Personal actors act in a real world and act in relationship to that world and to those who are in it. Their experience of positing actions in the real world enables them to know what objectivity is. In every act, furthermore, there is co-given with it, the experience of the self. As a self-conscious, self-determining cause of the acts I do, I come to understand what responsibility is and what is entailed in being responsible for my actions.[1]

Willing is even more central and exhaustively personal in his anthropology than knowing. Intellect takes in the whole scene, but it is will, acting on what the intellect has seen, which shapes and individuates the person because it is the will that determines this act or that. It is our will-determined acts that make us subjects among objects amid other subjects. By my acts I shape my existence and become a subject. My personhood can be found in the continuity of my discrete acts. To act is essentially to interact with the world around me. An act functions as a synthesis of the subjective and objective, the individual and the social, the immanent and the transcendent. We do not experience something external to us without experiencing ourselves experiencing it.

Human acts are acts of self-possession. In commenting on John Paul II's anthropology, Cardinal George notes: "Without self-possession, the person is less than human; his or her truth and dignity are destroyed at the root, even if a superficial array of choices remains open."[2] George continues in his rendering of Wojtyla's anthropology-turned-ethics: "The process of bringing personal subjectivity to objective self-knowledge and to full subjective self-consciousness involves knowing the objective truth, acting freely and rightly in surrender to it, and thus coming to self-awareness as a particular person in a community. . . ."[3] All human acts are intrinsically moral/immoral. Anthropology cannot be independent of ethics. If we do not see how acts make us who we are, we will not understand cultures which we create by our acts. Clearly this is the position of a philosophical anthropologist whose personal spirituality, moral convictions, and faith are very much part of the mix. Empirical anthropologist he is not, it should be obvious at this point.

II. THE CONTINUUM

When Wojtyla becomes Pope John Paul II, he continues to think in terms of personal subjectivity as his central category. In his first encyclical (*Redemptor hominis*, 1979), he writes: "The human person is the primary route that the Church must travel in fulfilling her mission. . . . This and this alone is the principle which inspires the Church's social doctrine" (n. 53). He continues with this hermeneutic although the social phenomenon of cultures becomes his favorite topic. For example, twelve years later in *Centesimus annus* (1991) he still insists that "at the heart of every culture lies the attitude a person takes to the greatest mystery, the mystery of God. Different cultures are basically different ways of facing the question of the meaning of personal existence" (n. 24).

Further evidence that this hermeneutic is still operative comes from the pope's 1995 address before the General Assembly of the United Nations, where he calls for a renewed reverence for the transcendent dimension of our humanity expressed in every authentically human culture. Specifically, he calls for a liberating culture of solidarity gathered around a vision of our humanity that sees each person as "a creature of intelligence and free will, immersed in a mystery which transcends our own being and endowed with the ability to reflect and to choose—and thus capable of wisdom and virtue."[4] To this audience of every conceivable culture, creed, and moral conviction, he insists: "Whatever diminishes man—whatever shortens the horizon of man's aspiration to goodness—harms the cause of freedom. In order to recover our hope. . . . we must regain sight of that transcendent horizon of possibility to which the soul of man aspires" (n.16).

III. CULTURE

In 1982, three years into his pontificate, he created the Pontifical Council for Culture with two purposes: the evangelization of cultures and the defense of cultures. On that occasion he wrote: "Since the beginning of my pontificate, I have considered the church's dialogue with the cultures of our time to be a vital area, one in which the destiny of the world at the end of the twentieth century is at stake."[5]

Other papal speeches show this same inclination to understand culture through the optic of personal subjectivity. In his UNESCO address of June 2, 1980 (entitled "Man's Entire Humanity is Expressed in Culture"), the pope explains that "man is the subject of culture as well as its object and purpose or goal."[6] He notes that we express ourselves in culture and objectify ourselves in it. By our acts we make the culture which then has a life of its own, while at the same time the culture makes us who we are by the life we have given it by our acts. For John Paul II, a culture seems to be the aggregate of a group's acts of self-determination. It is a two-way street: we make the culture, which in turn makes us who we are. A culture embodies the best and the worst in the human spirit, and the human spirit is constantly addressed by what has been embodied.

He repeatedly stresses that faith and culture need each other. The Gospel is truth about our humanity and is creative of cultures. When faith and culture reinforce one another, they are in right relationship with each other. Wherever the truth of our humanity as the Gospel teaches it is suppressed, the culture will become anti-human, as John Paul II had personally experienced from totalitarianism's impact on Poland. The Gospel brings a vision of self-sacrifice and therefore of self-transcendence that any culture needs: "The future of man depends on culture. . . . We rediscover ourselves in the ground of culture, the fundamental reality which unites us."[7]

Only if a culture is saddled with an ideology that enslaves us and that uses us for a goal other than human flourishing should we cease to assist in building that culture and begin to critique it. Further, "a faith which does not become culture is a faith that is not fully received, not entirely thought through, not faithfully lived."[8]

He distinguishes mass culture from traditional culture and the high culture of academic achievement and says that the faith must penetrate all three of these—in fact, all levels of experience. He begins to theologize culture with his insight that a culture is a "substratum waiting for the incarnation of Christianity."[9] If we are to become more human, the Gospel must permeate each of our cultures with its truth. Without it we are doomed to become less human. Further, the faith needs each culture to help us to know the full truth of Christ. Culture is that through which human beings become ever more human. The synthesis between the faith and culture makes culture more authentically human. The faith brings to culture the truth about our origins and our destiny. Each culture needs to be "healed, enabled, and perfected through Christ and the Gospel" (*RM*, n. 54).[10]

In general, we can locate John Paul II's great contribution to the faith/culture dyad better if we recall the few things that Vatican II said about them: that they need to be completed by faith (*LG*, nn.13, 17), perfected by faith (*GS*, nn. 53-62), and transformed by faith (*AG*, n.21), while we must respect each culture because it contains the *semina verbi* God has planted there (*LG*, n.11).

IV. INCULTURATION

Six months after *Redemptor hominis*, while writing his apostolic exhortation *Catechesi tradendae* (October 16, 1979), John Paul II used the word "inculturation": "Inculturation is the process whereby the faith becomes culture." It had not previously been used in a papal document.[11] As already noted, the pope posits a continuum within the process of inculturation, incarnation, and evangelization, a process which "will offer the different cultures the knowledge of hidden mystery and help to bring forth from their own living tradition an original expression of Christian life."[12] In the same place he also recommends going beyond the evangelization of individuals to the evangelization of cultures as a precondition for the redemption of both man and his culture. Since we are products of our cultures, in part at least, to live in an evangelized culture will increase the likelihood of our being the products of evangelization. Evangelization of cultures was a notion introduced by Pope Paul VI in *Evangelii nuntiandi*, n. 20.[13]

For John Paul II, Saints Cyril and Methodius are models of the introduction of the gospel to cultures. By their adroit evangelization and sensitive inculturation, Slav cultures came into the life of the Church. They were not absorbed nor fused into the Church, but became part of a communion which fostered the generous exchange of cultural and spiritual resources. This is also the pope's vision of the eventual communion of churches via cultures.[14] But what is not clear here is exactly what it is that is exchanged in this process.

In 1986 with his encyclical on the Holy Spirit, John Paul II notes several important pneumatological points about this matter. One of these is that no meaningful inculturation can be achieved without the assistance of the Holy Spirit. He also endorses here what Paul VI said in his apostolic exhortation on evangelization, that it is "through the Holy Spirit, the principal agent of evangelization, that the Gospel penetrates to the heart of the world."[15]

In the 1990 encyclical *Redemptoris missio* we again find the continuum of incarnation, inculturation, and evangelization: "Inculturation means the intimate transformation of authentic cultural values through their integration in Christianity and the insertion of Christianity in the various human cultures. . . . Through inculturation the Church makes the Gospel incarnate in different cultures and at the same time introduces peoples, together with their cultures, into her own community. She transmits to them her own values while at the same time taking the good elements that already exist in them and renewing them from within."[16] Christ is already hidden in the culture and the people. The original inculturation was the incarnation. By effective evangelization the word of God can become incarnate in all cultures. Hence, human agency continues what divine inculturation began.

V. THE TRUTH AND EVANGELIZATION

In some sense truth has been a preoccupation for John Paul II ever since he was ordained a bishop. The episcopacy and papacy have a special responsibility because the Church is "the social subject of responsibility for divine truth."[17] With Christ the truth has already been given in its entirety, but it becomes ever clearer as different cultures learn to express "better the unsearchable riches of Christ; hence daily we grow in our understanding of the truth already given in its entirety. . . . Therefore, there is growth of awareness in the Church of knowledge of the truth." Further, "it is by means of inculturation that one proceeds towards full restoration of the covenant with the Wisdom of God which is Christ himself."[18]

Continuing inculturation involves a recognition of how Christ is already present in those to be evangelized. Therefore, recognizing or "beholding the Lamb" already present among us is essential to evangelization too. The recognition must be followed by acknowledgment or proclamation. This act actualizes what has been latent in a culture since its inception because of the Incarnation.[19] The faithful evangelizer is one who experiences Christ already there through direct immersion in the culture's values, its language, and its ways—as was the case with Cyril and Methodius. Only by direct experience of the culture and its values "will the evangelizers be able to bring to the people the knowledge of the hidden mystery in a credible and fruitful way."[20] Evangelization, therefore, is not hauling the good news into a religious *tabula rasa*. Behind this assertion is the belief that the grace of God has been given to all, and so evangelization entails pointing out and teasing out and affirming the original inculturation already begun with Incarnation.[21]

To use the Gospel's metaphor, it seems that an act of evangelization is an act of harvesting what was already planted by God in a people; what is essential is bringing it to full actualization or fullness. "The fields are white with the harvest; pray the master to send harvesters." Thus, to proclaim what is discovered already to be there seems to be a major part of evangelization. If evangelization is bringing out the truth of the fact of the Incarnation as it is already present in a culture, then evangelization would look very different than importing *ab extra* those truths which people have to have in order to be part of the Church. Is this way of understanding evangelization the same as affirmation of what is good in a culture? How does it differ? Should there be a denunciation part for the evangelizer too? If that is permitted, how about the culture having the opportunity to denounce the cultural baggage which the evangelizers bring to their work?

If the evangelist always functions within a place where the Incarnation has already been working, then a divine inculturation process has already been going on everywhere. The good which the evangelizer sees in a culture, he or she is to link to the Incarnation of Christ in the culture. "The grace of God has been given to each and every human being . . . in every corner of the world."[22] If this is so, then evangelization is perceiving this and making the grace known. To miss this is to miss the truth of God already present and acting in a culture.

Evangelization has been misunderstood by many Christians because it has had the image of being an ectopic act that is trying to gain entrance where it has had no previous life. But John Paul II is changing evangelization by making it a more eductive act (a distinction that is mine, not his). The eductive evangelizer would, in effect, be saying to the evangelized: "Appreciate who you are in light of who made you who you are; appreciate what you do in light of the one who is co-authoring the good you do. You have been and are still being created by God—this is already true of you. You have been and still are being redeemed by Christ. You are living according to an account of the good which the spirit has put into your heart. Act on the basis of your perception of the good as your conscience teaches you. All that I the evangelizer want to do is to enable you to name the truth of who you already are and what you already do and who is behind these things you are and do." Inculturation has already been going on with the Author having been God. The evangelizer is bringing out the truth of what has been going on underneath the eyes and below the consciousness of the evangelized. By educing the truth, the evangelizer makes an epiphany that brings to light for the evangelized the truth of who they are, now named and seen more fully. The evangelizer must know that there is a continuum not to be severed between creation, incarnation, inculturation, and the mission of the church. Evangelization completes what divine inculturation began.

The same point has been made by the Second Vatican Council in *Gaudium et spes,* n. 22: "To all people of good will, in whose hearts grace is secretly at work. Since Christ died for everyone, . . . the Holy Spirit offers everyone the possibility of sharing in this Paschal Mystery in a manner known to God." When our better selves are acting, we speak the truth and act from the truth and seek out the truth. When this is done in sufficient numbers, the culture will reinforce our perceptions of what is true and therefore our better selves, as John Paul II says in *Centesimus annus,* n. 49: "Man remains above all a being who seeks the truth and strives to live in that truth, deepening his understanding of it through a dialogue which involves past and future generations. And from this open search for truth which is renewed in every generation the culture of a nation derives its character." Evangelization is truth-telling done by those whose knowledge of truth includes the faith. The truth which the evangelized need to know is that: "all is well and all manner of things will be well and you would be better off if you too could name why this is so. The Son and the Spirit were sent into the world and all that I the evangelizer am doing is naming what they have been sent to do, namely, to tell the truth to you about who you are." There is a difference between a field that is sown and a field that is harvested. The purpose of the sowing is the harvesting. An unharvested field is a field that is going to waste. The harvester/evangelizer brings out the truth hidden from the person's understanding of truth. The majority of human beings live in the world of still-to-be-articulated truth because the truth of who they are has not yet been named. Not seeing what is true leaves in the dark one who should be in the light; it leaves one living in the world of the half-lit implicit that should be the fully-lit explicit. There is a lack of freedom where there is a lack of truth. The fuller the truth, the fuller the freedom.

Pre-truth is also pre-kingdom; full truth is full kingdom. Now truth, therefore, is only kingdom—truth *in nuce* or aborning or already present but still opening out to a not yet full truth: "Working for the Kingdom means acknowledging and promoting God's activity, which is present in human history and transforms it. Building the Kingdom means working for liberation from evil in all its forms. In a word, the Kingdom of God is the manifestation and the realization of God's plan of salvation in all its fulness."[23] Thus, evangelization pulls back the veil and brings to consciousness and to recognition and to acknowledgment the implications of the already true that is only on its way to being the full truth. The (full) truth will make you (fully) free.

The same applies to cultures. They need to know that they are already good news by reason of their having come to be what they distinctively are as a given culture and by the victory won for them in Jesus Christ. They have something that the rest of the world and the final kingdom needs. That something will be enriching now if the account of the good that they act from derives from what is true about who they are. It will be destructive of themselves and of their own and possibly of other peoples if the account of the good they act from is untrue. A culture not open to truth about the good has a pervasively perverse effect on people. This is why true and good and culture belong together, because apart people are pulled in too many different directions.

John Paul II's doctrine on inculturation begins with God the Father and creation, and then continues with God the Son and incarnation, and finally crests with God the Holy Spirit and evangelization. His pneumatology is delightfully universal and unencumbered. For example, to the Aborigines of Australia he said: "But for thousands of years you have lived in this land and fashioned a culture that endures to this day. And during all this time the Spirit of God has been with you. Your 'dreaming,' which influences your lives so strongly that, no matter what happens, you remain forever people of your culture, is your own way of touching the mystery of God's Spirit in you and in creation. . . ."[24] If evangelization at its simplest is bearing witness to God, John Paul II does so here. He also explicitly uses Paul's speeches (e.g., in Acts 14, 15, and 17) as an example of inculturation by seeing how Paul entered into the cultures of the Athenians and the Lycaonians: "The Spirit who "blows where he wills" (Jn 3:8), who was already at work in the world before

Christ was glorified and who has "filled the world, . . . holds all things together [and] knows what is said" (Wis 1:7), leads us to broaden our vision in order to ponder His activity in every time and place. I have repeatedly called this fact to mind and it has guided me in my meetings with a wide variety of people."[25] This is not giving away the store—it is "finding God in all things." What then is the point of the Gospel? "Whatever the Spirit brings about in human hearts and in the history of peoples, in cultures and religions, serves as a preparation for the Gospel." Therefore, what is essential for those being evangelized is "to listen to the voice of the Spirit" since that voice is being spoken to them who do not yet accept the Gospel but who are being prepared to do so.[26]

How does one go about evangelization? The pope advises us to immerse ourselves in the culture, to learn the language and the cultural expressions, and to experience the values being newly expressed in order to locate the hidden mystery.[27] Is this not what Jesus did when He left His heavenly culture and immersed himself in Israel's and then gradually from within His immersion (the hidden life, for example) He began to see and eventually point to the all too hidden mystery of God's saving, active presence in Israel? He undertook a cultural solidarity with the people in order to point them to a solidarity of God's making, that is, the kingdom of God. Solidarity is the *telos* of inculturation in the sense that all things have to be brought into subjection to Christ in order to be restored to God. Inculturation is a very slow process.[28]

It is through dialogue with those who are not church that the Church can uncover the "seeds of the Word" or a "ray of truth which enlightens all people."[29] But at the same time inculturation is a difficult process, for it must in no way compromise the distinctiveness and integrity of the Christian faith, nor the "objective requirements of the faith itself."[30] Inculturation must be guided by two principles: compatibility with the gospel and communion with the universal Church.[31] There is a risk of passing uncritically from a form of alienation toward culture[32] to an over-estimation of culture. Since culture is a human creation and is therefore marked by sin, it needs to be healed, ennobled, and perfected. As Paul VI said to the people in Kampala: "It will require an incubation of the Christian mystery in the genius of your people in order that its native voice more clearly and frankly may then be raised harmoniously in the chorus of other voices in the universal church...." Inculturation needs an expression of the community's life, one which must mature within the community itself "and not be exclusively the result of erudite research."[33] This incubation is a very long process.

VI. The Underdeveloped Idea of Reciprocity

There is an interesting category in the writings of Pope John Paul II which only occasionally comes to the surface but is not spelled out. That category is reciprocity. For example, in *Slavorum apostoli* he defines inculturation as "the incarnation of the gospel in autochthonous cultures, and at the same time the introduction of those cultures into the life of the Church" (n. 21). There is much to ponder here. Was Vatican II's *Dignitatis humanae* an example of a culture's experience (in this case, the American experience of religious freedom) being introduced into the life of the Church? I believe it was. Will the subsequent experience of our American culture and of women's equality with men in it be a future example of a culture's experience being introduced into the life of the Church? I hope so. (I am aware of the two documents on women produced in recent times by the Vatican. Both of these are adroit but both are *a priori* analyses that do not give any indication of being informed by cultures.) But in both cases the process is far from simple. To return to the example of religious freedom which was the basis for the Conciliar endorsement of the doctrine of human rights, there has been since then much uncertainty within the Church about human rights, both individual/political and socio-economic rights. Once the principle is accepted, theory gets worked out very slowly. In the same way, my hope that an inductive, culturally attuned position on the equality of women will soon be introduced into the life of the Church. The UN's Beijing Conference on women's rights was both a start and an indication of the complexity of the issue. Not to be overlooked in saying this is that in many countries it is precisely the Church's standing up for women's rights that makes the Church unacceptable to the culture. The case of Ugandan mandatory dowries and the larger African example of polygamy are apposite here.

VII. Misgiving

There is a subtle distillation process that must be discerned in this matter of reciprocity. One can find an example, in the case of liberation theology. There were supposedly 100,000 base communities in Brazil, but they are now virtually non-existent. Why? Mull these two factoids together. There is a Vatican document on liberation that is light years ahead of much of the world and the local churches on the subject and still too visionary to be part of the thinking of the Church universal.[34] Where did its inspiration come from? From liberation theology! But this at a time when the episcopal appointments by the Vatican were of men who would be for the most part adverse to the direction being taken by base communities and by liberation theology.

What are we to make of this? The co-opting of liberation theology by the Vatican or the discernment of its genius for the universal Church? If one works from a hermeneutic of suspicion, it would be definitely the former; if from a hermeneutic of ultramontanism, the latter. If neither of these extremes, one needs to keep working at understanding the faith, and in this case reciprocity in particular. One does this knowing full well that the Vatican is itself very much a culture. This does not make its decisions wrong, unless it does not know that it is. Likewise, the pope hails from and is still very much marked by his own native culture. This does not make his decisions wrong, unless he does not know that he is.

I am sure that he knows that he is. What I am not always sure of is whether he knows when he uses the word "truth" or the word "faith" or the word "church" or the words "word of God," how culturally mediated each of these realities has been for him. Wherever there is faith or truth or church or Gospel, it is culturally mediated. These do not come down from above but come to us from a people, from particular people, all of whom have a history and a culture. This does not mean that they are merely a human product, but only that they are always in part so.

The theological point to be kept in mind here is that once the Word was made flesh, all subsequent mediations of the divine have come to us via humanly limiting and limited "flesh." The limiting factors are not only from one moment in history, but also through a limited cultural matrix. Let me use as examples two recent acts of the pope with respect to just one of the four realities mentioned above, namely, truth. Both of these acts and examples come from the culture of the Vatican and from the culture of the Polish pontiff. We read them by accepting these delimiting cultures with our own culturally delimited minds.

In his apostolic letter of June 30, 1998, the pope writes a new paragraph into Canon Law, n.750: "Each and every proposition stated definitively by the magisterium of the church concerning the doctrine of the faith or morals, that is, each and every proposition required for the sacred preservation and faithful explanation of the same deposit of faith, must be firmly embraced and maintained; anyone, therefore, who rejects those propositions which are to be held definitively is opposed to the doctrine of the Catholic Church."[35] Those who are to be punished and the penalties with which they are to be punished are then spelled out. How are we to interpret this move? I think that the best way is to see that as an attempt at consolidating "the integrity of the faith" so that cultures will know what it is that they are receiving when they are being evangelized by Roman Catholicism. That would be logical, given the pope's understanding of the relationship of "truth" to culture.

But there is an ever-present dialectic about inculturation. The thesis in this dialectic is the cultures. The antithesis is the integrity of the faith. The eductive side of evangelization belongs to the thesis. But evangelization is also a teaching of what cannot be known without the transmission of the "saving truth." This is where the antithesis enters into the picture. If this transmission is done without the Spirit's assistance or if it is done ineptly, the "saving truth" will be ectopic. If it is done in the Spirit, it will lead to the synthesis which happens when a person or a culture accepts the faith and its understanding of the truth. Would it not be helpful if a document like this which is focused on the integrity of the faith indicated what contribution is expected from the cultures that the pope has been urging the church to be open to and that the pope would like to "introduce into the life of the Church"? In *Slavorum apostoli* he spoke of "a generous exchange of cultural and spiritual resources" with the example of the fruit of the evangelization of Saints Cyril and Methodius in mind. He would be very comfortable, of course, attesting to and welcoming the cultural and spiritual resources of the Slavic cultures from his own personal experience and appreciation, since these are what nurtured his own faith. How open is he—or any of us for that matter—to being as multicultural as the Church is in its length and breadth? To what degree was it a deeper insight into the truth of the faith latent in cultures being evangelized that the pope was encouraging? Of course, if the Church already possesses the full truth, what is it that a new culture would contribute to the Church's growth in appreciation of the truth? Is the truth unfolding or is it already known? If it is unfolding, is our increase in knowledge of it locked up in and contingent on the evangelization of cultures, as John Paul II's pontificate seems to have implied? It would be helpful if the emphasis that the pope has placed on culture were better connected to what it is that he means by this integrity of the faith. How do these two fit together?

There are reasons to wonder whether the Vatican understands itself culturally or whether it believes it acts transculturally. To be specific, Cardinal Ratzinger's official explanation of the pope's letter cites Leo XIII's letter declaring the invalidity of Anglican ordinations as something to be held definitively. This was done without so much as consulting Cardinal George Basil Hume, the Primate of England, or Cardinal Cassidy, the President of the Pontifical Council for the Promotion of Christian Unity, before elevating this controversial letter to a truth "connected to revelation by historical necessity and to be held definitively."[36] This is hard to accept, given that the pope in *Crossing the Threshold of Hope* sees "the Petrine ministry as a ministry of unity which is carried out in the field of ecumenism. Peter's task is to search constantly for ways that will help preserve unity. Therefore he must not create obstacles but must open up paths." In the same place he writes: "Mutual respect is a prerequisite for authentic ecumenism."[37] This aforementioned action makes one wonder whether the nature of culture has been understood by those teaching its importance. It is heady stuff to believe that one is in some kind of transcultural relationship to truth while unsuspecting that one's own culture has a history of trying to make an order out of things that are not ready to be disposed of so tidily. I am referring here to the German culture.

An even more interesting and significant act of the present pope in this matter of insuring the integrity of the faith is his apostolic letter *Apostolos Svos* (May 21, 1998), on the role of bishops conferences around the world. As one news report has it, "Under the new rules, it would be almost impossible for the National Conference of Catholic Bishops in the United States, for instance, to issue binding statements on matters of doctrine or of public policy topics (like on nuclear weapons or the status of women) that diverged from the Vatican view."[38] One could ask: How will the cultures enrich the Church universal if the bishops conferences themselves are being distrusted to see what is essential to the life of the Church and its relationship to their own cultures? Cardinal Ratzinger explains the letter by noting: "We are talking about doctrine, that is to say, the truth. The truth is not arrived at by majority."[39] Nor, we might add, is it arrived at by ignoring the cultural and doctrinal discernments of those in place who are trying to be true to the understanding of culture of the Church and the pope.

This is a significant letter about ecclesiology, something that the press so far has completely missed. Its conclusions have been arrived at in part from ideas discussed at the Synod of Bishops of 1985 and in part from John Paul II's interpretation of both that synod and of the role of a bishop *vis-à-vis* the college of bishops. The episcopal conferences are the new kids on the block. Much more weighty juridically are "particular and provincial councils," which have history on their side and which the letter would like to see "revitalized." While limiting the power of episcopal conferences, the letter heightens two things. The one is the responsibility of the individual bishop for his own local church. The other is the responsibility of each bishop for and to the whole episcopal college with the pope as its head. The whole first part of the letter is most insistent on the unity and indivisibility of the whole episcopacy. The body of bishops *en bloc*, John Paul II believes, is at the heart of the integrity of the faith, and hence part of the antithesis mentioned above, rather than part of the thesis, as I had previously imagined and as many episcopal conferences were beginning to function. Without saying so in so many words, the letter implies that there has been an extreme in the way episcopal conferences were seeing their roles. This has already had two effects: first, limiting or intimidating individual bishops in the exercise of their office in their own diocese; the second, an erosion of the authority that might have been given to the positions taken by episcopal conferences. Although some measures are outlined to control these two unwanted effects, the overall direction of the letter is what we are interested in here.

There are many who see this as an effort at a new degree of control and centralization by making episcopal conferences subservient to the dominant culture of the Vatican. That would be an understandable interpretation. I do not believe that it is the best one. I believe that John Paul II's vision of the church *vis-à-vis* the cultures sees the need for a stronger dialectic. I believe that he saw the episcopal conferences as becoming too culturally particular. Perhaps he foresaw a danger in the Church losing sense of its universality. He is in no way de-legitimating the collaboration of bishops with one another in episcopal conferences. He is just spelling out in greater detail the limits of that collaboration and the *affectus collegialis* (collegial spirit) it engenders. Some would say that the pope was drawing in the reins on these episcopal conferences so that an individual bishop could become more a minion of the pope. But I do not think that such a reading would do justice to the letter's stress on the unity of the world's episcopacy. One might say rather that a far-seeing pope is envisioning this unity of the college of bishops as essential for and a harbinger of the future unity of the nations and that too great a power concentrated in the episcopal conferences might be generating a bloc ecclesiology. "The universal Church cannot be conceived as the sum of the particular churches, or as a federation of particular churches," the pope instructs. Hence, "a territorially based exercise of the episcopal ministry never takes on the collegial nature proper to the actions of the order of bishops as such" (n. 12).

Undoubtedly, the pope has an appreciation of the distinctiveness of each regional culture. By analogy he says as much from a response he gives in his own book *Crossing the Threshold of Hope*. In answering the question put to him on the reason for the Reformation, he opined: "Could it not be that these divisions have been a path continually leading the Church to discover the untold wealth contained in Christ's gospel and in the redemption accomplished by Christ? Perhaps all this wealth would not have come to light otherwise. . . . It is necessary for humanity to achieve unity through plurality, to learn to come together as one Church, even while presenting a plurality of ways of thinking and of acting, of cultures and civilizations. Would not such a way of looking at things be, in a certain sense, more consonant with the wisdom of God, with His goodness and providence?"[40] Indeed it would!

And if he is being consistent, there is another comforting insight into local self-determination in *Centesimus annus*. Invoking the long-hallowed principle of subsidiarity, the pope calls for "the subjectivity of society through the creation of structures of participation and shared responsibility."[41] Again, he is commenting on political ideas and entities, but should the people of God have any less participation and shared responsibility than people of a given nation? What kind of primacy should we expect if not one of trusting the presence of grace in all, not the least in both the individual bishops he himself has appointed and their collaborative bodies?

I reluctantly recall a stinging rebuke of this pope delivered by Bernard Häring, the famous Redemptorist moralist, on the occasion of the publication of *Veritatis splendor*. He expressed great distress over what he called "the many signs of his rooted distrust" in John Paul II's writings and he admitted to great discouragement because of "the manifold structures of distrust he has allowed to be established."[42] When I heard this several years ago, I thought it was unfair. Are these recent moves of the pope establishing "structures of distrust"? It is possible that these acts represent an old man fighting for control as he ages and that he is now reverting to the days of his youth when he had to fight structures he had good reason then to distrust. But I think that the more positive interpretation is the truer one. This pope is seeing farther than the rest of us and ordering course corrections to realign what he sees as having been veering slightly off course.

VIII. Final Comments

This is a great, sweeping heuristic we have here from John Paul II under the heading of culture stemming from a philosophical anthropology. This whole corpus on culture holds together and really is a profound vision of the Church's relation to the world. My main problem with it is that it does not seem modest enough. To be specific, the faith we proclaim is already a culture and (like all cultures) a limited "human creation." Our faith-culture (the hyphen is essential for our modesty) has a history not just of grace but of sin. Its history has made it *simul justus et peccator*, as Luther liked to put it. It still has traces, obviously, of imperialism, autocracy, patriarchy, intolerance, homophobia, racism, and sexism in it. Most of all, it has truths of faith that all cultures are in need of, but when it gets beyond the primordial truths of creation, incarnation, redemption, and the gradual, final recapitulation of all things in Christ, there is much dispute. Beyond these basic truths, not all that John Paul II insists upon is agreed upon nor are all truths in the peaceful possession of the faithful. It is more accurate to see ourselves as a pilgrim people trying to come to fuller truth and to an integrity of faith than a *societas perfecta* already possessing the truth and integrity. Part of the dispute that we have *ad intra* could be seen as focused on this question: What part of the truth that the Roman Pontiff would have us hold and proclaim is itself part of the Roman culture as well as the culture of his background, and what part is transculturally *de fide*? The cultural character of the faith being promoted here is not clearly seen and admitted. That faith-culture itself needs to undergo what the cultures John Paul II talks about have to undergo, namely, a radical conversion. Being aware of and self-critical about our own cultural baggage as a Church is the precondition of our credibility on the world stage. Vatican II was not loathe to admit that the Church is in continual need of purification.

Culture is a wonderful heuristic. Its strength is as a heuristic device, but this is also its weakness. It is not always clear where this reality is in any social analysis without the employment of very specific empirical methods. Nor is the culture of the perceiving analyst often clear to that analyst. It is much clearer to me, for example, that we both as a nation and in our more personal identities constitute a series of subcultures than that we are or represent a culture. A subculture is more like an interest group than a full-blown culture. It is interesting how much the pope insists on a long immersion by missionary evangelists in a culture in order for them to see God at work there, and yet he seems comfortable without any immersion at all when addressing cultures about what they must become or cease to become. This is perhaps a congenial way to proceed for philosophical anthropology, but it is not so for cultural anthropology, which is much more empirical and craves slow, detailed work. It is also congenial to ectopic evangelization and ectopic cultural normativity, not to eductive evangelization and eductive cultural normativity. So I go back again to the question: What did John Paul II mean when he wrote of "the introduction of evangelized cultures into the life of the Church"?

A final question is related to the spirit of the Vatican II document on the non-Christian religions, *Nostra aetate*. More specifically, do other faith traditions such as Islam, Judaism, Hinduism, and Buddhism have a role to play in their dominant cultures that is similar to the one being elaborated by John Paul II? He speaks about the need for knowledge of the political reality in order to have a sense of normativity that transcends it. Is it the faiths as such that have a specific role to play in nations and cultures? If so, it would be helpful to make more clear the great value to a state that is found in the culture-transcending nature of a religious faith. Further, that where there is more than one faith, it would be valuable to know about the role of Catholicism in the relationship of these faiths *vis-à-vis* the specific culture. Or is what he is saying of value to a culture only if it is the Catholic faith—as his non-advertence to the other faiths seems to imply?

NOTES

1. The best analysis of John Paul II's anthropology that I have seen is Francis George, O.M.I., *Inculturation and Ecclesial Communion: Culture and Church in the Teaching of John Paul II* (Rome: Urbaniana University Press, 1990), 31-38.
2. Ibid., 37.
3. Ibid., 38.
4. Quoted from George, *Inculturation*, 39.
5. Letter to Cardinal Agostino Casaroli, *L'Osservatore Romano*, 28 June 1982 (English-language edition), 19.
6. UNESCO address, *Acta apostolicae sedis*, 20 May 1982, 683.
7. Ibid.
8. This is his most quoted and frequently repeated comment about the relationship between faith and culture. For example, his January 16, 1982 address to the Congress of the "Movimento Ecclesiale di Impegno Culturale," quoted in *La Traccia*, vol. 3/1, p. 55.
9. Address to the bishops of Lombardy on their *ad limina* visit, *Acta apostolicae sedis*, 15 January 1982, 402.
10. This is a summary of my understanding of George, 45.
11. See S. Iniobong Udoidem, *Pope John Paul II on Inculturation* (Lanham: University Press of America, 1996), 27.
12. *Catechesi tradendae,* n. 53, quoted by Udoidem, 28.
13. See Udoidem, 28.
14. See *Slavorum apostoli,* n. 25.
15. *Evangelii nuntiandi,* n. 75.
16. *Redemptoris missio* (hereafter *RM*), nn. 52-53.
17. *Redemptor hominis,* n. 19.
18. *Familiaris consortio,* n. 10.
19. Udoidem, 55-57.
20. *RM,* n. 53.
21. Homily of John Paul II on 12 December 1979, quoted by Udoidem, 62.
22. This quotation is from the same Christmas homily referred to in note 21 above.
23. *RM,* n. 15.
24. Address of Nov. 29, 1986, quoted by Udoidem, 67.
25. *RM,* n. 29.
26. *RM,* nn. 29-30.
27. *RM,* n. 53.
28. *RM,* n. 52.
29. *RM,* n. 56.

30. *RM,* nn. 52-53.
31. *RM,* n. 54.
32. Recall H. Richard Niebuhr's typologies in *Christ in Culture* (Harper and Row, 1951), passim.
33. *RM,* n. 54.
34. *Libertatis conscientia* in *Origins* 15/44 (1986). It was prepared by the Congregation for the Doctrine of the Faith.
35. *Ad tuendam fidem* in *Origins* 28/8 (July 16, 1998): 115.
36. *The Tablet,* 11 July 1998.
37. *Crossing the Threshold of Hope (CTH),* 54.
38. *The New York Times,* 24 July 1998.
39. Ibid.
40. *CTH,* 153-54.
41. *Centesimus annus,* n. 11.
42. *National Catholic Reporter,* July 17, 1998.

The New Evangelization
of American Intellectual Culture:
Context, Resistances, and Strategies

Arthur R. Madigan, S.J.

The topic of this paper is the new evangelization of American intellectual culture.[1] Let me explain my terms. By "evangelization" I mean first of all the preaching or other presentation of Jesus Christ as Lord,[2] and then along with this the presentation of the existence and nature of God, the Church and its sacramental system, and the demands of a genuinely human and Christian existence.

By "new evangelization" I mean the evangelization called for by Pope Paul VI in *Evangelii nuntiandi* and then by Pope John Paul II in a variety of statements. The new evangelization is clearly not a matter of preaching a new Christ or a new gospel (cf. Gal 1: 6-9). What then is new about it? The evangelization called for is new in the conditions under which it occurs, new in the methods it employs, and, we may hope, new in its intensity.[3] The papal call for this new evangelization comes in the wake of what John Paul has spoken of as the "extraordinary grace" of the Second Vatican Council,[4] and can be understood as part of the Church's reception of the Council. The call for a new evangelization is issued, then, during the extended period of debate within the Church over the proper interpretation and reception of the Council's teaching. The call for a new evangelization has obviously not terminated this debate, but it can and should contribute to the debate by focusing attention on what we as a Church can say and must say to the contemporary world.

The documents on the new evangelization and the evangelization of culture insist on the need to evangelize not simply individuals, but also the cultures in which those individuals grow up and are formed.[5] They point to a number of salient features, both strengths and weaknesses, of contemporary culture in general and American culture in particular.[6] They focus on the crucial difficulty presented by the widespread denial of objective truth about the human person and morality.[7] They call attention to the troubling influence of the culture of death on American culture.[8] I agree with the analysis found in these documents. My task, as I see it, is to extend the analysis to the particularly difficult case of American intellectual culture, thus fleshing out the general descriptions and prescriptions in the writings of John Paul.

I accept the very general notion of culture found in the second chapter of Vatican II's pastoral constitution *Gaudium et spes*, summarized by Avery Dulles as "a socially constituted environment in which certain ideas, attitudes, values, and modes of behavior are transmitted to new generations."[9] Nonetheless I will often use "culture" as a collective noun designating a group of people who share certain ideas, attitudes, values, and modes of behavior, as in the phrase "American intellectual culture."[10]

American intellectual culture is not an officially structured body, and the criteria for membership in it are correspondingly imprecise. Many members of the intellectual culture hold college or university appointments, but it also includes unaffiliated writers and scholars, fellows and associates in think tanks, members of the various artistic establishments, substantial numbers of journalists and other media people, members of professions such as law and medicine, bioethicians, and then a wide range of observers. To use an analogy from the world of athletics: American intellectual culture includes players, coaches, reporters, and broadcasters, but also spectators, some of whom hold season tickets, while others just attend the occasional game, and still others tune in sporadically. The line between the core members of the intellectual culture and the secondary participants is not, and for present purposes need not be, totally clear; and the same is true of the line between the secondary participants in the intellectual culture and the population at large. This paper will focus on the core members of the intellectual culture, both because their peculiarities are not yet well recognized or articulated in the growing papal and ecclesiastical literature on the new evangelization and the evangelization of culture, and because what is true about them, and about the prospects of evangelizing them, will apply *mutatis mutandis* to the much greater numbers of secondary participants whom they influence.

I shall speak first about the *context* of the new evangelization of the intellectual culture, and then about the special *resistances* that the intellectual culture puts up against evangelization.[11] I will conclude by suggesting some *strategies* that we might follow in the new evangelization of American intellectual culture.

CONTEXT: SALIENT FEATURES OF
AMERICAN INTELLECTUAL CULTURE

For a believing Catholic, American intellectual culture is difficult to understand, almost as difficult as the Chinese culture of the sixteenth and seventeenth centuries was for the Jesuit missionaries of that day. That all parties are speaking English only veils the difficulty. In some respects we are so far from American intellectual culture that we can hardly comprehend its mentality, while on the other hand we are so close to American intellectual culture that we may not identify its assumptions clearly.

American intellectual culture is, first of all, a modern culture, in the senses of modernity delineated by Charles Taylor in *Sources of the Self*.[12] It affirms the value of the ordinary life of work and family, and rejects any claims of special status for privileged estates such as knights or nobles, priests or bishops, monks or nuns. It affirms the obligations of universal benevolence and beneficence, generally understood in terms of minimizing or eliminating pain. It affirms the goods of self-responsible freedom and individual self-expression. It rejects the ascetic ideal and the monkish virtues. It is (as Taylor notes in *Sources of the Self* and again in "A Catholic Modernity?") beset by a deep underlying conflict between the claims of self-responsible freedom and self-expression on the one hand and the claims of universal benevolence and beneficence on the other.[13]

American intellectual culture is a *liberal* culture. I gloss the word "liberal" as follows: the culture affirms the freedom of enlightened individuals; it takes for granted the basic correctness of the eighteenth-century Enlightenment, especially its criticism of authority and tradition; and it accepts the Whig interpretation of history as a story of ongoing progress. American intellectual culture is a culture of individual freedom. In terms that I borrow from the intellectual historian David Hollinger, it is a culture that privileges voluntary affiliation over permanent identity.[14] Such anti-liberal, anti-Enlightenment, anti-Whig interpretation figures as Leo Strauss, Allan Bloom, and Alasdair MacIntyre are essentially outsiders to American intellectual culture, whereas Peter Gay and Martha Nussbaum are essentially insiders. As MacIntyre has pointed out, what are currently presented as debates between liberals and conservatives are really for the most part debates between liberal liberals and conservative liberals.[15]

American intellectual culture is in large part a *post-Protestant* culture. In his book *Without God, Without Creed*, the Notre Dame historian James Turner has chronicled the intellectual itinerary of American Protestant intellectuals from

Calvinism and Enlightenment Deism down to the late nineteenth century, when the total abandonment of belief in God become a live option for the generality of American Protestant intellectuals.[16] The post-Protestant aspect of the intellectual culture poses particular difficulties for the new evangelization, partly because of residual anti-Roman bias, but more importantly because of the widespread assumption that Christianity in any of its traditional forms is intellectually bankrupt—that it has already been tried and found wanting.[17]

American intellectual culture is, like American culture in general, a distinctly *political* culture. That is, the basic framework of the American political system is integral to the culture in a way that could not be said of, say, French or German or Japanese cultures, which have maintained their cultural continuities even through radical changes of political constitution. Of course, it is widely admitted that the American political framework has been and is continually evolving, and it is almost as widely admitted that the framework ought to evolve over time. Still, the ideas of representative government, separation of legislative, executive, and judicial powers, and the limitation of state power by judicially enforceable individual rights are taken as axiomatic, not simply as political arrangements but as elements of a worldview whose bedrock values include equality, respect for privacy, and the toleration of differences. This politically based worldview has little in common with Roman Catholic ecclesiology, canon law, or administrative practice.[18]

American intellectual culture has a strong strain of *pragmatism* and *anti-foundationalism*. While the clash between the intellectual and the practical man of business is a commonplace in American tradition, the commercial and technical orientation of the general culture finds many a parallel in the intellectual culture, in the pragmatic outlook canonized by John Dewey, but also in the neo-pragmatic outlook represented in different ways by Willard Van Orman Quine,[19] Hilary Putnam,[20] Richard Rorty,[21] and Stanley Fish.[22] "Pragmatist" is not a polite word for a crude philistine. The central notion is not crudity but anti-foundationalism, a rejection of the idea that there are fixed points of basic truth, and so, a rejection of any epistemic strategy that tries to secure such basic truths and then to derive other truths from them.[23]

There are many ways to illustrate this anti-foundationalist tendency, but let me offer one example that bears on the topic of evangelization. Christian apologists have long supposed that there is a certain natural or logical succession of issues that a person confronts on the path towards faith, conversion, and baptism—the existence of God, then the mission and divinity of Jesus Christ, next the claim of the Church to represent Jesus Christ, and finally the sacramental and moral consequences of accepting the claims of Christ and the Church—with each earlier step paving the way for those that follow and each later step presupposing the steps before it. To someone steeped in a pragmatic or anti-foundationalist outlook, this linear approach is neither obvious nor compelling. In a pragmatic or anti-foundationalist approach, you can begin anywhere along the line, or rather at any point in the web of belief (that change of metaphor from line to web is important), and then move to other points on the web, without needing to justify these moves by reference to supposed logically prior foundations. To express the anti-foundationalist position in Aristotelian-scholastic terms: there is no such thing as priority *quoad se*, only priority *quoad nos* or *quoad me*. The Church's magisterium, if I understand correctly, says that if we thoroughly understand what the priesthood instituted by Jesus Christ is and does, we are bound to recognize that women cannot in the nature of the case be priests. This is a good foundationalist approach: what Christ did is basic and normative. But someone steeped in an anti-foundationalist mentality might feel equally justified in starting from some other point on the web of belief and saying, for instance, "No one who refuses to ordain women can credibly claim to be speaking for God."

The mention of Richard Rorty and Stanley Fish invites the question, Is American intellectual culture a post-modern culture? Of course, the word "post-modern" is notoriously slippery.[24] I would answer with a set of conditionals. If being post-modern means using jargon of the kind common in certain brands of literary criticism, then only a small part of the intellectual culture is post-modern. American intellectual culture speaks, by and large, decent English.[25] If being post-modern means rejecting modernity and the Enlightenment, then the intellectual culture is definitely not post-modern.[26]

If being post-modern means denying the reality of objective truth, then the culture is not post-modern; the prestige of the natural sciences and technologies counts in favor of the possibility of objective truth. And, to go out on a limb, I think the intellectual culture as a whole respects the possibility of attaining truth in moral matters. The difference between the intellectual culture and John Paul II is not that the culture rules out the possibility of truth in the moral area, but that the culture has different rules or standards for evaluating truth-claims, and that it privileges individual differences to a much higher extent than John Paul does. To put the matter in terms of Aristotelian logic, the intellectual culture affirms a great many particular propositions, and even some universal propositions, but it tends to be suspicious of universal propositions and to insist on a great deal of evidence and argument before accepting them. Where John Paul might charge the intellectual culture with skepticism about the possibility of attaining truth, representatives of the intellectual culture might reply that they were not skeptical, just careful. The culture has been strongly influenced by what James Turner has identified as an "ethics of belief," according to which it is morally wrong to believe what one does not know and morally virtuous to face the world without the comforts of religious belief.[27]

Back to the question about post-modernity: to the extent that post-modernity continues and intensifies the modern revulsion from metaphysics, from a teleological view of nature, from the understanding of natural teleology as morally normative, the intellectual culture is decidedly post-modern. And if being post-modern means taking a functional or genealogical view of metaphysical and moral claims, considering them not first of all as truth claims but first of all as measures of social control, expressions and reinforcements of power relationships, then there is at least a strong post-modern current in the American intellectual culture.

The mention of power and power relationships brings up another facet of American intellectual culture: it is shaped not only by the academy, but also in important ways by the *influential professions*. Law schools turn out lawyers, some of whom become judges, some of whom shape public policy in the light of their legal theories. Undergraduate departments and graduate programs turn out economists, whose focus on economic concerns comes to dominate the political forum, and whose instrumental conception of rationality (finding the most efficient means to given ends, not reflecting on the ends themselves) comes to pervade the culture generally. The interactions among the professions, the academy, and the culture are complex. Richard Posner, Chief Judge of the United States Court of Appeals for the Seventh Circuit, embodies a certain economic understanding of rationality in his judicial opinions, but also, building both on economic rationality and on legal rationality, goes on to address a variety of topics in books such as *Sex and Reason*.[28] Martha Nussbaum, a classicist and Aristotelian philosopher, collaborates with the Nobel Prize economist Amartya Sen on issues of development.[29] Later she secures a professorship in the University of Chicago Law School (with cross-appointments in Philosophy and Divinity) and publishes widely on the issues of the day.[30] The crucial field of bioethics is a meeting place of different disciplines and rationalities: philosophy, religious ethics, medicine, law, administration.[31]

Consider the therapeutic professions, in particular medicine, psychiatry, and psychology. The American intellectual culture of freedom and self-development represents, in the words of Philip Rieff, *The Triumph of the Therapeutic*.[32] Of course, there is also resistance to the prestige of the therapeutic professions, and these professions themselves appear to be in a process of change, in part due to economic factors. Still, they are immensely influential on the intellectual culture and the culture generally. A particularly telling, or chilling, instance, if one can credit it, comes from the book *The Brethren*, in which Bob Woodward and Scott Armstrong suggest that admiration for the doctors of the Mayo Clinic was a significant factor in the formation of Justice Blackmun's majority opinion in *Roe v. Wade*.[33] Priests and religious, whose formation years spanned the transitional period of the late 1960's and early 1970's, are aware of the extent to which presuppositions drawn from psychology and psychiatry have modified or even superseded earlier understandings of asceticism, spirituality, and vocation.[34]

My point here is not to deplore the influence of law, economics, and the therapeutic professions. It is to bring out that many people in the culture, even many in the intellectual culture, derive their notions of rationality from the genuine but limited rationalities of these professions, whereas John Paul II in *Fides et ratio* is advocating a broader and more adequate rationality that transcends these partial viewpoints. The core issue between John Paul II and American intellectual culture is not whether one is for or against rationality, objectivity, and truth, but rather what one understands by rationality, objectivity, and truth.

American intellectual culture is shaped not only by the academy and the professions, but also by the world of the *imaginative arts*. Of course, it is typical of human beings generally to be influenced by the arts. My non-expert impression is that American intellectual culture is marked by deep differences about norms for evaluating works of art; what one observer finds innovative and liberating, another finds petty and derivative. The artistic subculture harbors a fair amount of hostility towards institutional religion, as witness Andres Serano's *Piss Christ* and Sinead O'Connor's performance tearing up a photograph of John Paul II. This hostility is in large part a reaction against Christian and Catholic teaching in the area of sexuality.[35] But apart from these overtly anti-religious manifestations, a good deal of contemporary art tends to undermine the awareness of a stable, teleologically oriented human nature and to replace it with an imaginative vision of human nature as almost infinitely malleable. Take, for example, the four-person marital arrangement known as "sedoretu" in Ursula K. Le Guin's "Another Story, or A Fisherman of the Inland Sea."[36] The details of sedoretu are not important here, and the story is not even slightly pornographic, but it uses the imagination in a way that relativizes the statistically normal and what might be thought of as the normatively natural, institution of marriage. Art can and often does operate as a relativizing force, and the relativizing impulse in our culture is not only intellectual, as in Michael Warner's book, *The Trouble with Normal*,[37] but artistic as well.

American intellectual culture is *marked by debates*, by four debates in particular. First is the political debate between the claims of liberty or autonomy and the claims of equality or entitlement. This is really shorthand for a whole series of debates, and members of the intellectual culture do not feel obliged to line up on the same side in each of them. It is common, for instance, to stress the claims of autonomy and privacy in the areas of sexuality and reproduction, while accepting a considerable degree of regimentation in other areas, e.g., redistributive taxation, mandatory recycling, the restriction of handguns, and the prohibition of certain forms of speech. A second debate, well outlined by David Hollinger in his *Postethnic America*,[38] is between the claims of particular allegiances to family, church, region, and ethnic group and the cosmopolitan claims that all humans be treated alike and that decisions be taken from the viewpoint of humanity as such. Hollinger finds that the cosmopolitan element in American culture (and I take it this includes most of the intellectual culture) privileges voluntary affiliations over permanent identities.[39] A third debate, or cluster of debates, is over the theory and practice of education, including the recent "culture wars," as well as the current debates over school choice and public funding of access to private education. A fourth sphere of debate is sexuality, including the understanding of the sexes, the pros and cons of the various feminisms, the status and prospects of marriage and the nuclear family, and the theoretical and practical issues raised by the sexual minorities. Of course, all these debates extend out into American culture at large. But my sense is that the intellectual culture is, on balance, more inclined than the general culture to take the cosmopolitan over the particularist view, more inclined to settle educational questions on the basis of the cosmopolitan point of view, and more inclined to settle the debates about gender and sexuality on the basis of individual freedom.

My main point, however, is that we should not misconstrue these debates, as though they heralded a crisis of American intellectual culture, or as though they were cries for help, cries to which the new evangelization would be the longed-for answer. They are no such thing. As Alasdair MacIntyre has pointed out, it is perfectly normal for a living tradition to be characterized and in part constituted by a continuing argument about the goods that it recognizes and that it serves to protect.[40] For all its internal conflicts, American intellectual culture remains liberal, post-Enlightenment, and progress-oriented. It is, despite periodic warnings of crisis, a confident culture. One sign of this confidence is the intellectual culture's tendency to embrace cultural diversity as an educational ideal. That embrace is possible precisely because the culture is supremely confident that nothing in the way of cultural diversity can or will successfully challenge, either in practice or at the level of theory, its own liberal, progressive, cosmopolitan, post-Enlightenment presuppositions.

American intellectual culture has great assimilative power. The stories told in George Marsden's *The Soul of the American University*[41] and in James Burtchaell's *The Dying of the Light*[42] are not simply tales of the sloth, stupidity, or cowardice of various Protestant and Catholic academics and administrators. They are also, and perhaps even more importantly, stories of the immense assimilative power of the dominant intellectual culture. Those of us who are academics, and especially members of religious communities that have had a major role in the founding and development of colleges and universities, need to reflect on the extent to which American intellectual culture has worked its assimilative wonders on us: on us as individuals and on the mentalities that prevail in what many Jesuits still speak of as "our" educational institutions.[43]

RESISTANCES OF THE INTELLECTUAL CULTURE TO THE NEW EVANGELIZATION

I have said enough to suggest that American intellectual culture will be less than receptive to the new evangelization. I shall now attempt to list some particular points of resistance, organizing them around the four foci of conversion mentioned above.

First, then, it is not easy for someone steeped in the American intellectual culture to affirm that there is a God in anything like the sense proposed by the Bible and by Catholic tradition. Factors in this resistance include: the general anti-metaphysical tendency of the culture; the post-Protestant critique of biblical images of God; the influence of popularized science or pseudo-science[44]; the influence of genuine natural science, when taken as the sole model of rationality; and the notion, expressed in sociological terms, that belief in God is a "survival," a relic of an earlier and unenlightened age, and that religious believers are a cognitive minority.[45] These points of resistance also help to explain why American intellectuals who believe in God so often keep that belief under wraps.

Second, it is not easy for someone steeped in the American intellectual culture to affirm that Jesus Christ is his or her resurrected Lord, much less that Jesus of Nazareth is God in the sense found in the scriptures and elucidated by the Councils of Nicaea and Chalcedon. Factors in this resistance include: intellectual disagreement with, and visceral revulsion from, fundamentalist Protestantism; suspicion of the development and the supposed Hellenization of doctrine within the Roman Catholic tradition; in some quarters, a positivist approach to history. A particular difficulty is the understandable reluctance to rest anything on the biblical word when its credentials and interpretation are so widely and, it appears, interminably disputed. Here I am thinking of such books as John S. Spong's *Born of a Woman*[46] and *Resurrection, Myth or Reality?*[47] and John Dominic Crossan's *The Historical Jesus*,[48] but also of the periodic re-visitations of the quest for the historical Jesus by the weekly news magazines. How can you bet your life on something that changes with each Christmas or Easter issue of *Time* or *Newsweek*? These points of resistance also help to explain why American intellectuals who believe in Jesus Christ so often keep that belief under wraps.

Third, it is not easy for someone steeped in American intellectual culture to commit himself or herself to the Roman Catholic Church. Factors in this resistance include: the residual Protestantism that characterizes much of the intellectual culture; the Enlightenment critique of authority and tradition as sources of truth; the ethos of individual freedom and self-realization; the sociological view of the Church as a survival (and a particularist survival that arrogantly parades itself as universal and asserts universal claims!). This constellation of factors also helps to explain why American intellectuals who are Catholics tend to be, or to present themselves as, "cafeteria Catholics," picking and choosing among Catholic beliefs and practices.

Fourth, it is not easy for someone steeped in the American intellectual culture to accept the demands of human moral life as that life is presented by the Bible and interpreted by Catholic tradition. I do not pretend that living a human moral life is easy for anyone, but people steeped in the American intellectual culture will have additional difficulties. They will be used to the modern affirmation of self-responsible freedom and individual self-expression, to the ethos of self-development and the therapeutic culture. They will be acquainted with sciences or techniques of selfhood and development that rival the Christian understanding. They will be familiar with a rich psychological vocabulary for talking about the human situation, but unfamiliar with, or even repelled by, the language and tone of magisterial pronouncements. To someone brought up on Freud, or to someone brought up on Henry James or Virginia Woolf or John Cheever or Iris Murdoch, papal and ecclesiastical pronouncements about personhood and moral life can appear not so much false as childishly simple and naïve. Of course, one can use a rich vocabulary to talk nonsense, even pernicious nonsense, and the difficulties of Christian moral life are not reducible to difficulties of language. However, the difficulties of language and cultural background are serious obstacles to the new evangelization in the area of morality.

Taken together, these resistances are not only a formidable set of obstacles to the new evangelization, but also a veritable counter-evangelization, continually undermining the faith and practice of believers.[49] I do not pretend for a moment that these resistances can all be dispelled, or that these obstacles can easily be made to disappear. Some of them will simply have to be confronted, and the virtues of the evangelist will have to include the courage to confront them. But the confrontation and the evangelization will go better to the extent that we realize how genuinely difficult it can be for representatives of the intellectual culture to accept God, Jesus Christ, the Catholic Church, and the fullness of the moral life.

My procedure in these sections has been inductive, and thus is open to two questions: whether the data I have selected are in fact representative of the culture, and if they are, whether I have interpreted them correctly. Much of what I have said could easily be disputed or qualified. I have not said a word about the powerful influence of Christianity on African-American intellectual culture, or about the perceptions of Christianity by American Jewish intellectuals. And the American scientific establishment is hardly a hotbed of anti-foundationalism or post-modernism. But a more detailed and nuanced account would on the whole confirm the impression of a profound gulf between American intellectual culture and the gospel of Jesus Christ. Permit me, then, to end this long but superficial survey with some lines from Rachel Attwater's biography of the Jesuit missionary to China, Johann Adam Schall: "After three long years of waiting, Adam Schall was very ready for his mission. Through his study of the language that had such beautiful characters and such differing basic concepts from the tongues of the West, he was gaining an insight into the complexities of the Chinese mind and a comprehension that there could be no entry for the West as such into the Celestial Empire."[50]

STRATEGIES FOR EVANGELIZING AMERICAN INTELLECTUAL CULTURE

The obstacles in the way of evangelizing American intellectual culture are daunting. Nonetheless, there are significant openings or opportunities for evangelizing the culture. The ethos of freedom and self-development is an opportunity, if we can find a way to speak the language of freedom and self-development effectively and in an authentically Christian way. The debates that divide the intellectual culture are opportunities, provided that we can intervene in them to some purpose. The influence of the professions is an opportunity, if we can understand the types of rationality involved in the professions and make plain their strengths and their limitations. The plurality of fora in which the intellectual culture can be encountered (colleges and universities, think tanks, the various media) is an opportunity. There is no lack of opportunities to evangelize the intellectual culture. The question is whether we will exploit them.

The new evangelization of American intellectual culture will require elements of pre-evangelization, that is, discourse aimed at removing obstacles to the reception of the gospel message. My first suggestion, then, is: *let's not be afraid of apologetics*, that is, of a frank statement of the contents of Catholic belief and of their presuppositions, together with arguments for the truth or at least the reasonableness of these beliefs and presuppositions. In recent years "apologetics" has become something of a pejorative term in Catholic circles. But Paul Griffiths has argued forcefully that apologetics is necessary for meaningful interreligious dialogue, and I think the same is true for the new evangelization.[51]

My second suggestion is: *don't just think isms, think people*. The encyclical *Fides et ratio* and the other documents that bear on intellectual culture and the new evangelization speak in necessarily general terms about tendencies and trends of thought (positivism, fideism, rationalism, nihilism, and so on). But people are always more than instances of isms. To put the evangelization of culture into practice, we need to supplement our grasp of general principles with particular and concrete knowledge of significant figures in American intellectual culture. If each of us could become thoroughly conversant with one or two of these people, and with the obstacles that make it difficult for them to be converted or to profess the Christian faith in its fullness, that would be a great advance.

Third, we have to articulate, more thoroughly and more expressively than we have done, a Christian interpretation of the *culture of freedom*. John Paul II, following long tradition, has been speaking of genuine freedom and contrasting it with spurious freedom.[52] An authentically Christian conception of freedom could make a strong appeal to the intellectual culture and to American culture generally, but the Holy Father's idiom and tone sometimes make his message almost inaccessible to American intellectual culture. Here let me borrow from the Protestant writer Kathleen Norris. Her *Amazing Grace* may not be a great book, but it illustrates the kind of revival and freshening of language that we need if we are to communicate to the intellectual culture.[53]

Fourth, it will be important for us to study and intervene in the culture's *debates* over liberty and equality or autonomy and entitlement, over particularism and cosmopolitanism, over the theory and practice of education, over gender and sexuality. For example, Catholic elementary and secondary education, currently the stuff of cheap satire and low humor, but also of political debate, may in the long run be a crucial piece of evidence for the truth about human beings, evidence of a kind that people in the intellectual culture ought to take seriously; and if so, that is more important than the current agitation about public funding for Catholic education. And for that matter, how many people currently know, or care, what the Catholic tradition might have to say about the World Bank, the IMF, the WTO, or other aspects of the contemporary international capitalist economy?

It is of course crucial that those of us who intervene in these debates have something to say that is both informed by our Catholic commitments and that genuinely advances the discussion. As a Jesuit in training, I was often reminded about Matteo Ricci and Adam Schall and the other Jesuit missionaries in China. For the most part, the moral drawn from these reminders was the need to be adaptable. Without prejudice to adaptation, I would draw a different moral. Ricci and Schall gained entry to the court of China because they knew things that the Chinese elite wanted to know, namely mathematics and astronomy. We will more likely gain access to the present-day courts of American culture if we can address the concerns of the culture (politics and economics, particularism and cosmopolitanism, education, gender and sexuality) with contributions that are both authentically Catholic and genuinely illuminating.[54]

Hence, in the fifth place, it will be important to study and intervene in the fields of *law, economics, medicine, and the other therapeutic professions*. Here the aim must be to influence the professions precisely by understanding and articulating their particular aspects of human rationality, challenging the professions to implement these ideals, and at the same time challenging the claims of any profession to have grasped the whole of rationality. We have some promising models to follow, such as Mary Ann Glendon in law[55] and John Piderit in economics.[56] In the context of the professions and the scholarly disciplines, I would like to point to a problem that I cannot solve. Participation in a profession or a scholarly discipline tends to come at the price of a certain compartmentalization ("if you ask me as a professional, my answer is . . . ; but if you ask me as a believer, my answer is . . . ").[57]

In part this compartmentalization reflects a just respect for the autonomy of the various disciplines; in part it is a practical necessity for anyone seeking the acceptance and recognition of other professionals in the field. Still, we need to do more thinking about how the apostolate of presence, acceptance, and recognition in a profession or scholarly discipline can contribute to evangelization.[58]

Sixth, it will be important to cultivate the *liberal arts and philosophy*, precisely in order to challenge and broaden the genuine but limited rationalities of the various influential professions. This rationale for the study of philosophy and the liberal arts has nothing to do with classicist or antiquarian bias. In the context of the new evangelization, John Paul's exhortation in *Fides et ratio,* n. 81, to recover the sapiential dimension of philosophy "as a search for the ultimate and overarching meaning of life" takes on a special urgency.

Seventh, it will likewise be important to cultivate the *literary, visual, and performing arts*. The new evangelization will be stillborn or stunted if we try to present Jesus Christ or the truth about the human person simply in terms of concepts and judgments. Even intellectuals are human beings, and human beings are moved and touched by the vivid particulars of stories, pictures, music, dance, and drama. True, many practicing artists are disaffected with or hostile towards religion. This situation needs to be healed, and I do not know how to heal it.[59] I have no expert judgment on the visual and performing arts, but I hope that Paul Johnson is correct that the arts are on the brink of transformation,[60] and that they may in our time become more expressive of the truth about humanity. I also hope that we may see a renewal of authentic religious art, meaning by that not so much art with an explicitly religious subject matter as art that expresses the human aspiration towards transcendence.[61]

Eighth, it might well help the new evangelization if the Society of Jesus and the Catholic Church generally were to develop and foster more *public intellectuals*, that is, men and women whose names and ideas are known not just in a particular discipline but in American intellectual culture generally. So far as I can see, the Catholic episcopate has not had a public intellectual since Fulton Sheen. Asked to name the current American Catholic public intellectuals, I would reply with names like Cardinal Avery Dulles, S.J., Mary Ann Glendon, Alasdair MacIntyre, Richard John Neuhaus, John Noonan, Michael Novak, Andrew Sullivan, Charles Taylor, George Weigel, Garry Wills, and perhaps Lisa Sowle Cahill, Robert Drinan, Andrew Greeley, David Hollenbach, Monika Hellwig, Richard McBrien, David O'Brien, Walter Ong, and Thomas Reese. We could use a good many more. Of course, the making of a public intellectual is a delicate task. It requires intelligence (though not necessarily profound scholarship), a readiness to speak not just in a technical style to professional colleagues but in a style accessible to non-specialists, certain gifts of personality, and, let us be frank, a certain acceptance by the influential media. When I say that the episcopate has not had a public intellectual since Fulton Sheen, part of what I mean is that the relevant media have not elected to make any other bishops public intellectuals. Indeed, the influential media tend to select as public intellectuals those Catholics who are perceived, rightly or wrongly, as sharing the presuppositions of the dominant intellectual culture or of important groups within it. There is, then, no simple way to produce more Catholic public intellectuals. But it will help the new evangelization of intellectual culture if we can identify Catholics who might make good public intellectuals and help them along.

Ninth, while the importance of Catholic higher education is obvious and is affirmed in a series of papal pronouncements,[62] I believe it would help the new evangelization of American intellectual culture if we became more *sophisticated about Catholic higher education.* The debate over the implementation of *Ex corde ecclesiae* and Canon 812 has focused attention on the supervision of Catholic theological teaching, on the academic freedoms of faculty, and on the powers and immunities of college and university administrations. These are all legitimate issues, but the topic of evangelizing American intellectual culture places them in a broader context, in which the central facts are: that Catholic colleges and universities are economically dependent on the student market; that hence they are involved in a contest for recognition and prestige; that this contest for recognition and prestige conditions the processes of hiring, tenure, promotion, assignment of administrative responsibility, and the allocation of scarce resources; and that most of the referees and judges in the contest for recognition and prestige belong to the dominant intellectual culture.[63]

Largely as a result of this contest and its effects, Catholic colleges and universities have indeed become places of dialogue between faith and culture, but in a rather different sense from that envisioned by *Ex corde ecclesiae,* nn. 43-47. That document presupposes Catholic institutions of higher learning that are secure and unambiguous in their Catholic identities and invites them to address the concerns of their surrounding cultures. In the American Catholic university, however, believers and unbelievers meet as equals. Whether or not they ever talk with one another about religion and faith, they may well meet on the level of academic politics, in the practical political arguments whose outcomes influence the policies and will in the long run determine the identities of the institutions. This is an untidy and at times a painful situation, especially for those of us who grew up unprepared for the political dimensions of their college or university apostolate. But academic politics can be more than just a tedious necessity, a dispiriting rear-guard action. It can be an important locus of evangelization. The core requirement is that we be able, at the right moment and in the right setting (not necessarily a plenary meeting!), to articulate to colleagues the *deepest reasons* why we want to see our department or college or university develop in certain ways and not in other ways. Obviously this requires great tact and discretion; it cannot be a matter of brow-beating or of love-bombing. But if we cannot learn to evangelize our colleagues in this way—if the right moment and the right setting never come—then there is not much reason to think that we will evangelize American intellectual culture at large.

Tenth, we need to reflect on the role of *American Catholic* theology in the evangelization of the intellectual culture. This evangelization has to be theologically grounded and theologically sophisticated. Hence the American Catholic theological community would seem to be an important, even an indispensable, resource for the new evangelization. But there are difficulties. One is that in American academic culture members of the learned professions understandably resist taking their marching orders from any source outside their respective professions.[64] Another is that, for all their funding and faculty positions, theology, divinity, and religious studies are minor, if not marginal, disciplines within American intellectual culture at large. What are we to do, if the new evangelization of the intellectual culture has to be theological, but academic theology as currently organized cannot or will not carry the ball? Just so that the point is quite clear: here I am not talking about the issue of orthodoxy versus theological dissent, but about the relevance of theology, whether completely orthodox or partially in dissent, to American intellectual culture. This difficulty may also be an opportunity. Perhaps we need to refine current forms of theological education, or develop new forms, to impart the kind of theological formation needed by people who will move in the intellectual culture.[65] An orientation towards engagement with the intellectual culture might even be a helpful stimulus to theology. We are familiar with theological programs that are oriented towards pastoral ministry, towards religious education, and towards spirituality. Why not a theological program committed to engaging the best of American culture?

Eleventh, and here I return to a point already made, part of any strategy for the new evangelization of American intellectual culture must be to remain continually alert to the *influence of that culture on ourselves*. Let us not be surprised if we are changed by the encounter with the dominant intellectual culture. It will have things to teach us. Let us not expect that the new evangelization will leave the evangelists unchanged.

Twelfth, and last, let me raise a most delicate question, the question concerning the liturgy, especially the *liturgy* of the Eucharist. I do not suggest that we need to rework the liturgy of the Eucharist to accommodate the needs of the new evangelization. The Eucharist has already been made the instrument of enough causes and crusades for us to know that it is best understood as the worship of God, period.[66] Let me suggest, however, that a reverent and worshipful mode of Eucharistic celebration, oriented towards and expressive of God's transcendent mystery, might in its own mysterious way evangelize those members of the American intellectual culture who come into contact with Catholic worship.[67]

This long list of recommendations might give the impression that the new evangelization is first and foremost a task that we are called on to perform. That would be a serious error. We might all bear in mind the counsel of St. Ignatius Loyola that the means that unite a human instrument with God and so dispose it to be wielded dextrously by God's divine hand are more effective than those that equip it in relation to other human beings.[68]

It is God's to touch the mind, God's to touch the heart, God's to give the increase.[69]

PAPAL TEACHINGS AND RELATED DOCUMENTS CONCERNING CULTURE AND EVANGELIZATION

A. PAPAL TEACHINGS:

Paul VI, Apostolic Exhortation *Evangelii nuntiandi* (December 8, 1975), in *On Evangelization in the Modern World* (Washington, D.C.: United States Catholic Conference, 1976).

John Paul II (in chronological order):

Address to the Presidents of Catholic Colleges and Universities, The Catholic University of America (October 7, 1979), in *The Pope Speaks to the American Church*, ed. Cambridge Center for the Study of Faith and Culture (San Francisco: HarperSanFrancisco, 1982), 105-08.

Post-Synodal Apostolic Exhortation *Catechesi tradendae* (October 16, 1979), in The *Post-Synodal Apostolic Exhortations of Pope John Paul II*, ed. J. Michael Miller, C.S.B. (Huntington, Ind.: Our Sunday Visitor Publishing, 1998), 67-118.

Address to UNESCO General Conference, Paris (June 2, 1980), "Man's Entire Humanity Is Expressed in Culture," in *The Church and Culture since Vatican II*, ed. Joseph Gremillion (Notre Dame, Ind.: University of Notre Dame Press, 1985), 187-200.

Address to the Pontifical Council for Culture (January 18, 1983), in *The Church and Culture since Vatican II*, 201-06.

Address to the Pontifical Council for Culture (January 16, 1984), in *The Church and Culture since Vatican II*, 207-09.

Annual Christmas Message to the College of Cardinals (December 21, 1984), in *The Church and Culture since Vatican II*, 213-22.

Address to the Pontifical Council for Culture (January 15, 1985), in *The Church and Culture since Vatican II*, 210-12.

Address to Leadership of Catholic Education, New Orleans (September 12, 1987), in *The Pope Speaks to the American Church*, 193-99.

Post-Synodal Apostolic Exhortation *Christifideles laici* (December 30, 1988), in *The Post-Synodal Apostolic Exhortations of Pope John Paul II*, 361-462.

Opening Address to the Archbishops of the United States (March 8, 1989), in *Evangelization in the Culture and Society of the United States and the Bishop as Teacher of the Faith* (Washington, D.C.: United States Catholic Conference, 1989), 5-7.

Closing Address to the Archbishops of the United States (March 11, 1989), in *Evangelization in the Culture and Society of the United States and the Bishop as Teacher of the Faith*, 152-56.

Apostolic Constitution *Ex corde ecclesiae* (August 15, 1990) (Washington, D.C.: United States Catholic Conference, n.d.).

Encyclical Letter *Redemptoris missio* (December 7, 1990).

Post-Synodal Apostolic Exhortation *Pastores dabo vobis* (March 25, 1992), in *The Post-Synodal Apostolic Exhortations of Pope John Paul II*, 493-616.

Opening Address to the Fourth General Conference of Latin American Bishops (October 12, 1992), in Fourth General Conference of Latin American Bishops, *New Evangelization, Human Development, Christian Culture* (Washington, D.C.: United States Catholic Conference, 1993), 3-24.

Encyclical Letter *Veritatis splendor* (August 6, 1993).

Encyclical Letter *Evangelium vitae* (March 25, 1995).

Encyclical Letter *Fides et ratio* (September 14 , 1998).

Thirteen *ad limina* addresses to the bishops of the United States (1998), in *Springtime of Evangelization*, ed. Thomas D. Williams, L.C. (San Diego: Basilica Press/San Francisco: Ignatius Press, 1999).

Post-Synodal Apostolic Exhortation *Ecclesia in America* (January 22, 1999) (Washington, D.C.: United States Catholic Conference, 1999).

Letter to Artists (April 4, 1999) (Boston: Pauline Books and Media, 1999).

B. RELATED DOCUMENTS:

Evangelization in the Culture and Society of the United States and the Bishop as Teacher of the Faith, Meeting of His Holiness John Paul II with the Archbishops of the United States

(March 8-11, 1989) (Washington, D.C.: United States Catholic Conference, 1989).

Fourth General Conference of Latin American Bishops (October 12-28, 1992), *New Evangelization, Human Development, Christian Culture* (Washington, D.C.: United States Catholic Conference, 1993).

John Paul II, *Crossing the Threshold of Hope* [Answers to questions posed by Vittorio Messori], ed. Vittorio Messori, trans. J. McPhee and M. McPhee (New York: Alfred A Knopf, 1995).

Pontifical Council for Culture, *Towards a Pastoral Approach to Culture* (May 23, 1999) (Washington, D.C.: United States Catholic Conference, 1999).

NOTES

1. The principal sources of papal teaching drawn on in this paper are listed in chronological order at the end of this paper. The endnotes will cite these documents by title and section number, and, when the document is most easily found in a collection or anthology, by page number in that collection or anthology.

2. The primary content of evangelization is Jesus Christ, the Son of God, who became incarnate, died, and rose from the dead: see (in chronological order) Paul VI, Apostolic Exhortation *Evangelii nuntiandi*, n. 27, in *On Evangelization in the Modern World* (Washington, D.C.: United States Catholic Conference, 1976), 21; John Paul II, *Catechesi tradendae*, nn. 5-6, in *The Post-Synodal Exhortations of John Paul II*, ed. J. Michael Miller, C.S.B. (Huntington, Ind.: Our Sunday Visitor Publishing, 1998), 70-71; *Christifideles laici*, nn. 33-34, in *The Post-Synodal Exhortations of John Paul II*, 409-14; *Redemptoris missio*, nn. 2-4; *Ecclesia in America*, n. 66; "Called to the New Evangelization" section 2, in *Springtime of Evangelization*, The Complete Texts of the Holy Father's 1998 *Ad Limina* Addresses to the Bishops of the United States, ed. Thomas D. Williams, L.C. (San Diego: Basilica Press/San Francisco: Ignatius Press, 1999), 54-55.

3. *Evangelii nuntiandi* remains the fundamental text on the new evangelization. Building on it, John Paul II has repeatedly emphasized the need for evangelization, re-evangelization, and a new evangelization; see *Christifideles Laici*, nn. 33-34; *Ecclesia in America*, n. 66, which quotes from his Address to the Assembly of CELAM III (March 9, 1983): "new in its ardor, methods and expression." *Christifideles laici*, n. 34, speaks explicitly of a re-evangelization in areas where Christianity was formerly strong but now is challenged by secularism, atheism, and indifference to religion. *Redemptoris missio*, nn. 33 and 37, situate this new evangelization within the overall context of the the Church's mission. The new evangelization is one of the principal themes of the *ad limina* addresses in *Springtime of Evangelization* (cited above in note 2). See also Pope John Paul's interview "What is the 'New Evangelization'?" in *Crossing the Threshold of Hope*, ed. Vittorio Messori (New York: Alfred A. Knopf, 1995), 105-17.

4. See "The Mystery of the Church" section 2, in *Springtime of Evangelization*, 46.

5. See in particular (in chronological order) *Evangelii nuntiandi*, n. 20; *Ex corde ecclesiae*, nn. 48-49; *Evangelium vitae*, nn. 78, 95-100; "Called to the New Evangelization," esp. section 6, in *Springtime of Evangelization*, 53-60; *Ecclesia in America*, nn. 70-72.

6. See in particular *Evangelii nuntiandi*, n. 55; *Ecclesia in America*, nn. 13-25, 52-65 (speaking of the Americas in general, not only about the United States).

7. See in particular *Veritatis splendor*, esp. nn. 4, 32, 83, 87-88, 106-07; *Fides et ratio*, nn. 80-88.

8. See in particular *Evangelium vitae*, nn. 11-24; "Building a Culture of Life," in *Springtime of Evangelization*, 120-28; *Ecclesia in America*, n. 63 (speaking of the Americas in general, not only about the United States).

9. "Faith and Culture in the Thought of John Paul II," in *Prophecy and Diplomacy: The Moral Doctrine of John Paul II. A Jesuit Symposium*, eds. John J. Conley, S.J. and Joseph W. Koterski,

S.J. (New York: Fordham University Press, 1999), 176. Dulles's essay (*Prophecy and Diplomacy*, 175-89) gives an invaluable summary of John Paul's understanding of the relations between faith and culture.

10. I hope I may be pardoned for using the adjective "American" with primary reference to the United States.

11. In these respects I hope to extend the helpful analysis of American culture by John Cardinal O'Connor, "The Bishop as Teacher of the Faith," in *Evangelization in the Culture and Society of the United States and the Bishop as Teacher of the Faith*, Meeting of His Holiness John Paul II with the Archbishops of the United States (March 8-11, 1989) (Washington, D.C.: United States Catholic Conference, 1989), 18-31.

12. See *Sources of the Self: The Making of the Modern Identity* (Cambridge: Harvard University Press, 1989).

13. See *Sources of the Self*, esp. 495-521, as well as "A Catholic Modernity?," in *A Catholic Modernity: Charles Taylor's Marianist Award Lecture*, with responses by William M. Shea, Rosemary Luling Haughton, George Marsden, Jean Bethke Elshtain, ed. James L. Heft, S.M. (New York/Oxford: Oxford University Press, 1999), 13-37.

14. See David A. Hollinger, *Postethnic America: Beyond Multiculturalism* (New York: Basic Books, 1995), 116-24.

15. See *After Virtue: A Study in Moral Theory*, 2nd ed. (Notre Dame: University of Notre Dame Press, 1984), 222; "Politics, Philosophy and the Common Good," in *The MacIntyre Reader*, ed. Kelvin Knight (Notre Dame, Ind.: University of Notre Dame Press, 1998), 244.

16. *Without God, Without Creed: The Origins of Unbelief in America* (Baltimore/London: Johns Hopkins University Press, 1985).

17. One sample of the mentality that now confronts the new evangelization comes from the Harvard logician and philosopher of science Willard Van Orman Quine, who, asked what philosophy can usefully say about God, replied "What my own philosophy can say about God is that there is no such thing, at any rate in any ordinary sense of the word; and there is no answering for extraordinary senses." See *Key Philosophers in Conversation: The Cogito Interviews*, ed. Andrew Pyle (London/New York: Routledge, 1999), 23. Another sample comes from the poem "In That Desert," written by the poetess and science-fiction writer Ursula K. Le Guin for the AIDS Wall in Portland, Oregon: "A lizard with no tail / looked at me and its flicked tongue / said: Belief in punishment / is punishment, belief / in sin is sin." The poem appears in her *Going Out with Peacocks and Other Poems* (New York: Harper Perennial, 1994), 24. An older sample, but still worth study, is the portrait of the Catholic intellectual Caleb Wetherbee in George Santayana, *The Last Puritan: A Memoir in the Form of a Novel* (New York: Charles Scribner's Sons, 1936), 182-203; in the critical edition (Cambridge and London: MIT Press, 1994), 181-201.

18. There is at least an implicit recognition of this problem in John Paul's complaint about a tendency to understand, or rather to misunderstand, the Church by construing the exercise of Church authority in political terms: see "The Mystery of the Church," section 4, in *Springtime of Evangelization*, 48-49, as well as "Canon Law in the Life of the Church," section 3, in *Springtime of Evangelization*, 139-41. It is no accident, however, that American media tend to focus on the political dimensions of theological issues.

19. See W. V. Quine and J. S. Ullian, *The Web of Belief* (New York: Random House, 1970).

20. Putnam entitles his theory of knowledge "internal realism." See his *The Many Faces of Realism* (La Salle, Ill.: Open Court, 1987), and *Realism with a Human Face* (Cambridge, Mass./London: Harvard University Press, 1990).

21. An easy way into this aspect of Rorty's thought is his essay "Postmodernist Bourgeois Liberalism," in his *Objectivity, relativism, and truth: Philosophical Papers*, vol. I (Cambridge: Cambridge University Press, 1991), 197-202; this is also available in the first edition of *The American Intellectual Tradition, Vol. II: 1865 to the Present*, eds. David A. Hollinger and Charles Capper (New York/Oxford: Oxford University Press, 1989), 271-76, but not in the second (1993) or third (1997) editions.

22. Fish is best known as a literary critic, but the titles of two of his books hint at the broader implications of his anti-foundationalism: *There's No Such Thing as Free Speech, and It's a Good*

Thing Too (New York: Oxford University Press, 1994) and *The Trouble with Principle* (Cambridge and London: Harvard University Press, 1999).

23. I am using the terms "foundationalism" and "anti-foundationalism" somewhat loosely. For their use in contemporary analytic theory of knowledge, see Robert Audi, *Epistemology* (London/New York: Routledge, 1998), 188-89, 205-08.

24. For John Paul II's cautious assessment of post-modernity, see *Fides et ratio,* n. 91. A brief sketch of post-modernity can be found in Roger Haight, S.J., *Jesus, Symbol of God* (Maryknoll, N.Y.: Orbis Books, 1999), 330-34. For a more detailed presentation, see Kenneth L. Schmitz, "Postmodernism and the Catholic Tradition," *American Catholic Philosophical Quarterly* 73 (1999): 233-52, followed by comments by John Caputo (253-59), Thomas R. Flynn (261-66), and James L. Marsh (267-75), and a response by Schmitz (277-90); also Nancey Murphy, *Anglo-American Postmodernity: Philosophical Perspectives on Science, Religion, and Ethics* (Boulder, Colo.: Westview Press, 1997).

25. It would be worthwhile to probe the linguistic and stylistic differences between the standard American English of the intellectual culture and the type of English found in translations of papal and ecclesiastical documents. My sense is that the very style of these documents can be an obstacle to a cultured American reader, and that an important work of translation remains to be done. For an analogous case, consider the young Augustine's contempt for the Latin of the Scriptures: see *Confessions* III.5.9.

26. A particularly vigorous defense of modernity and the Enlightenment against post-modernist and other challenges is Peter Gay, "The Living Enlightenment," in *The Tanner Lectures on Human Values* 19 (1998): 69-90.

27. See *Without God, Without Creed* (cited above in note 16), 203-25, esp. 214. Charles Taylor draws on and develops Turner's work in *Sources of the Self* (cited above in note 12), 401-10, esp. 404-05. For the origin of the phrase "ethics of belief," see W.K. Clifford, *The Ethics of Belief and Other Essays* (Amherst: Prometheus Books, 1999), 70-96. Clifford's essay was first published in 1877.

28. (Cambridge and London: Harvard University Press, 1992). An accessible introduction to Posner's work is "The Outrageous Pragmatism of Judge Richard Posner," *Lingua Franca* 10/4 (May-June 2000): 26-34.

29. See their co-edited book, *The Quality of Life* (Oxford: Clarendon Press, 1993)

30. Professor Nussbaum's interventions on the issues of the day are too numerous to list here. Among her contributions are: *Cultivating Humanity: A Classical Defense of Reform in Liberal Education* (Cambridge/London: Harvard University Press, 1997), *Sex and Social Justice* (New York/London: Oxford University Press, 1999), and *Women and Human Development: The Capabilities Approach* (Cambridge: Cambridge University Press, 2000).

31. For a denunciation of American bioethics, see Wesley J. Smith, "Is Bioethics Ethical?," *The Weekly Standard* (April 3, 2000), 26-30. For a more adequate view of what bioethics can be, see Mark G. Kuczewski, *Fragmentation and Consensus: Communitarian and Casuist Bioethics* (Washington, D.C.: Georgetown University Press, 1997). In a widely circulated letter of February 28, 2000, the Baylor University ethician H. Tristram Engelhardt, Jr., wrote: "As a Catholic philosopher, you have undoubtedly noticed that many of the battles of the culture wars are fought in health care. In part, these battles have a secular expression. In great measure, they are rooted in conflicting understandings of religion, indeed, of Christianity."

32. Philip Rieff, *The Triumph of the Therapeutic: Uses of Faith After Freud* (New York: Harper and Row, 1966).

33. *The Brethren: Inside the Supreme Court* (New York: Simon and Schuster, 1979), 167, 174-75.

34. See Joseph Becker, S.J., *The Re-Formed Jesuits: A History of Changes in Jesuit Formation During the Decade 1965-1975,* vol. 1 (San Francisco: Ignatius Press, 1992), 249-52. One need not accept all of Becker's analysis to recognize the influence of contemporary psychology and psychiatry on Jesuit formation.

35. I speculate that the acceptance of homosexual activity in the artistic subculture has been key to its acceptance in the intellectual culture and to its growing acceptance in the general culture.

36. In her *A Fisherman of the Inland Sea: Science Fiction Stories* (New York: Harper, 1994), 147-91. On the positive side, Le Guin's story "The Ones Who Walk Away from Omelas" is one of the

most vivid and effective statements in contemporary American literature against consequentialist ethics; it can be found in Le Guin's *The Wind's Twelve Quarters: Seventeen Stories of Fantastic Adventure* (New York: Harper, 1975), 345-57.

37. Michael Warner, *The Trouble with Normal: Sex, Politics, and the Ethics of Queer Life* (New York: Free Press, 1999), recommended by Martha Nussbaum in *The Front Table: Noteworthy Titles from the Seminary Co-op Bookstore* (Winter 1999), 21-22.

38. Cited above in note 14.

39. *Postethnic America*, 85-86.

40. See Alasdair MacIntyre, *After Virtue* (cited above, note 15), 222. The positive contribution that argument and conflict make to tradition remains insufficiently appreciated in Catholic circles.

41. George M. Marsden, *The Soul of the American University: From Protestant Establishment to Established Unbelief* (New York/Oxford: Oxford University Press, 1994). Marsden provides a convenient summary of its thesis in "What Can Catholic Universities Learn from Protestant Examples?," in *The Challenge and Promise of a Catholic University*, ed. Theodore M. Hesburgh, C.S.C. (Notre Dame/London: University of Notre Dame Press, 1994), 187-98.

42. James Tunstead Burtchaell, C.S.C., *The Dying of the Light: The Disengagement of Colleges and Universities from their Christian Churches* (Grand Rapids/Cambridge: William B. Eerdmans, 1998).

43. Contemporary American Catholic thinkers pass differing judgments on contemporary American culture. If I read correctly, the majority take a basically favorable view of the culture, or at least a favorable view of Catholic involvement with the culture. See Michael Novak, *The Spirit of Democratic Capitalism* (New York: Simon and Schuster, 1982), *Freedom with Justice: Catholic Social Thought and Liberal Institutions* (San Francisco: Harper and Row, 1984), and *Free Persons and the Common Good* (Lanham, New York, London: Madison Books, 1989); Richard John Neuhaus, *The Catholic Moment: The Paradox of the Church in the Postmodern World* (San Francisco: Harper and Row, 1987). A minority take a more critical view of the culture. See Matthew Lamb, "Inculturation and Western Culture: The Dialogical Experience Between Gospel and Culture," *Communio* 21 (1994): 124-44; Glenn W. Olsen, "The 'Catholic Moment' and the Question of Inculturation," in *Catholicity and the New Evangelization*, ed. Anthony J. Mastroeni (Corpus Christi: Fellowship of Catholic Scholars, 1994), 17-53. See also George Weigel, "Thoughts on Some Mid-Course Corrections," in his *Soul of the World: Notes on the Future of Public Catholicism* (Washington, D.C.: Ethics and Public Policy Center/Grand Rapids: William B. Eerdmans, 1996), 1-10. It would be worthwhile, in this context, to research the legacy of John Courtney Murray, S.J. (1904-1967). Murray was an extraordinarily perceptive and articulate man, who lived at a time when the harmony between Catholic commitments and American values was closer than ever before (and perhaps closer than ever since his time), and who was quite alert to problematic trends in the culture. How Murray might have evaluated American culture in the era following *Roe v. Wade* is a matter for speculation. My sense is that, thirty-plus years on, his legacy is more often invoked to assert the harmony of Catholicism with American culture, or to hush the articulation of difficulties in the relationship between Catholicism and American culture, than to encourage a candid exploration of such difficulties. It is of crucial importance that both Catholics who take a basically favorable view of the culture and Catholics who take a more critical view should be involved in the new evangelization.

44. See, for instance, Carl Sagan, *The Demon-Haunted World: Science as a Candle in the Dark* (New York: Ballantine Books, 1996). In his biography of Sagan, William Poundstone relates that one Norman Horowitz, having detected signs that his grandson was finding religion, sent him *The Demon-Haunted World* in an attempt to dissuade him. See *Carl Sagan: A Life in the Cosmos* (New York: Henry Holt, 1999), 343. If Sagan was not highly regarded by his scientific peers, that did not prevent him from becoming an influential member of the intellectual culture—arguably more influential than most of his scientific peers.

45. See Peter Berger, *A Rumor of Angels: Modern Society and the Rediscovery of the Supernatural* (Garden City: Doubleday Anchor, 1970), 6-8.

46. John Shelby Spong, *Born of a Woman: A Bishop Rethinks the Birth of Jesus* (San Francisco: HarperSanFrancisco, 1992).

114

47. John Shelby Spong, *Resurrection, Myth or Reality: A Bishop's Search for the Origins of Christianity* (San Francisco: HarperSanFrancisco, 1994).

48. John Dominic Crossan, *The Historical Jesus: The Life of a Mediterranean Jewish Peasant* (San Francisco: HarperSanFrancisco, 1991).

49. This indeliberate but pervasive counter-evangelization is, I suspect, far more damaging than the explicitly anti-religious or anti-supernatural polemics found in, for example, *Challenges to the New Enlightenment: In Defense of Reason and Science*, eds. Paul Kurtz and Timothy J. Madigan (Buffalo: Prometheus Books, 1994).

50. Rachel Attwater, *Adam Schall: A Jesuit at the Court of China, 1592-1666*, adapted from the French of Joseph Duhr, S.J. (Milwaukee: Bruce, 1963), 41.

51. Paul J. Griffiths, *An Apology for Apologetics: A Study in the Logic of Interreligious Dialogue* (Maryknoll: Orbis Books, 1991).

52. See *Evangelium vitae*, n. 96: "No less critical in the formation of conscience *is the recovery of the necessary link between freedom and truth*" (emphasis in the official translation); *Ecclesia in America*, n. 34: "There can be no rule of law, however, unless citizens and especially leaders are convinced that there is no freedom without truth"; see also "Freedom and the Moral Law," especially sections 2-5, in *Springtime of Evangelization*, 110-17. See also Avery Dulles, S.J., "The Truth about Freedom: A Theme from John Paul II," in *Veritatis Splendor and the Renewal of Moral Theology*, eds. J. A. DiNoia, O.P., and Romanus Cessario, O.P. (Princeton: Scepter Publishers/ Huntington, Ind.: Our Sunday Visitor/Chicago: Midwest Theological Forum, 1999), 129-42.

53. Kathleen Norris, *Amazing Grace: A Vocabulary of Faith* (New York: Riverhead Books, 1998).

54. To belabor the obvious: it would be helpful if Catholics, especially Catholic academics and intellectuals, were more familiar with the major texts of Catholic tradition, such as the documents of the Second Vatican Council.

55. Mary Ann Glendon, *The New Family and the New Property* (Toronto: Butterworths, 1981), *Abortion and Divorce in Western Law* (Cambridge, Mass.: Harvard University Press, 1987), *The Transformation of Family Law: State, Law, and Family in the United States and Western Europe* (Chicago: University of Chicago Press, 1989), *Rights Talk: The Impoverishment of Political Discourse* (New York: Free Press, 1991), and *A Nation under Lawyers: How the Crisis in the Legal Profession is Transforming American Society* (New York: Farrar, Straus and Giroux, 1994).

56. John J. Piderit, S.J., *The Ethical Foundations of Economics* (Washington, D.C.: Georgetown University Press, 1993).

57. For a good example of this kind of professional compartmentalization, see William W. Meissner, S.J., M.D., *Ignatius of Loyola: The Psychology of a Saint* (New Haven/London: Yale University Press, 1992), xxiv-xxv: "If the theologian allows that Ignatius was the recipient of great mystical graces and that the miraculous course of his inspired saintly career was the work of God's grace guiding and inspiring him at every step of the way, on this subject the psychoanalyst can say neither yea nor nay. That interpretation lies beyond the scope of his methodology and theory. The psychoanalyst is concerned only with those aspects of his subject that reflect basically human motivation and the connections of psychic meaning—whether or not the patterns of behavior have religious or spiritual meaning."

58. In his response to Charles Taylor's "A Catholic Modernity?," George Marsden says: "[I]t is often easier for senior academics who are recognized in their fields to take off the secular humanist garb than for younger and less established scholars to do so" ("Matteo Ricci and the Prodigal Culture," in *A Catholic Modernity* [cited above in note 13], 91).

59. While John Paul's 1999 *Letter to Artists* is an important resource in this area, we need to do more than make the letter widely available. It is crucially important that believers who are artists find ways to speak with other artists about faith and religion.

60. Paul Johnson, "The Arts / Towards Recovery," *National Review* 52/1 (January 24, 2000): 37-41.

61. I take this distinction from W. Norris Clarke, S.J., "The Metaphysics of Religious Art: Reflections on a Text of St. Thomas Aquinas," in *Graceful Reason: Essays in Ancient and Medieval Philosophy Presented to Joseph Owens, C.Ss.R.*, ed. Lloyd P. Gerson (Toronto: Pontifical Institute of Mediaeval Studies, 1983), 301-14, esp. 301-02, 313-14.

62. Paul VI's *Evangelii nuntiandi* is curiously reticent about the place of higher education in evangelization, but John Paul II has more than made up for this: see his "Address to the Presidents of Catholic Colleges and Universities" (The Catholic University of America, October 7, 1979), in *The Pope Speaks to the American Church* (San Francisco: HarperSanFrancisco, 1992),105-08; *Ex corde ecclesiae*, nn. 48-49; *Ecclesia in America*, n. 71; "The Church's Educational Mission," sections 6-7, in *Springtime of Evangelization*, 85-88. See also the Pontifical Council for Culture, *Towards a Pastoral Approach to Culture*, n. 29.

63. In referring to these academic matters, I do not intend to slight the importance of high-visibility athletics as sources of publicity and prestige.

64. For signs that this may be changing in the natural sciences, and for signs of resistance to the change, see Eyal Press and Jennifer Washburn, "The Kept University," *Atlantic Monthly* 285/3 (March 2000), 39-54.

65. Here I am borrowing and extending what John Paul II says about priestly formation in *Pastores dabo vobis*, n. 55, in *The Post-Synodal Exhortations of John Paul II*, 574-76.

66. See John Paul II, "Authentic Liturgical Renewal," in *Springtime of Evangelization*, 129-36.

67. See Aidan Nichols, O.P., "Re-enchanting the Liturgy," in *Christendom Awake: On Re-energising the Church in Culture* (Edinburgh: T. & T. Clark, 1999), 21-39. Of course, there is a great difference between Nichols, who proposes to restore Christendom in some form, and Charles Taylor, who sees the disappearance of Christendom as a good thing (see "A Catholic Modernity?" [cited above in note 13], 17-18, 36-37). In a lecture that deserves prompt publication and wide readership, M. Francis Mannion has argued for a renewal of liturgy on the levels of eschatology, cosmology, and doxology.

68. *Constitutions of the Society of Jesus*, trans. with an introduction and commentary by George E. Ganss, S.J. (St. Louis: Institute of Jesuit Sources, 1970), 332.

69. In the preparation of this paper I have profited from Aidan Nichols, O.P., *Christendom Awake* (cited above in note 67), from several of the essays in *The New Catholic Evangelization*, ed. Kenneth Boyack, C.S.P. (New York/Mahwah: Paulist Press, 1992), and from several of the papers in *Catholicity and the New Evangelization* (cited above in note 43). Helpful background can be found in George M. Marsden, *Religion and American Culture* (San Diego: Harcourt Brace Jovanovich, 1990). I have also profited from the comments of Christopher Cullen, S.J., Richard Cobb-Stevens, John Laurance, S.J., Harriet Luckman, Gabriela Martínez, and Thornton Lockwood.

A Response to Arthur R. Madigan, S.J.

Christopher M. Cullen, S.J.

INTRODUCTION

After his 1831 tour of the young American republic Alexis de Tocqueville wrote: "The religious atmosphere of the country was the first thing that struck me on arrival in the United States . . . . It was religion that gave birth to the English colonies in America. One must never forget that . . . . America is still the place where the Christian religion has kept the greatest real power over men's souls."[1]

Tocqueville's observation reminds us of the deep religious roots of American culture, and it is important to realize to what an extent Tocqueville's observation still holds true within a large segment of American culture. We have only to call to mind the continuing vitality of evangelical Christianity and Roman Catholicism in this country. But where the situation has changed completely since Tocqueville's day is among the cultural elite. It is about the cultural elite that Madigan is speaking in his very fine paper analyzing American intellectual culture. He is speaking about the movers and shakers of society, the opinion-makers, indeed, our own contemporary puppeteers; and it is about this group that Madigan has provided us with a clear-sighted, excellent, and refreshingly realist analysis. It is due time for such forthright and truly enlightening analysis for two fundamental reasons: first, because we are easily and subtly shaped by the values of this cultural elite without realizing it, and, second, we cannot evangelize a culture without analyzing its deep philosophical assumptions. We must drag those often unspoken premises into the light of day.

Madigan's analysis is essential in the face of two fundamental facts: first, John Paul II calls us to a new evangelization—a new evangelization that has become the defining program for his entire pontificate; and, second, religion is the heart and soul of any culture. Religion transforms culture. But in order for John Paul's new evangelization to succeed, we must take account of the culture in which we live and work.

117

In my brief remarks, I would like to do three things: first, I would like to comment on the context outlined in Madigan's paper; secondly, with regard to the twelve different strategies, I would like to comment on Madigan's call to cultivate the liberal arts and philosophy, and on this point, I would like to call attention to a philosophical school that Madigan did not mention, but which I think has singularly unique contributions to make both to the evangelization of American intellectual culture and the Church; and, thirdly, I would like to second Madigan's comments on the liturgy and briefly expand on them.

THE CONTEXT: RESISTANCES

MODERNS AND POST-MODERNS

Madigan presents many of the characteristics of American intellectual culture. It seems to me to be a very accurate and fairly comprehensive analysis. He has provided just the sort of exhaustive list we need in dealing with a patient as troubled as modern American intellectual culture; he has accurately described the majority branch of contemporary American intellectual culture. However, I think it is important to take cognizance of the other branch of contemporary American intellectual culture, namely, the post-moderns.

There are some important distinctions between the moderns and post-moderns in contemporary culture. This is not the place to enumerate all of those differences in detail, but on one issue in particular it is necessary to comment, and that is on the issue of the possibility of attaining truth. Moderns tend to accept the Enlightenment by and large and, as a result, hold that truth can be attained in certain fields of human inquiry, namely, the natural and/or social sciences. In other words, in those fields that employ an empirical scientific method, moderns tend to hold that truth can be attained. The post-moderns, on the other hand, tend not to believe in the possibility of attaining objective truth. Moderns with their scientistic views—the view that the empirical scientific method as practiced in the contemporary natural and social sciences is the only valid means of attaining a systematized body of objective knowledge—tend to be found in the natural sciences, in mathematics, and in the medical and legal professions. Post-moderns are found mostly in the humanities, especially in literary studies and in certain select philosophy departments. The distinction between these two groups is important to bear in mind because those who do not believe in the possibility of attaining any sort of objective truth are going to be far harder to convert to Christianity, if it is possible at all. The post-moderns do not accept the Enlightenment settlement; these "tenured radicals" (as Roger Kimball calls them in his book on the cultural revolution of the 1960s)[2] will prove deeply resistant to Christianity in any of its forms or to any authentically religious worldview.

With this distinction in mind, however, it is also important to see a point of unity between moderns and post-moderns, and this is on the possibility of attaining truth in philosophy in general and in metaphysics in particular. Both moderns and post-moderns view metaphysics and natural philosophy with deep suspicion. Indeed, both groups tend to accept Kantian or post-Kantian critiques of metaphysics; they share a foundational skepticism on the most important issues of human life. This foundational skepticism leads often to the conclusion that the human intellect cannot attain truth in metaphysical speculation and so is not born for the contemplation of higher things. Efforts of the intellect to find ultimate fulfillment in truth and contemplation are vain. It is Kant himself who compares the search for the inner nature of things (*noumena*) behind the phenomena to the follies of mariners who abandon the island under their feet for the hope of a never-never land:

> We have now not merely explored the territory of pure understanding, and carefully surveyed every part of it, but have also measured its extent, and assigned to everything in it its rightful place. This domain is an island, enclosed by nature itself within unalterable limits. It is the land of truth—enchanting name!—surrounded by a wide and stormy ocean, the native home of illusion, where many a fog bank and many a swiftly melting iceberg give the deceptive appearance of farther shores, deluding the adventurous seafarer ever anew with empty hopes, and engaging him in enterprises which he can never abandon and yet is unable to carry to completion.[3]

As a result of such metaphysical skepticsm, the sapiential dimension of human life is largely lost. The human being is not an agent of truth; on the contrary, the human being is little more than a clever ape—the animal who makes better and more sophisticated tools than any other and, as a result, has a higher standard of living than any other. No matter how great his technological achievements or how sophisticated his electronic toys, the human being is merely a clever animal. I do not mean to suggest in any way that the problem is found in science or technology themselves; the problem is in the closing of the mind to the higher things. The closing of the mind follows from this underlying metaphysical skepticism.

RELATIVISM

What accompanies the scientistic attitude of moderns or the nihilism of the post-moderns is a radical relativism when it comes to subjects outside the domain of the physical sciences. Morality and metaphysics are both subjects of sheer opinion where objective truth, by and large, cannot be obtained. Hence, although he was speaking specifically of the problems of relativism in theology, Ratzinger is quite right when he says, "relativism has thus become the central problem for the faith at the present time."[4]

MATERIALISM

Another element of the context of American intellectual culture, which is in the background of Madigan's analysis and is obliquely referred to, needs to be dragged out into the light of day—the pervasive influence of modern materialism. (Perhaps, physicalism is a better term.) Materialism is now the dominant cosmology in the West.[5] We need to recognize this. Materialism poses increasingly grave challenges to a Christian or even religious view of life because it attacks the very foundation of any religious life. In the materialist view the human being is little more than ninety-eight cents worth of chemicals, mere atoms in motion. Materialism's challenge is especially acute in terms of certain strictly materialistic theories of evolution and in the whole burgeoning field of cognitive science.

STRATEGIES

Madigan mentions twelve different "strategies" or actions to advance John Paul II's new evangelization in the context of American intellectual culture. I largely agree with those strategies and would second them. I would like, however, to comment in particular on his call to cultivate the liberal arts and philosophy, and then I would like to expand on the twelfth way of contributing to the new evangelization that Madigan mentions, namely the liturgy.

CULTIVATING THE LIBERAL ARTS AND HUMANITIES: CLASSICIZING THE MODERN MIND

Cultivating the liberal arts is important for many reasons; I would like to mention here two in particular. First, without the liberal arts, education becomes a matter of acquiring some skill or technological know-how and not asking the philosophical questions about the meaning of life. Without the liberal arts, education becomes a purely pragmatic affair: education means merely acquiring the skills to get a job and to gain success (however it may be defined). Such an education, as America's and the West's has increasingly become, marks the triumph of the sophistic view of life: life is about being successful and getting what you want, not about truth or the contemplation of the higher things. Such an education too readily produces "hollow men,"[6] or "souls without longing."[7]

In this regard the land-grant college movement in America has marked a sort of triumph for sophistic education. The founding of land-grant colleges in order to produce engineers and agricultural technicians fits very well in such a view. These land-grant colleges have been a mixed blessing. On the one hand they have accomplished or produced technological marvels. American agriculture at the beginning of the twenty-first century has made it possible for the American farming industry to produce enough food to feed every man, woman, and child on the planet. But the land-grant colleges have also re-oriented higher education away from a focus on the liberal arts and the humanities to technology.

Secondly, cultivating the liberal arts in the humanist tradition has been an education that helped open the mind to Christian revelation. American intellectual culture was formed for many generations by the same texts and disciplines that nearly every educated Westerner had studied since at least the Renaissance.[8] It is important to bear in mind that Renaissance humanism has been thrown out as the principal means of educating the best and brightest of America's youth only in the twentieth century.[9] Of course, there was an important difference between the humanism of Protestant or secular colleges and Catholic colleges: the Catholic colleges were far more steeped in medieval scholasticism and philosophy, while the former was more strictly classical and literary. Nevertheless, the education received in the schools of the West, whether Protestant or Catholic, has been fundamentally similar over the last four centuries.[10] We have now seen the first generations of intellectuals formed apart from that classical humanist tradition, and it is not a pretty sight.[11] As intellectuals who by-and-large work in academia, the task before us, I would suggest, is to recover the West's patrimony.

Why is this so valuable for John Paul's new evangelization? Because by presenting minds with the great texts of antiquity and the Middle Ages (and some of the best of modernity), we help open minds at least capable of considering the claims of revelation. The ancient pagan mind—steeped in Hellenism—was far more open to Christianity and revelation than is that of the modern nihilist or technocrat.

Perhaps, one can only understand the value of education in the classics if one considers the perennial threats to a Christian mind: materialism and nominalism. The ancient literary texts present us the ideals of a heroic culture that regarded man as something significantly more than a clever animal—as a noble creature capable of heroic virtues. Indeed, human beings are the sort of creatures that routinely converse with the gods. Moreover, the ancient literary texts often grapple with philosophical questions and prompt the reader to search for wisdom. We have only to think of the philosophical questions that loom so large in classical Greek tragedy or the deeply philosophical character of Vergil's *Aeneid* or Seneca's letters.

Our Jesuit forebears thought that reading the great books of the ancient world helped prepare the mind for the Christian, indeed specifically Catholic sacramental worldview. The intellectual history of the West has been a story of repeated appropriations of the legacy of classical antiquity, for various purposes, whether theological, philosophical, or political. The task of opening the American mind may well lead through classical antiquity's Hellenism and its progeny.[12]

CULTIVATING PHILOSOPHY: DON'T FORGET SCHOLASTICISM

Madigan calls for cultivating philosophy. On this point, however, I think we should be more specific. One of the best ways of challenging the very foundations of modern secularism and materialism is found in a specific philosophical school—scholasticism. I think this was the great insight that Leo XIII expressed in his encyclical, *Aeterni Patris* (1879). Leo was calling us out of the fortress mentality; he was calling the Church to move beyond a siege-mentality and to engage intellectual assumptions that seemed to render Christianity either pernicious or irrelevant. Leo called the Church to rediscover her roots, her patrimony.

Chesterton's well-known comment that metaphysics has buried all its undertakers can also be applied to scholasticism. Scholasticism in its realist branches has the philosophical and intellectual tools to address the modern ailments, such as nominalism, metaphysical skepticism, materialism, the loss of transcendence and the concomitant loss of meaning. In particular, scholastic hylomorphism is uniquely able to address the challenges presented by modern materialism.

Scholasticism retains enormous vitality. To point to just a few signs of that vitality, I could mention Alasdair McIntyre's revival of the tradition of the virtues in what has been one of the most influential books of the past twenty years, his *After Virtue* (1984). In his latest book, *Dependent Rational Animals: Why Human Beings Need the Virtues* (1999), McIntyre has presented the importance of natural philosophy to ethics. I could mention William Wallace's brilliant attempt to synthesize natural philosophy and a philosophy of science in his book, *The Modeling of Nature: Philosophy of Science and Philosophy of Nature in Synthesis* (1996), or Catherine Pickstock's *After Writing* (1998), which is both an attack on post-modernism that uses the latter's own categories and a vigorous defense of various Thomistic doctrines. There are also a number of analytic philosophers who have done considerable work on Aquinas and other scholastics, e.g., Brian Davies, *The Thought of Thomas Aquinas* (1992). In fact, this group has become a sort of school in its approach, as can be seen in *The Monist*'s recent issue devoted to "Analytic Thomism."

From Leo XIII's scholastic turn to John Paul II's new evangelization, the papacy has attempted to re-evangelize the West. And at least in this regard, there is a certain continuity over the last century of papal initiatives. The pontificate of Leo XIII marks a significant strategic shift: he led the Church away from its defensive and hostile stance towards modern Western culture and initiated an attempt to reclaim Western culture after the defeats of the previous two-and-a-half centuries.

LITURGY: RE-DISCOVERING THE TRANSCENDENT

Madigan quite rightly talks about the importance of prayerful liturgies that open believers to the transcendent. The importance of a renewed liturgy to the new evangelization cannot be overstated. Religion transforms culture, but among the various elements of religion that have the most transformative effect, none can be ranked of greater importance than religious ritual or cult. Ritual establishes what is important, what is really real. Ritual orders things: what is sacred, what is man, what is his place in the cosmos, what he is to hope for. Ritual involves life in communion with transcendence.

Modernity defined itself as the conscious rejection of transcendence, as the conscious rejection of divine revelation and revelation's guardian, the Church. Transcendence has been rejected, and with it, a sacramental view of reality. In rituals things are symbols, and so, living the sacramental life reveals the symbolic nature of reality. Understood in this way, modernity is profoundly, radically antithetic to Catholic Christianity because of its rejection of transcendence and the sacramental worldview. In the ancient world Pliny wanted the Christians to give up their assemblies. The Christians replied: *Sine dominica non possumus vivere*, "Without the liturgy, we cannot live."

NOTES

1.   Alexis de Tocqueville, *Democracy in America*, eds. J. P. Mayer and Max Lerner, trans. George Lawrence (New York: Harper & Row, Publishers, 1966), 271, 291.

2.   Roger Kimball, *Tenured Radicals: How Politics Has Corrupted Higher Education* (New York: Harper and Row, 1990).

3.   Immanuel Kant, *Critique of Pure Reason*, trans. Norman Kemp Smith (Boston: Bedord/St. Martins, 1969), 257.

4.   Joseph Cardinal Ratzinger, "Relativism: The Central Problem for the Faith Today" in *Origins: CNS Documentary Service* 26 (October 31, 1996): 311.

5.   For a fine presentation of the views of contemporary materialists, see Paul K. Moser and J. D. Trout, eds., *Contemporary Materialism: A Reader* (New York: Routledge, 1995).

6.   Charles J. Sykes, *The Hollow Men: Politics and Corruption in Higher Education* (Washington, D.C.: Regnery Gateway, 1990).

7.   Michael Platt, "Souls without Longing," *Interpretation: Journal of Political Philosophy* 18/3 (1991): 415-65.

8.   Françoise Waquet describes the dominance of classical education in colonial America: "Latin was not only the daily bread of collegians in Europe, but in the New World as well: the school system established in the American colonies was modeled on what was done in England" (*Latin, or the Empire of Sign from the Sixteenth to the Twentieth Century*, trans. John Howe [New York: Verso, 2001], 22). In the nineteenth century Latin's dominance began to decline in the U.S., and its prevalence became more "variable" than in contemporary Europe where Latin retained its hegemony throughout the nineteenth century. Nevertheless, in the United States, "Latin still had an enviable place in the secondary schools in 1900, being studied by half the pupils" (Waquet, 29). Indeed, in the U.S., Latin retained a dominance until it was dropped as a requirement for admission to college; once it was no longer necessary for admission to college, it declined rapidly. In 1931 Yale dropped Latin as a requirement for applicants, and many other institutions followed suit (Waquet, 30). See also, Meyer Reinhold, *Classica Americana: The Greek and Roman Heritage in the United States* (Detroit: Wayne State University, 1984).

9.   "The place of classical studies in American education in the early twentieth-century was superficially secure . . . . Latin was required for admission to practically every traditional liberal arts college or university and widely required for the bachelor of arts degree, though there was now a Latin-less bachelor of science. Largely because of the college requirements, Latin was strong in secondary schools" (Reinhold, 337). This is not to deny, of course, the intense struggle that went on throughout the nineteenth century between defenders of classical education and those who called for a more "useful" education. See Meyer, "The Quest for Useful Knowledge in Eighteenth Century America," 50-93, and "Opponents of Classical Learning in America during the Revolutionary Period," 116-41, both sections in *Classica Americana*.

10. Classical humanism's influence in Protestant education began early; it was Luther's follower, Melanchthon, who helped already shape a Protestant humanism in the sixteenth century: "With the exception of religion . . . schooling in Brunswick and, it seems, throughout Lutheran Germany was very similar to its equivalent in Catholic countries. The situation hardly altered in the seventeenth century" (Waquet, 21). "Catholic or Protestant, seventeenth-century schoolboys throughout Europe all did Latin. And so of course did their Orthodox contemporaries. In Peter the Great's Russia there appeared schools copied from the Jesuit colleges" (Waquet, 22). "The Protestant colleges that existed in France at the beginning of the seventeenth century provided an education that, from our point of view, hardly differed from the one supplied by Jesuit establishments. Latin took up the majority of school time; pagan 'classical' authors formed the bulk of the curriculum; the same textbooks were used. . . . Nevertheless the resemblances are more striking than the differences: the same humanist approach predominated in both systems, and the difference became even less marked over the century as the study of Greek and Hebrew declined in the Protestant academies" (Waquet, 10).

11.   The eighteenth century was marked by increasing challenges to Latin's hegemony, which nevertheless remained largely intact, even though weakened. Waquet discusses at length, however, the humanist revival of the nineteenth century that took place throughout Europe: "[T]he ancient languages were honored everywhere, and everywhere they were the distinguishing mark of educational establishments for the elite . . . . In England, where the cult of the classics reached a peak in the nineteenth century, ancient languages came to represent half or even three quarters of the timetable at some public schools" (27). Waquet explains how Latin revived in French schools in the nineteenth century after a brief interlude in the Revolutionary period: "The *baccalauréat*, set up in 1808, confirmed the dominance of Latin in French nineteenth-century secondary education; the subject was compulsory for all candidates until 1882, when the *baccalauréat de l'enseignement spécial* was instituted. After that, it was possible to take the *baccalauréat* without Latin; but not until 1902 did the 'modern' *baccalauréat* secure official equality with the classical one" (13). "Education historians agree on the major place occupied by Latin in secondary education until as late as the 1880s" (Waquet, 13). Waquet describes the vicissitudes of Latin in twentieth-century France (16-19).

12.   For an interesting discussion of the debate in American culture over our relationship to the tradition of Western civilizations, see Michael Allen Gillespie, "Liberal Education and the Idea of the West," in *America, the West, and Liberal Education*, ed. Ralph C. Hancock (New York: Rowman & Littlefield, 1999), 1-25.

Pope John Paul II
and the New Age Movement

Mitchell Pacwa, S.J.

Pope John Paul II has maintained a lively interest in culture, promoting that which elevates the human person to a share in the holiness for which God has created all persons. Though he criticizes that which dehumanizes, depersonalizes and distracts from holiness, at the same time he looks for the positive impulses which may lie behind the negative manifestations. In "Beyond New Age Ideas: Spiritual Renewal,"[1] his *ad limina* address to the bishops from Iowa, Kansas, Nebraska and Missouri (May 28, 1993), John Paul II addressed his concerns about the New Age movement within the context of the call to holiness which the Church was ordained to promote.

He began with a characteristic expression of hope for the American Catholic witness to holiness, as evidenced in the variety of American saints: a native American, Blessed Kateri Tekakwitha, an immigrant St. John Neumann, and a convert born in America, St. Elizabeth Ann Seton. They demonstrate the Scriptural call[2] to holiness championed by the Second Vatican Council.[3] However, he is concerned that in the midst of the secularization of life, the recent quest for spirituality from the New Age movement "includes some very ambiguous elements which are incompatible with the Christian Faith."[4]

These incompatible elements include a desire to come to God through knowledge or experience based on Eastern mysticism and psychological techniques. They are pantheistic and "replace personal responsibility to God for our actions with a sense of duty to the cosmos." They lack attention to revelation and relativize religious doctrine "in favor of a vague worldview expressed as a system of myths and symbols dressed in religious language." Neither do they include a "true concept of sin and the need for redemption through Christ."[5]

At this point a fuller definition of the New Age movement may be useful before examining John Paul's recommended responses to this movement. I have proposed a four point definition which is able to organize the disparate fads which are included under the New Age umbrella.[6]

First, the New Age is a movement rather than an organization since it lacks a structure and unified leadership. Though some Christian critics have attempted to identify leadership and organization, this attempt typically becomes a form of conspiracy theory reminiscent of the tradition of Jesuit conspiracies to take over the world. New Age theorists disagree with each other's ideas so radically that even the casual reader notices the contradictory claims for crystal power, tarot card interpretation, spirit channeling and angelology, etc., even within the same occult field. More significantly, the New Age practitioners compete for the same customers, which leads to divisions and even lawsuits among them.

Despite this lack of unity, the pope is correct to view the movement as a significant influence within American culture. A rough survey of religion in the early 1990s indicated that only 2% of Americans considered themselves New Agers. However, the New Age book industry includes fifty publishing houses, in addition to the mainline publishers who included lucrative New Age books. Large sections of the mainstream book dealers and about two thousand specifically New Age and occult bookstores account for billions of dollars in book sales. Some estimates claim that the New Age seminars made about the same amount, though that figure may be lower at the beginning of this century due to the significant slowdown or demise of the larger seminar businesses. Still financially significant are the television offers for occult advice over 1-900 numbers, which can range from $180 to $240 and $300 dollars an hour. Astrological advice appears in nearly every newspaper and a large industry of astrologers, tarot card readers and psychics operates throughout the country. In the 1990s the angels were a seven billion dollar a year industry. Such a lucrative industry is not financed by the 2% of the population which admits to being New Age. Rather, many millions of people dabble in New Age and occult practices, spending money freely as they move from one fad to another.

The second basic idea in the New Age movement is experiential monism. While Spinoza and other philosophers developed a monist theory based on rational speculation, the New Agers avoid the rational and seek to experience the oneness of all being. Like many modern people, the New Agers fear that the divisions among governments, peoples, religions and philosophies may destroy all life on the planet through war, disease, or pollution. They assert that these disputes arise from the divisions caused by rational thinking. Reason analyzes reality and necessarily takes the world apart by defining entities. Therefore the New Age solution to these divisions is to move away from rational thinking and from defining the world into illusory individual entities so that people can experience the oneness of all reality.

New Agers back up their suspicion of reason with a theoretical avoidance of the left side of the brain, where logic dominates, in favor of the right side of the brain, which is supposedly holistic, mystical, and creative. The most commonly recommended means of short-circuiting the rational functions of the left brain are ingesting hallucinogenic drugs, yoga, breathing exercises, and hypnosis. Each technique or "psycho-technology" gives a person the much sought "altered state of consciousness" which offers a feeling of oneness with the whole universe. Such an altered state of consciousness opens the New Ager to reality and closes the curtain on the illusions which come from reason. Of course, the irony is that the rejection of reason would make verbal communication impossible, thereby causing the radical isolation of individuals in their own worlds. The New Age pursuit of monism would not unify but atomize all who make it the touchstone of their personal reality.

The third defining element of the New Age flows logically from its monism: if everything is one being, then that one being is divine. The majority of New Agers hold a radical pantheism in which everything is a part of or, using an analogy from physics, a vibration of God. A variety of doctrines, usually the most dangerous ones, flow from this pantheistic belief.

Pantheism is the basis for the denial of a true concept of sin which John Paul criticized.[7] New Agers believe that since everything is God, then everything and everyone is good. Evil does not exist, every person and thing is already perfect, so no one can judge another behavior as wicked in any manner. Even Hitler and Stalin are divine, so they are beyond moral criticism. Rather than judge behavior to be evil, all deeds are lessons from which a person can learn. Some lessons are difficult, such as murder, rape, theft—the deeds which have traditionally been considered sins—because they entail difficult karma. Karma is the law of cause and effect which underlies traditional Hindu moral thought. Every action causes its effect—evil deeds have an evil effect in this life or in a future reincarnation, and likewise with good deeds. Since New Agers deny the existence of evil and sin (contrary to traditional Hindu belief), they reject any notion of karma as punishment. Rather, karma causes an effect which educates the person by teaching correspondingly difficult lessons: the murderer will eventually get murdered, not as punishment but simply to teach the other side of this difficult lesson. Similarly, the rapist will get raped, and so on for all deeds. Of course, such a belief entails a subtle placement of responsibility for painful experiences on the victims, since New Age reincarnation teaches that each individual exercises his or her divine power in choosing each incarnation and the kind of karma it will entail. Each victim chooses to become incarnate in a body that will experience murder, rape, cancer or any other "difficult lesson" from karma.

Life is not always so fair in distributing the yin and yang, the obverse and reverse sides of these lessons, so New Agers believe that reincarnation is necessary to further the education of the soul. Since each person is already perfect, the purpose of these lessons is not moral perfection but rather a growth in awareness of the divinity and the perfection which already exists within. Redemption by Jesus Christ is not needed, since sin does not exist. Rather, growing awareness of full divinity and perfection through each person's many incarnations will bestow the same consciousness of being the Christ which Jesus attained after His many incarnations. New Agers do not want to judge Christian worship of Jesus as God, but they warn that worship of Jesus as Christ slows down an individual's ability to develop a full awareness of being Christ.

In order to advance their progress toward awareness of their divinity, many New Agers engage in various forms of the occult. Spiritual experiences are sought from traditional occult sciences such as astrology. They use eighteenth-century tarot card reading and they invent New Age tarot decks. Nineteenth-century seances have been transformed from parlor trick consultation of spirits at floating tables to hypnotic trance channeling of spirits who possess their "channels" (e.g., J. Z. Knight, Elizabeth Montgomery, et al.). Some New Agers seek hypnosis to learn about their past incarnations and gain self-understanding or improvement. A declining interest in channeled spirits was replaced by channeling angels in the 1990s. Both spirits and angels dictated hundreds of books through their mediums, to reveal the purpose of life, the nature of God, and the meaning of Jesus Christ. Precisely in these writings can one find the incompatibility with Sacred Scripture and Christian tradition. All of these versions of Christ, from Edgar Cayce's readings to *A Course In Miracles*, channeled by "Jesus" through Helen Schucman, reject the gospel's only begotten Son of God who became man to redeem sinners in favor of a New Age avatar who has evolved into a superior "Christ-consciousness."

The fourth element of the New Age movement is its astrologically based millennialism. The precession of the earth's axis is the basis for defining the sidereal ages: as the axis precesses, it points toward one of the twelve signs of the zodiac for approximately 2,160 years. The axis has pointed toward Pisces for the past 2,000 years. Pisces is symbolized by two fish. One stands for Jesus Christ, as Christians have noted by using the Greek word *Ichthus* meaning fish but acting as a Greek anagram for Jesus Christ Son of God and Savior. The other fish stands for Satan, whom many New Agers consider to be Jesus's brother, or even the fourth person of the Trinity, as C. G. Jung noted in *Answer to Job*. However, the axis of the earth is moving toward Aquarius, a water sign. This age of Aquarius will begin a new millennium in which spiritually minded people will learn to use their right brain to overcome the dualism caused by rationalistic, left brain activity. In the age of Aquarius, all people will be reincarnated as New Age believers who can communicate telepathically, not only among humans, but also with space travelers, dolphins (who are reincarnated beings from Atlantis), the spirits of the dead, etc. This millennial hope motivates some people to forsake "the ultimate hope" of the "resurrection of the dead and life everlasting" proclaimed in the Apostles' Creed and the *Catechism of the Catholic Church* (nn. 988-1065), as John Paul notes in his *ad limina* address on the New Age, n. 3.

In addition to the general New Age subculture, John Paul mentioned that New Age ideas enter "preaching, catechesis, workshops, and retreats, and thus influence even practicing Catholics" (n. 2). He did not mention any specific names or movements, but a few Catholics have gained prominence through their introduction of New Age thought. Matthew Fox, formerly a Dominican priest and presently an Episcopalian priest, has been a prime leader of Catholic New Age influence. He writes of the need to replace left brain thinking with right brain mysticism in order to take Christians beyond the dualistic thought introduced by St. Augustine and Isaac Newton. Instead of original sin, which Fox claims was an idea invented by St. Augustine in his controversy with the Celtic monk Pelagius, Fox calls Christians to center on the original blessing with which God created the universe. His goal is a more positive attitude toward the world, a living cosmology wherein science, mysticism, and art come together to encourage "deep sexuality; deep communication between young and old; deep creativity in lifestyles, work and education; deep worship; deep ecumenism and interaction among all religions of the planet."[8] The most basic goal will be "an awakening to the sacred." He rejects a theology of the fall into sin which led to a need for redemption and proposes a Cosmic Christ. Jesus Christ is the "second person" of the Trinity and also the Cosmic Christ. However, "Cosmic Christ is the divine pattern that connects in the person of Jesus Christ (but by no means is limited to that person)."[9] Fox's importance stems not only from his strong book sales, but also from the graduates of his Institute for Creation-Centered Spirituality, who have been teaching his ideas under many Catholic auspices, as the pope noted in his address to the bishops.[10]

Pope John Paul II does not encourage fear but, characteristically, he looks for the positive meaning behind the New Age Movement and then makes suggestions about responses to it. First, he asked the bishops to "detect the authentic thirst for God and for an intimate, personal relationship with him. . . . [T]he search for meaning is the stupendous quest for the truth and goodness which have their foundation in God himself, the author of all that exists."[11] He had noted this pattern in *Pastores dabo vobis:* "In the more specifically religious and Christian sphere, ideological prejudice and the violent rejection of the message of spiritual and religious values are crumbling and there are arising new and unexpected possibilities of evangelization and the rebirth of ecclesial life in many parts of the world. . . . The thirst for God and for an active meaningful relationship with him is so strong today that, where there is a lack of a genuine and full proclamation of the Gospel of Christ, there is a rising spread of forms of religiosity without God and the proliferation of many sects."[12]

In response to this "authentic thirst for God," the pope asks Christians to examine their own consciences whether their witness to Christ has been credible.[13] Have pastors, and all Christians, paid enough attention to the spiritual thirst of the human heart? Have they insisted on the spiritual dimension of the faith which recognizes the supernatural dimension where persons meet Christ the redeemer who offers the only satisfaction for human spiritual thirst?[14] Do Christians demonstrate that they are authentic teachers of the spiritual life by answering spiritual thirst as people whose lives are "hid with Christ in God" (Col 3:3). Is the Christian's hope in the resurrection of the body and eternal life clearly preached so as to offer a hope and a future which exceeds the Aquarian millennialism? Does the Christian proclaim a cold, rationalistic religion which ignores deeply felt religious thirst or psychological pain? Does it ignore sensitivity to the ecology and a love of the beauty of nature? The Christian's examination of conscience in these regards can lead to the proclamation of the Gospel which is both sensitive to the needs of New Age seekers and faithful to the truth of salvation in Jesus Christ.

John Paul summons Christians to proclaim those spiritual goods and truths which will provide an antidote to the New Age syncretism of Eastern spirituality, psychological techniques, and the occult. While the New Age monism moves toward the peaceful unity of the human race, the rejection of the rational precludes the verbal communication which aids in that unity by a common search for the truth. The New Age's radically isolated individualism is best countered with that hiddenness in Christ which offers ecclesial, communal intimacy with God as the basis of human unity.[15]

John Paul especially recommends "more vigorous preaching and catechesis on eschatological themes" as an antidote to the New Age Aquarian millennialism. Instead of belief in reincarnation which reduces the significance of "the absolute uniqueness of each human person and the finality of death," Christians preach that life in the body has a transcendent goal. Relevant to this is the importance of the soul's immediate judgment after death, the need to pray for the purification of souls before seeing God, and the existence of an eternal hell.[16] The New Age temptation to ignore the reality of sin and the possibility of damnation leads them "to think of salvation as a right and as a foregone conclusion." The Church's evangelical task is "to remind people of the awesome reality of human freedom, the price of salvation (cf. 1 Cor 7:23) and the riches of divine mercy (cf. Eph 2:4)." In this the New Age movement will find not condemnation but the basis for human dignity.[17]

Though his *ad limina* address turns toward the issue of vocations to the priesthood and religious life, a basic point remains relevant to evangelization of the New Age movement. He reminds the bishops that "the call to holiness" is an invitation to everyone (Eph 1:4). Successful preaching to the New Age will not entail an attempt to incorporate New Age beliefs and practices into the Church so as to make them feel comfortable with their already held beliefs. Such an attempt by Matthew Fox, his school and others simply waters down the Church's teaching and confuses the people of God with syncretism. Instead, Catholics can evangelize the New Age by offering the fullness of the Gospel, the hope of eternal life, and its deep ennoblement of each person before God. Such is the task which John Paul leads through his own willingness to preach and teach to any and all in the world, whether through apostolic visits or his writings. This is the task he hands over to all Catholics in regard to the New Age movement and all others who need Jesus Christ the Redeemer.

NOTES

1.   John Paul II, "Beyond New Age Ideas: Spiritual Renewal" [hereafter "Beyond"] in *Origins* 23/4 (10 June1993): 59-61.

2.   For example, 1 Peter 1:15-16: "But as He who called you is holy, be holy yourselves in all your conduct; since it is written, 'You shall be holy, for I am holy.'"

3.   John Paul II, "Beyond," n. 1.

4.   John Paul II, "Beyond," n. 2.

5.   Ibid.

6.   See M. Pacwa, S.J. *Catholics and the New Age* (Ann Arbor: Servant Press, 1992), where this definition is expanded, and New Age ideas common to Catholic circles are developed.

7.   John Paul II, "Beyond," n. 2.

8.   Matthew Fox, *Coming of the Cosmic Christ* (San Francisco: Harper and Row, 1988), 161, 8.

9.   Ibid, 135. See also Pacwa, for further critique of Fox and other New Age influences within Catholicism.

10.   John Paul II, "Beyond," n. 2.

11.   John Paul II, "Beyond," n. 3.

12.   John Paul II, *Pastores dabo vobis*, Apostolic Exhortation On the Formation of Priests in the Circumstances of the Present Day (25 March 1992), n. 6.

13.   Ibid.

14.   John Paul II, "Beyond," n. 3.

15.   *Lumen gentium,* n. 1: "Christ is the light of humanity; and it is, accordingly, the heartfelt desire of this sacred Council, being gathered together in the Holy Spirit, that by proclaiming His Gospel to every creature (see Mk 16:15), it may bring to all men that light of Christ which shines out visibly from the Church. Since the Church, in Christ, is in the nature of sacrament—a sign and instrument, that is, of communion with God and of unity among all men—she here purposes, for the benefit of the faithful and of the whole world, to set forth, as clearly as possible, and in the tradition laid down by earlier Councils, her own nature and universal mission."

16.   John Paul II, "Beyond," n. 4.

17.   Ibid.

John Paul II and Interreligious Dialogue

Joseph A. Bracken, S.J.

In his introduction to a set of essays by non-Christians on Pope John Paul II's approach to interreligious dialogue, Harold Kasimow notes: "John Paul II, who is sincerely dedicated to interfaith relations as a means of promoting justice and peace and mutual understanding among religions, is at the same time the most devoted and influential Christian missionary of our century."[1] While this might seem to some as a high compliment paid to the pope by a Jewish scholar, it actually reflects feelings of deep ambiguity on his part toward the role of John Paul II in contemporary interreligious dialogue. For, as he shortly thereafter explains, there is a tension here between the overall intent of interreligious dialogue and the goal of proclamation of the Gospel, which is apparently not felt by the pope but is deeply felt by many non-Christians. As Kasimow comments, "the aim of mission [or proclamation of the Gospel] is not just to enrich the other person, to make him or her a more spiritual member of his or her community. The aim of mission is to convert the person to Christ."[2] In effect, then, Kasimow is questioning whether Pope John Paul II is unconsciously working at cross-purposes with himself in making dialogue and proclamation co-constituents of the Church's overall mission. Either he should focus exclusively on proclamation of the Gospel and not pretend to engage in dialogue with the representatives of other religions, or he should give himself fully to the task of interreligious dialogue and effectively give up the task of proclamation of the Gospel.

Yet, the pope clearly does not admit the existence of this dichotomy. As he says in *Redemptoris missio*, "Interreligious dialogue is part of the Church's evangelizing mission. . . . The Church sees no conflict between proclaiming Christ and engaging in interreligious dialogue."[3] Furthermore, many Christians (including most Jesuits) would likewise feel profoundly uncomfortable with a forced choice between evangelization and dialogue as the way to implement their Christian vocation in life. Yet, credibly to maintain the complementary character of evangelization and dialogue within one's life and mission, one should have at hand a theoretical understanding of the nature and function of interreligious dialogue which legitimates that complementarity. My task in this paper will be to offer such a schema, quite tentative, to be sure, but perhaps sufficiently articulated to provoke further reflection and discussion among the participants at this conference. Accordingly, I will first review Pope John Paul II's comments in a recent address entitled "A Dialogue of Peace and Brotherhood" where he makes quite clear once again the link between evangelization and dialogue. Then I will summarize the work of James L. Fredericks in a recently published book *Faith among Faiths* wherein he proposes a new approach to interreligious dialogue in terms of what he calls comparative theology.[4] But, since Fredericks regards comparative theology simply as "a process or practice, not a theory,"[5] I will in the third part of this essay attempt a theoretical justification of the "practice" of comparative theology on the basis of my understanding of the world of intersubjectivity in which we all live. Finally, in the fourth part of the essay, I will indicate how, as I see it, Pope John Paul II's approach to interreligious dialogue fits into this new scheme as set forth by Fredericks and myself.

I. POPE JOHN PAUL II ON INTERRELIGIOUS DIALOGUE

In a "catechesis" dated September 9, 1998 and subsequently published in the *Newsletter of the Jesuit Secretariat for Interreligious Dialogue* (1999, n. 6), Pope John Paul II first makes reference to *Nostra aetate*, the Second Vatican Council's Declaration on the Relation of the Church to Non-Christian Religions: "The Catholic Church rejects nothing of what is true and holy in these religions. She has a high regard for the manner of life and conduct, the precepts and doctrines which, although differing in many ways from her own teaching, nevertheless often reflect a ray of that truth which enlightens all men" (*Nostra aetate,* n. 2). Commenting upon this passage, the pope first notes that this is an ancient doctrine of the Fathers of the Church. "The 'seeds of truth' present and active in the various religious traditions are a reflection of the unique Word of God, who 'enlightens every man coming into the world' (cf. Jn 1:9) and who became flesh in Christ Jesus (cf. Jn 1:14). They are together an 'effect of the Spirit of truth operating outside the visible confines of the Mystical Body' and which blows where it wills (Jn 3:8; cf. *Redemptor hominis,* nn. 6, 12)."

The pope concludes therefrom that "every quest of the human spirit for truth and goodness, and in the last analysis for God, is inspired by the Holy Spirit. The various religions arose precisely from this primordial human openness to God." The Holy Spirit was, accordingly, silently at work in the religious experience of the founders of the various world religions, is reflected even now in the doctrines and rituals of those same religions, and finally comes to expression in the prayers of believers, both Christian and non-Christian, throughout the world. Poignant witness to this Spirit-filled power of prayer was provided by the World Day of Prayer for Peace at Assisi on October 27, 1986, when the pope gathered with the leaders of many world religions, each to pray in his own way for world peace. Furthermore, given the omnipresence of the Holy Spirit not only in the minds and hearts of individuals but also in the customs and practices of entire peoples, one must likewise conclude that non-Christians will be saved in and through the devout practice of their own religions. As John Paul notes, normally "it will be in sincere practice of what is good in their own religious traditions and by following the dictates of their own conscience that the members of other religions respond positively to God's invitation and receive salvation in Jesus Christ, even while they do not recognize or acknowledge him as their Savior (cf. *Ad gentes,* nn. 3, 9, 11)."

What Pope John Paul II is claiming here, of course, is what makes Harold Kasimow and others like him uneasy: namely, that their salvation is to be found in Christ even against their own better judgment and conscious intention. The pope is equivalently saying that he knows something about the true import and meaning of their religious beliefs which they themselves do not know (as yet). Inevitably, this appears as an unconsciously patronizing attitude toward them on the part of the pope even though he clearly wants to avoid that impression. For, as he says in that same catechesis, "the attitude of the Church and of individual Christians towards other religions is marked by sincere respect, profound sympathy, and, when possible and appropriate, cordial collaboration." But then, of course, John Paul immediately adds: "This does not mean forgetting that Jesus Christ is the one Mediator and Savior of the human race. Nor does it mean lessening our missionary efforts, to which we are bound in obedience to the risen Lord's command: 'Go therefore and make disciples of all nations, baptizing them in the name of the Father and of the Son and of the Holy Spirit' (Mt 28:19)." With this comment, the discomfort of Kasimow and others returns. Keeping in mind this psychological impasse between individuals of obvious good will toward one another, let us now turn to Fredericks's notion of comparative theology (as opposed to what has been generally termed theology of religions).

137

II. A NEW PARADIGM FOR INTERRELIGIOUS DIALOGUE

At the beginning of *Faith among Faiths*, Fredericks lays out the three classical approaches to interreligious dialogue, namely, exclusivism, inclusivism, and pluralism, and he indicates how all three are defective in terms of his own criteria for an adequate Christian theology of religions. These two criteria can be phrased as questions. First, is the theory in question faithful to the overall Christian tradition or, on the contrary, does it effectively deny some of its basic tenets? Secondly, does the theory assist Christians to deal creatively with their non-Christian friends? That is, will Christians as a result not only learn about these other religions but also learn from them so as to enrich their own Christian faith? Perhaps the more important of these two criteria for Fredericks is the second since in his mind the basic problem with interreligious dialogue at present is that very real differences both in doctrine and in ritual between the various world religions are being ignored in the search for similarities or common ground. In any event, in the next few paragraphs, I will summarize the main lines of Fredericks's argument.

Karl Barth is, in Fredericks's eyes, a representative of the policy of exclusivism in dealing with non-Christian religions because he insists that "there can be no knowledge of God apart from his special revelation within history: Jesus Christ."[6] All religions, including Christianity, are "foolish, sinful attempts to justify ourselves apart from the grace of God."[7] Christianity, to be sure, has served as the historical vehicle for God's free self-revelation; hence, it may be counted as the one true religion but only in virtue of divine grace, not because of anything that Christians have done to earn that distinction. In any event, "[o]nly those who profess faith in Jesus Christ, the final and unsurpassable revelation of God to the world, can be saved."[8] As Fredericks sees it, Barth's approach to theology of religions is flawed both because it implicitly denies the universal salvific will of God (cf. 1 Tm 2:4) and because it offers no incentive for Christians to learn about, still less to learn from, the other world religions.

Karl Rahner, on the other hand, offers a notable example of an inclusivist approach to interreligious dialogue. With his "theology of the anonymous Christian," for example, he affirms, on the one hand, that Christianity is the "absolute religion" in the sense that in Jesus Christ God has made a final and unsurpassable self-revelation and that God intends the Church to be the religious home for every human being.[9] But, on the other hand, says Rahner, God is genuinely at work in the beliefs and practices of various non-Christian religions; accordingly, non-Christians who are faithful to their own religious beliefs and practices will still enjoy salvation through the saving merits of Jesus Christ.[10] Hence, non-Christians who are faithful to their own religions can be thought of as "anonymous Christians." Rahner's approach to non-Christian religions clearly has much in common with that of Pope John Paul II as summarized above. Nonetheless, Fredericks finds Rahner's theory (like that of Karl Barth) unacceptable. For, in terms of the criterion of continuity with the Christian tradition, Fredericks asks whether membership in the institutional Church loses all significance if conscientious non-Christians can be counted as "anonymous Christians."[11] Likewise, in terms of helping Christians to deal creatively with their non-Christian neighbors, Rahner's theory is defective because it implicitly eliminates the need for Christians to study carefully the beliefs and practices of non-Christians. In effect, Christians already know the deeper meaning and value of those beliefs and practices since in the final analysis they are only preparatory for the fullness of divine revelation to be found in Christ and the Church.

Turning then to one of the pluralist theologians, John Hick, Fredericks notes, first of all, that Hick's own position on the proper approach to interreligious dialogue changed over the years. Initially, Hick advocated what he called a theocentric (as opposed to a Christocentric) approach to religious diversity: "All religions, doctrines, concepts, and symbols point beyond themselves to the incomprehensible and inexpressible mystery of the divine itself. Therefore, contrary to exclusivist and inclusivist views, no religion can claim to occupy the center of the universe of faiths."[12] Later, however, he adopted a "reality-centered" focus for interreligious dialogue: "Each of the great religions offers human beings a way of freeing themselves from the prison of their own ego for a life lived in unity with reality itself, however this unity may be interpreted within the religious traditions themselves."[13] In both cases, of course, the divinity of Jesus has to be seen as mythological rather than factual; that is, the Gospel story of the life, death and resurrection of Jesus is "a model or paradigm for understanding in a nonliteral fashion realities that are considerably more complex."[14] Likewise, taking this mythological approach to what counts as Ultimate Reality in the various world religions, Hick, like Rahner, implicitly claims to know more about the various world religions than the orthodox believers in each case: that is, "all religious believers, no matter what they might actually say about themselves, are really talking about the same transcendent Absolute" under different names.[15] Hence, just as with the exclusivism of Karl Barth and the inclusivism of Karl Rahner, Hick's pluralist position does not encourage Christians first to learn about the various non-Christian religions and then to learn from them in terms of enriching their own Christian faith.

Fredericks turns next to Paul Knitter as still another distinguished proponent of the pluralist position. In contrast to John Hick, Knitter argues for "the need to incorporate the justice concerns of the theology of liberation into Christianity's view of non-Christian religions."[16] Hence, as Knitter sees it, "Jesus did not preach about himself as the incarnation. Jesus preached the liberation of every human being in the coming of God's kingdom."[17] Jesus, accordingly, should be seen as only one of many religious figures who have proclaimed a message of salvation to their followers. What is precisely meant by salvation, of course, will differ from one religion to another since salvation is never available to human beings in the abstract, but always in terms of "a particular path, practice, sacrament, ritual, or savior figure."[18] Yet, the basic notion of salvation as concern for "the well being of humans and the earth" clearly serves as a criterion for Knitter in his judgments about the efficacy of various religions in the cause of global peace and justice.[19]

In this way, Knitter avoids total relativism in his approach to world religions. But, as Fredericks points out by way of critique, he equivalently converts salvation into a metaphysical Absolute which tends to submerge the very real differences between the world religions in matters of doctrine and ritual. Implicitly, therefore, Knitter is urging on members of non-Biblical religions a vision of justice and peace grounded in the notion of the Kingdom of God as found in the Bible. But does he thereby fully respect the integrity of these other religions? In the eyes of a Christian or Jew, for example, the caste system in India would seem to be a glaring example of social injustice, whereas for Hindus the same caste system, at least in its overall configuration, is sanctioned by the Vedas, the sacred writings of their religion. In brief, then, Knitter like Hick seems to fall into the "trap" of judging the various world religions in terms of an extrinsic common denominator (for Hick, Reality; for Knitter, salvation). Yet this strategy, as Fredericks sees it, has the double negative consequence of oversimplifying both their own religious tradition, namely, Christianity, and the doctrine and practices of the other world religions. As a result, there is little or no challenge for Christians to study deeply the actual beliefs and practices of members of other religions in the hope of ultimately enriching their own religious heritage.

The ground is thus prepared for presentation of what Fredericks means by comparative theology in which Christians remain loyal to their own faith-tradition and yet acquire new resources for understanding and appreciating that same faith-tradition in the light of the beliefs and practices of other world religions. He offers two examples of such an approach to non-Christians religions, only one of which I will summarize and comment upon here. In the Buddhist tradition, life and death are not viewed as opposites but rather as complementary features of one and the same reality. Hence, one will never really live fully without accepting the inevitability of one's death, and one will always fear death until one sees death as a necessary part of the life-process. Initially, such a perspective on life and death appears to be totally opposed to the Christian worldview. For, the whole point of the Christian vision is to proclaim the conquest of death in terms of Christ's resurrection from the dead and the promise of eternal life for us as His followers (cf. Rom 5:12-21). Thus Buddhism and Christianity would seem to be basically opposed in their respective attitudes toward life and death. But, says Fredericks, there are still other passages in Paul's letters and in the New Testament generally which affirm that the power of Christ's resurrection is at work in the minds and hearts of Christians even now, well in advance of their eventual death and personal resurrection. As Paul notes in Colossians 2:12, for example, through Baptism Christians are both buried with Christ and rise with him to new life as members of the Christian community.

Fredericks's point in all this, of course, is that the Buddhist notion of the complementary or "non-dual" character of life and death can be very helpful for Christians in bringing them to realize the full dimensions of their own Christian belief in the resurrection. In this sense, one can learn not only about Buddhism but also from Buddhism in order to enrich one's own Christian faith. This is what comparative theology aims to accomplish. At the same time, Fredericks carefully notes that the overall world views of Buddhism and Christianity are quite different, even opposed on key issues. Whereas Buddhists, for example, focus on the present moment so as to be attentive to persons and things in their "suchness," Christians view the present moment both in itself and in terms of an eschatological future: "Dying and rising with Christ means becoming a new creation, here and now. But at the same time dying with Christ also means becoming heir to the resurrection as a future promise that will become real 'on the last day.'"[20] Thus, while Christians inevitably experience a tension between what already is and what someday will be, Buddhists instinctively view with suspicion any diversion, however pious, from complete absorption in the present moment.[21] Buddhists and Christians, therefore, must learn to appreciate and value their differences as well as their commonalities in terms of doctrine and ritual.

III. A Philosophical Justification

Before exploring how Fredericks's approach to interreligious dialogue matches up with the approach taken by Pope John Paul II, I want to set forth something like a philosophical justification for Fredericks's stance. For, even though Fredericks himself sees his approach as simply a strategy for dealing with a theoretical impasse among students of the various world religions, namely, the inability of exclusivists, inclusivists, and pluralists to reach agreement on the necessary presuppositions of effective interreligious dialogue, I believe that this move on Fredericks's part can be theoretically justified in terms of an incipient metaphysics of intersubjectivity. That is, if dialogue among members of different world religions inevitably takes place in an intersubjective context, then new insight or objectivity is achieved more through shared perspectives or consensus on a given issue than simply through appeal to rational argument. Reason, in other words, always operates within the context of a personal set of beliefs, only some of which can be subjected to re-examination at any given moment.[22] No matter how forcefully I present arguments in support of my beliefs, these arguments will be persuasive to others only to the extent that my beliefs somehow make sense within their own belief-systems or worldviews. A basic consonance or compatibility between at least some of my beliefs and some of the beliefs of my dialogue-partners must take shape if the conversation is ultimately to bear fruit.[23] This is not to exclude, of course, the possibility of a religious conversion on the part of an individual so that he or she may eventually change belief-systems and thereby become am adherent of another religion. But the far more common assumption would seem to be that individuals, while remaining within their antecedent belief-systems, will slowly come to appreciate and value the belief-systems of others, see in these other worldviews or belief-systems unexpected resources for enriching their own religious beliefs.[24]

If we shift now to the level of interreligious dialogue between entire communities or faith-traditions, then in my judgment the same guidelines still apply. That is, even more than with individuals, religious communities will possess an antecedent set of beliefs which define their religious identity. In their dealings with other religious groups with different belief-systems, they will be receptive to those beliefs characteristic of other faith-traditions which are somehow consonant or compatible with their own cherished beliefs; on the other hand, they can be expected to reject or at least view with suspicion those beliefs set forth by other religious groups which clash with their own beliefs. Likewise, just as with individuals, religious communities can be expected to undergo some limited transformation in their belief-systems through dialogue with other religious groups. But, unlike individuals, religious communities cannot be expected to undergo a religious conversion to the belief-system or worldview of another religious community and thereby to give up their historical self-identity. The very fact that their corporate self-identity is maintained through an ongoing discernment and evaluation with respect to goals and values which they all in principle endorse argues very strongly against the group as a whole abruptly deciding to abandon one worldview and embrace another.

Implicit here in my thinking is what I call a metaphysics of intersubjectivity whereby subjects of experience in dynamic interrelation create structures of intelligibility or ongoing patterns of thinking and action for their mutual exchange. Objectivity in terms of what is considered good and true is thereby generated in and through sustained intersubjectivity.[25] Appeals to right reason and/or divine revelation as totally independent criteria for what is considered true and good, therefore, are not logically possible within this scheme since what is understood to be eminently reasonable and/or of divine origin has to be received subjectively and transmitted to others intersubjectively. Put in other terms, what is proclaimed as true and good on the basis of right reason and/or divine revelation ultimately has to be received and evaluated in terms of what the individual or community already understands to be true and good. If individuals or communities find these claims unreasonable or not in accord with divine revelation as they previously have understood it, then they will reject or view with great suspicion such a proclamation of what is true and good, even when it comes from an otherwise very reputable source. Realistically, they cannot do otherwise since what is implicitly under attack is the underlying network of beliefs by which they define their ongoing individual and collective self-identity.[26] This is, of course, not to deny the objective validity of right reason and divine revelation for the guidance of both individuals and communities, but only to claim, as noted above, that within this metaphysical scheme both right reason and divine revelation are inevitably received subjectively and transmitted to others intersubjectively. Pure objectivity with respect to truth and goodness would seem to be an illusion.[27]

IV. JOHN PAUL II'S APPROACH TO INTERRELIGIOUS DIALOGUE

At this point we may briefly reconsider Pope John Paul II's approach to interreligious dialogue in which, as noted earlier, he consciously links dialogue with proclamation of the Gospel. As I see it, he is fully entitled to make that claim, both in terms of his personal beliefs as a conscientious Christian and in view of his position as head of the Roman Catholic Church. Those non-Catholics who take offense at this stance of the pope are not sufficiently taking into account the implicit network of beliefs out of which the pope is operating in making that claim. Pope John Paul II is presumably what we have considered above an inclusivist, one who is personally convinced that Jesus Christ is the Savior of the world and that all well-intentioned human beings, regardless of their religious affiliations, will ultimately be saved in and through the merits of Christ. Hence, it makes perfectly good sense for the pope simultaneously to engage in friendly dialogue with adherents of the other world religions and at the same time tirelessly to preach the message of the Gospel to them in the hopes of bringing about their eventual conversion to Christ, either in a public or in a strictly private way. For him to do anything else would be in his mind to betray his own duty as a faithful Christian and as head of the Catholic Church.

On the other hand, in my judgment, the pope himself could perhaps be more sensitive to the way in which his announced campaign for evangelization in the new millennium will almost inevitably be received by non-Christians, above all, Hindus, Buddhists, Confucians, Taoists, and so on in South and East Asia. They will surely reserve to themselves the judgment how much of the Gospel message they can and should incorporate into their own network of religious beliefs stemming from their membership in a specific non-Christian religious community. They will, accordingly, almost certainly resist any overt attempt at mass conversion to Catholicism by the pope or any other well-intentioned Roman Catholics. Quite the contrary, their interest in and attraction to the teachings of the Catholic Church will be presumably conditioned upon what they perceive as a corresponding interest in the teachings of their religions on the part of the pope and other Roman Catholics. In this respect, the strategy laid down by James Fredericks in *Faith among Faiths* is very judicious. Instead of trying directly to convert the other parties in interreligious dialogue to one's own religious world view, one should aim, first, through dialogue to learn about these other religions and then to learn from them for the enrichment of one's religious tradition.

The results of such cautious interreligious exchange, of course, will in all likelihood not be immediately evident. But one may surmise that in the end the long-range success of the pope's campaign for the conversion of Asia in the twenty-first century may be largely dependent upon the successful implementation of such a strategy. My wager, in other words, is that Catholicism will be successful in both interreligious dialogue and proclamation of the Gospel in South and East Asia to the extent that Catholics show themselves as truly open-minded in their appreciation and appropriation of the religious insights and values of classical Hinduism, Buddhism, Taoism, Confucianism, etc. Non-Catholics in those parts of the world, in other words, will presumably feel quite "at home" within Roman Catholicism because so many of their own cherished religious beliefs and values have somehow found a "home" within the doctrines and rituals of the Catholic Church both in Asia and elsewhere around the world. Whether this will result in significantly increased numbers of personal conversions to Catholicism remains to be seen since conversion is ultimately a matter of personal response to divine grace. But such a strategy for the continued linkage of dialogue and evangelization would seem to be, in my judgment, a truly humane and Christian way to proceed.

To sum up, then, I think that Pope John Paul II has done admirable work in using his role as head of the Roman Catholic Church to foster dialogue among the adherents of the various world religions on different occasions, notably at Assisi in Italy on October 27, 1986. Likewise, it is clear that he retains not only a deep respect but also an affection for those individuals with whom he has thus engaged in dialogue. All that seems to be lacking is perhaps a greater willingness on his part both to learn about and to learn from these other world religions. Some of his remarks on various occasions have been sharply criticized by non-Catholics as basically wrong or at the very least insensitive to the religious feelings of those to whom they were addressed.[28] All this can be remedied in due time if Pope John Paul II and/or his successor reflects more deeply on what we mentioned earlier, namely, that truth and goodness, even though obviously tied both to right reason and to divine revelation, nevertheless can only be received subjectively and transmitted to others intersubjectively. One must respect the different ways in which other human beings determine what is true and good for the conduct of their lives.

NOTES

1. Harold Kasimow, introduction to *John Paul II and Interreligious Dialogue,* eds. Byron L. Sherwin and Harold Kasimow (Maryknoll: Orbis Books, 1999), 6.
2. Kasimow, 7.
3 John Paul II, *Redemptoris missio,* n. 55, cited in Kasimow, 7.
4. James L. Fredericks, *Faith among Faiths: Christian Theology and Non-Christian Religions* (New York: Paulist Press, 1999), 6-11.
5. Fredericks, 9.
6. Fredericks, 17
7. Fredericks, 17.
8. Fredericks, 17.

9. Fredericks, 24.
10. Fredericks, 25.
11. Fredericks, 30.
12. Fredericks, 40.
13. Fredericks, 48.
14. Fredericks, 42.
15. Fredericks, 109.
16. Fredericks, 56.
17. Fredericks, 56.
18. Fredericks, 64.
19. Fredericks, 69.
20. Fredericks, 158.
21. Fredericks, 159. See also the reply of the noted Buddhist scholar Thomas P. Kasulis to the "realized eschatology" set forth by Ruben Habito, a Christian scholar, in "The Momentous and the Momentary," *The Sound of Liberating Truth: Buddhist-Christian Dialogues in Honor of Frederick J. Streng*, eds. Paul O. Ingram and Sallie B. King (Surrey: The Curzon Press, 1999), 239-43.
22. See Bruce D. Marshall, *Trinity and Truth* (Cambridge: Cambridge University Press, 2000), 144-45.
23. Marshall, *Trinity and Truth*, 154-55.
24. Marshall, *Trinity and Truth*, 176-79. Marshall makes clear how more intensive study of Jewish belief in the divine election of the people of Israel has illuminated Christian belief in Jesus as the Incarnate Word of God. That is, God's predilection for the people of Israel is reflected for Christians in the fact that Jesus was a Jew who in His own way carried forward the teachings of Judaism.
25. See my *The One in the Many: A Contemporary Reconstruction of the God-World Relationship* (Grand Rapids: Eerdmans, 2001).
26. Marshall, *Trinity and Truth*, 149: "A communal belief system will thus have assimilative power to the extent that it can incorporate novel truth claims without making the community give up its own most central beliefs, and so abandon its identity-constituting epistemic priorities." Certain beliefs, in other words, are crucial for the self-identity of both individuals and communities; to give them up is equivalently to give up one's previous individual or corporate identity in favor of still another individual or corporate self-identity.
27. See my article "Authentic Subjectivity and Genuine Objectivity," *Horizons* 11 (1984): 290-303, where I argue that objectivity and intersubjectivity mutually condition one another.
28. Consider, e.g., a response of the Dalai Lama to the controversial critique of Buddhism by John Paul II in his book *Crossing the Threshold of Hope* (New York: Alfred Knopf, 1994), in which the pope characterizes Buddhism as "atheistic" and "indifferent to the world, which is the source of evil" (85-86): "I [the Dalai Lama] have not felt that his view of Buddhism is very deep. His remarks about the Dharma [Buddhist doctrine] in his book are both sad and amusing. They are sad because his approach moves in the direction of polemics, and amusing because so superficial. Buddhism does not regard the world as evil; the world is basically neutral. What is really a problem, or can be evil, is the attitude of grasping, or attachment, selfish attachment stemming from ignorance" (*John Paul II and Interreligious Dialogue*, 87). At the same time, the Dalai Lama professes his admiration for and friendship with Pope John Paul II because of their common concern both for social justice and for growth in spirituality.

A Response to Joseph A. Bracken, S.J.

Earl C. Muller, S.J.

Joseph Bracken begins his essay entitled "John Paul II and Interreligious Dialogue" by noting the ambiguity felt by the Jewish scholar, Harold Kasimow, at the conjunction between evangelization and interreligious dialogue in the thought of the pontiff. He wonders whether John Paul is not "working at cross-purposes with himself" in this. The principal thrust of Bracken's own effort is to establish "a theoretical understanding of the nature and function of interreligious dialogue which legitimates that complementarity." To this end Bracken evokes a metaphysics of intersubjectivity. "Reason," he observes, "always operates within the context of a personal set of beliefs." He does not refer to Hans-Georg Gadamer here, although he could have. All of our understandings take place within the context of a particular horizon of meaning. Achieving an understanding of a 'text' formulated within a different horizon of meaning requires a fusing of horizons in which one's own horizon is expanded to include the horizon in which the text was formulated. Here "text" is understood broadly to mean the verbal or behavioral affirmations of members of a different religion. Bracken concludes that "non-Catholics who take offense at this stance of the pope are not sufficiently taking into account the implicit network of beliefs out of which the pope is operating in making that claim." He then closes out his essay with a suggestion for an evangelical strategy that is more effective in the light of the metaphysics of intersubjectivity that he has set out.

I am in substantial agreement with Bracken's methodological proposal and with his conclusions. For this reason I propose to offer in the following remarks complementary considerations on the conjunction between evangelization and interreligious dialogue rather than a detailed analysis of Bracken's argument. There are two unequal points focused around the evangelistic dynamic of the Church (which will be treated very briefly) and the good represented by the religions of the world in themselves. This latter will follow and critique the discussion provided by Jacques

Dupuis, S.J. in a recent work, *Toward a Christian Theology of Religious Pluralism.*[1]

From the side of evangelization, I would suggest that effective missionary activity requires a complete inculturation of the Gospel. Such an inculturation, even as it purifies and transforms the culture into which it is entering, cannot prescind from the religious structure of that culture since culture and religious structure are not neatly separable from one another. Effective evangelization requires detailed and sympathetic knowledge of a given culture and, accordingly, detailed and sympathetic knowledge of the religious structure of that culture. From the side of those being evangelized, a detailed and sympathetic knowledge of Christianity (and of the cultures in which it arose and grew) is likewise required if any conversion is to take place. The acquisition of this two-sided knowledge so useful for conversion requires dialogue. Of course, the dialogue partners can, for their part, also have missionary agenda motivating their participation in such talks. In this regard even evangelically motivated talks can be understood as mutual rather than one-sided. Obviously this would be less true in instances where one dialogue partner was not missionary in its outreach.

If the rationale for engaging in genuine dialogue for the sake of evangelization is fairly straightforward in the sense that conversion requires at some point an exchange of knowledge, the rationale for engaging in dialogue because of the positive good to be found in the world religions requires a more detailed theological grounding. The history of the Church's reflection on the possibility of good being found in non-Christian religions has been mixed and generally negative. A very brief sketch of some of the issues and the positions taken is necessary to frame our discussion properly. This will be drawn largely from Dupuis's work.[2] There are two interrelated questions at issue: whether individuals can be saved outside the visible confines of the Christian Church and whether non-Christian religions have any salvific value.

The fundamental structure of the answer given through the centuries was provided by the Church's reflection on the history of humankind and of Israel prior to the advent of Christ. Enoch was taken up into heaven. Abraham was justified by his faith. The God of Jesus Christ was the God who led Israel out of Egypt, the God who gave the Law to Israel. The answer to both of the questions posed in the preceding paragraph was positive. The Church, however, had to reconcile this view with its even more fundamental conviction that there was no salvation apart from Jesus Christ (Acts 4:12). The salvation of individuals outside of the Church and the salvific efficacy of non-Christian religions had to be related to Christ and, by implication, to His Church.

This was easily accomplished with regard to Israelitic or Jewish religion prior to Christ. The rituals and laws given to Israel by God foreshadowed Christ and His salvific work. God, in Judaism, was preparing the way for the coming of His Son and for the establishment of the Church. What was promised beforehand in Judaism was fulfilled in Christ and in Christianity. The saving efficacy of Jewish sacrifices was grounded in this intrinsic forward-looking reference to Christ.

This notion of Judaism as a *praeparatio evangelica* was, *mutatis mutandis,* applied also to the Greco-Roman world. Hellenistic philosophical thought was of central importance in this broadened application of the principle of Gospel preparation. If the pagan philosopher was indeed able to arrive at truth, it was because he had access to the truth, either in terms of a covert reliance on the inspired Scriptures or, more importantly, in terms of the availability of the Logos to the mind of every human individual. Christians quickly identified this philosophical Logos with Jesus, the very Word of God. The philosophical activity of the pagan world prepared the way for the Christian message. Even the more religious elements of the Hellenistic world were pressed into this sort of service—the Christian adaptation of the Sibylline Oracles is simply one instance of this.[3]

The work of preparation, however, is over once the reality prepared for appears on the scene. If the principle continued to be valid in the period of Christian expansion, it was widely understood to be no longer relevant once Christianity had become the official religion of the empire. The Gospel had been preached to all the nations and those who still refused to accept Christ and enter the Church, or who had departed from the Church through heresy, were thought to be lost. It is in this period that the principle *extra ecclesiam nulla salus* was formulated. In explicit form it goes back to St. Cyprian, although elements of it are found as early as Ignatius of Antioch. Cyprian, and certainly Ignatius, had heretics and schismatics in view. Augustine, and especially his disciple Fulgentius of Ruspe, extended the principle to cover Jews and pagans as well.

Cyprian and Fulgentius are the usual sources used by subsequent councils and official documents of the Church. Those statements are fairly explicit in their use of the principle. Innocent III insisted on a confession of faith in the Waldensian crisis which affirmed that outside the Roman Church "no one can be saved."[4] The Fourth Lateran Council, against the Albigensians and Cathars, asserted that "there is indeed one universal church of the faithful, outside of which nobody at all is saved."[5] Boniface VIII's bull of 1302, *Unam Sanctam,* is even stronger. Not only is there no salvation outside of the Church, but Boniface concludes with a doctrinal declaration: "that it is absolutely necessary for the salvation of all men that they submit to the Roman Pontiff."[6] The Council of Florence, in the sixth part of the bull of union with the Armenians where the Athanasian Creed is cited, asserted that "whoever wills to be saved, before all things it is necessary that he holds the catholic faith. Unless a person keeps this faith whole and undefiled, without doubt he shall perish eternally."[7] In the bull of union with the Copts, the Council quoted Fulgentius to the effect "that all those who are outside the Catholic Church, not only pagans but also Jews or heretics and schismatics, cannot share in eternal life . . . unless they are joined to the Catholic Church before the end of their lives; . . . and that nobody can be saved, no matter how much he has given away in alms and even if he has shed his blood in the name of Christ, unless he has persevered in the bosom and the unity of the Catholic Church."[8]

Within fifty years of Florence, the New World was discovered. This event served to crystallize earlier attempts at enunciating broader perspectives and led over the next few centuries to various proposals for what Dupuis refers to as "'substitutes' for faith in Jesus Christ and Church membership for salvation."[9] There had been early speculation among some of the Fathers of the Church that one of the purposes for Christ's descent into hell was to preach the Gospel to those who had lived before Him. This never gained much currency because it "would contradict the Christian doctrine according to which the eternal fate of souls is fixed at death."[10] Others, even as late as Cardinal Billot, suggested an intermediate place in the afterlife, limbo, where virtuous pagans as well as unbaptized children would dwell. This, in Dupuis's view is a "desperately negative solution."[11]

Thomas had provided three different avenues that theologians would exploit. Although he insisted on explicit faith in the Trinity and in the Incarnation of the Word as necessary for salvation, he hedged this with regard to those who had gone before Christ and spoke of an implicit faith present which grounded their salvation. Secondly, Thomas developed the notion of a baptism of desire which was sufficient for salvation which included even those who had not heard about Christ but "whose desire to conform to the will of God afforded them the faith and charity which justify."[12] Finally, Thomas held that coming to the age of reason involved "a firm moral decision before God, aided by grace." This "included implicit faith in Jesus Christ as well as an implicit desire of baptism."[13]

This latter was developed by theologians into the notion of the fundamental option. The former two notions were developed, especially by the theologians at the University of Salamanca and the Roman College, into a developed theory of implicit faith. Coincidentally the Council of Trent explicitly allowed for salvation through a baptism of desire, and the condemnations of Baianism and Jansenism made it clear that the Church accepted the notion of the presence of grace outside the confines of the visible Church. Papal pronouncements in the wake of the Enlightenment were generally oriented to the condemnation of indifferentism with regard to the world religions which in various ways reaffirmed the necessity of the Church. Pius IX, in the allocution *Singulari Quadam*, set out invincible ignorance as subjectively excusing individuals from the requirement to enter the Church for salvation. Salvation is denied only those who culpably refuse to become members of the Church. It was Pius XII, in the encyclical *Mystici Corporis*, who first developed at length in a magisterial document the notion that non-Catholics can be ordained to the mystical Body of Christ "in desire resolution (*etiamsi inscio quodam desiderio ac voto ad mysticum Redemptoris Corpus ordinentur*)."[14] The condemnation of Leonard Feeney followed a few years after this. In that condemnation the need for an orientation toward the Church was reaffirmed, but it was explained that visible membership was not absolutely required.[15]

Dupuis singles out two major approaches among Catholic theologians leading up to Vatican II. The first, which he calls the fulfillment theory, is represented by figures like Jean Daniélou, Henri de Lubac, and Hans Urs von Balthasar. "Daniélou draws a sharp distinction between nature and the supernatural, or equivalently between religion and revelation. 'Non-Christian' religions belong to the order of natural reason, the Judeo-Christian revelation to the order of supernatural faith."[16] De Lubac identified Christianity as the single axis of the divine plan. Like Daniélou, he would understand the relationship between the world religions and the Judeo-Christian tradition in terms of a correlation between nature and the supernatural. For von Balthasar, Christ is the "Concrete Universal." He contrasted the personal God of the religions of the book to the impersonal divine reality which characterizes the God of Eastern religions. In his own way von Balthasar echoed the nature-supernatural structure which characterizes the positions of Daniélou and de Lubac. The mysticism of the East "proceeds from man and sets out in the direction of God," whereas the mysticism of Christianity is characterized by a God who reaches out to men.

It is more accurate to characterize this first approach by this contrast between the natural and the supernatural rather than by the focus on Christianity as the fulfillment of all human religiosity. A number of writers following the second approach would likewise understand Christianity as the fullest or fulfilling revelation of God. The key difference between the two approaches is the assessment that is made of the intrinsic worth of non-Christian religions. Theologians of the former group see no salvific value as such. Salvation requires supernatural faith, and this cannot be obtained by any purely natural striving for God. Non-Christian religions at best provide only the spatio-temporal occasions for God's grant of saving grace to individuals; they in no way mediate that grace.

The second approach, as Dupuis puts it, refuses to separate nature from grace. Rahner's "supernatural existential" is typical. Abstractly considered, the natural desire to see God grounds an obediential potency to self-transcendence in God but this is not grace. However, God concretely wills the salvation of all and by grace has built into each individual a graced dynamic that is inherent in all human actions, including the construction of a religion. Efforts by non-Christians to achieve union with God are already graced from, as it were, within nature. It would follow that non-Christians can be saved not simply because of a grace that comes to them apart from their natural efforts but precisely in them. This "supernatural existential inherent in them in their concrete historical reality constitutes the a priori condition for the possibility of the incarnation." This implies, of course, that God's self-revelation in Christ is "the perfect realization, the absolute fulfillment, of anthropology."[17]

Variants of this approach are found in the works of Raimon Panikkar, Hans Küng, and Gustave Thils. Küng, in particular, is dependent on Rahner's work though he goes further in seeing the world religions as the ordinary means of salvation for their members. Thils argues that natural knowledge of God is already a revelation of God. Insofar as this cosmic revelation lies at the base of the world religions, salvation is possible within them. Thils's distinction between this cosmic revelation and the supernatural revelation of the Judeo-Christian tradition is close to the distinction between nature and the supernatural of the first approach. The difference is that he allows a mediation of grace through this natural revelation. The most problematic of this group of theologians is Panikkar. In looking to the reality behind the Jesus-myth as being the Christ who is also found in Hinduism, he severely qualifies the uniqueness of Jesus Christ and approaches those theologians who propose a theocentric rather than a Christocentric foundation for a theology of religious pluralism.

Vatican II did not declare itself for either theological view, though there was development over previous magisterial statements in the explicitness of the expectation of the availability of the grace of salvation outside the Church. There are a number of relevant statements. The first is found in *Lumen gentium,* nn. 16-17:

> Finally, those who have not yet accepted the gospel are related to the people of God in various ways. . . . There are others who search for the unknown God in shadows and images; God is not far from people of this kind since He gives to all life and breath and everything, and the Savior wishes all to be saved. There are those who without any fault do not know anything about Christ or His Church, yet who search for God with a sincere heart and, under the influence of grace, try to put into effect the will of God as known to them through the dictate of conscience: these too can obtain eternal salvation. Nor does divine Providence deny the helps that are necessary for salvation to those who, through no fault of their own, have not yet attained to the express recognition of God yet who strive, not without divine grace, to lead an upright life. For whatever goodness and truth is found in them is considered by the Church as a preparation for the gospel and bestowed by Him who enlightens everyone that they may in the end have life.

There are several things to notice about this passage. First, salvation is placed within the twin context of a relationship or orientation toward the people of God, the Church. Second, the universal salvific will of God is the ground for the possibility of salvation outside the Church. This salvific will is specified as the will of the Savior, Jesus Christ. Third, salvation is always a result of human response to the grace of God and is never apart from that grace. Fourth, all that is good and true of those who are outside the Church is understood as a *praeparatio evangelica.* The doctrine is thus very traditional even as it is far more optimistic about salvation outside the visible confines of the Church than previous documents. It is also to be noted that this statement is compatible with either side in the preceding theological discussion—salvation as understood in terms of grace given to individuals who follow the dictates of their conscience or salvation understood as mediated by good and true means found providentially provided by God (e.g., in the various world religions). This last is made a bit more explicit in the decree *Nostra aetate*:

The Catholic Church rejects nothing of those things with are true and holy in these religions. It regards with respect those ways of acting and living and those precepts and teachings which, though often at variance with what it holds and expounds, frequently reflect a ray of that truth which enlightens everyone (n. 2).

The second text of interest is *Gaudium et spes,* n. 22:

This [reception of the Spirit] applies not only to Christians but to all people of good will in whose hearts grace is secretly at work. Since Christ died for everyone, and since the ultimate calling of each of us comes from God and is therefore a universal one, we are obliged to hold that the Holy Spirit offers everyone the possibility of sharing in this paschal mystery in a manner known to God.

The Council does not specify the manner in which this offer is made to non-Christians. The manner is known to God, not to the Council Fathers. That God is active through non-Christian religions themselves is not closed out. What is clear is that such mediations are mediations of the paschal mystery of Christ even if this is in no way explicit.

The next set of texts are from the Decree on Missionary Activity, *Ad gentes*:

This all-embracing plan of God for the salvation of the human race is accomplished not only as it were secretly in their souls, or through the efforts, including religious efforts, by which they see God in many ways . . . . for these efforts need to be guided and corrected, even though in the loving design of God's providence they can at times be regarded as leading towards the true God or as paving the way for the gospel message (*praeparatione evangelica*).

Missionary activity is nothing other and nothing less than the manifestation or epiphany of God's plan and its fulfilment in the world and in its history. . . . Whatever truth and grace are already to be found among peoples—a secret presence of God, so to speak—it frees from evil infections and restores to Christ their source. . . . Accordingly, whatever good is found to be sown in the minds and hearts of human beings or in the particular rites and cultures of peoples, not only does not perish but is healed, elevated and perfected, to the glory of God, the confusion of the devil and the happiness of humankind.

In order that they may be able to give this testimony to Christ fruitfully, they should associate with these people in a spirit of respect and love. . . . They should be familiar with their national and religious traditions; they should with joy and reverence discover the seeds of the Word which lie hidden in them. . . . Just as Christ Himself searched into the hearts of people, and by a genuinely human dialogue led them to the divine light, so too His followers, profoundly animated by the Spirit of Christ, should know the people among whom they live and should associate with them, so that they themselves, by sincere and patient dialogue, may come to know what riches a generous God has distributed to the nations. At the same time, however, let them strive to illustrate these riches with the light of the Gospel, to set them free and to restore them to the dominion of God the savior.[18]

Religious efforts on the part of non-Christians are explicitly named and described as possibly leading to God and serving as a preparation for the Gospel. Where God is active among non-Christians, that activity is ordered to liberation from sin and union with Christ, which is to say, it is salvific. Whatever is good, including religious rites, is to be preserved, healed, elevated, and perfected. Missionary activity is essential, in part because it manifests the structure of the saving grace that is available to everyone. Finally, and quite importantly as will be made clear later, one of the motivations for interreligious dialogue is so that Christians themselves may come to know the riches that God has distributed to the nations.

Paul VI did not advance beyond the Council. Indeed, his characterizations of the world religions as "natural," as having "their arms stretched out towards heaven," clearly place his view within the first of the pre-conciliar Catholic approaches discussed above. It is only in Christianity that the human movement upward toward God is met by a downward movement, with God reaching down to humanity.[19] There is thus an exclusivity to Christianity; all other religions are simply understood as a preparation for the religion of Jesus.

John Paul II, however, has made a "singular contribution . . . in the emphasis with which he affirms the operative presence of the Spirit of God in the religious life of non-Christians and the religious traditions to which they belong."[20] The texts are numerous and echo the more positive elements of Vatican II. Bracken mentions the catechesis dated September 9, 1998. Dupuis examines several others. We will examine them in roughly chronological order.

In *Redemptor hominis* (1979) the pope wrote that "the firm belief of the followers of the non-Christian religions . . . is also an effect of the Spirit of truth operating outside the visible confines of the Mystical Body."[21] A little later, citing *Ad gentes,* n. 11, he noted that the Council Fathers had seen "in the various religions as it were so many reflections of the one truth, 'seeds of the Word,' attesting that, though the routes taken may be different, there is but a single goal to which is directed the deepest aspiration of the human spirit as expressed in its quest for God."[22] In the next paragraph, reflecting on the dignity of the individual, he wrote that the missionary must respect "everything that has been brought about in him [the non-Christian] by the Spirit, which 'blows where it wills.'" This same point is made in the catechesis which, as Bracken noted, concludes with the affirmation that "every quest of the human spirit for truth and goodness, and in the last analysis for God, is inspired by the Holy Spirit." It is this which led to the rise of the various religions.

Bracken makes note of the Assisi prayer meeting held in 1986. John Paul's comments on the Spirit are of interest in the present context: "Every authentic prayer is under the influence of the Spirit . . . . We can indeed maintain that every authentic prayer is called forth by the Holy Spirit, who is mysteriously present in the heart of every person."[23] The pope had already expressed this sentiment in his "Message to the People of Asia" (Manila, 21 February, 1981): "We trust that wherever the human spirit opens itself in prayer to this Unknown God, an echo will be heard of the same Spirit who, knowing the limits and weakness of the human person, Himself prays in us and on our behalf . . . . The intercession of the Spirit of God who prays in us and for us is the fruit of the mystery of the redemption of Christ, in which the all-embracing love of the Father has been shown to the world."[24] John Paul did not explicitly say that this activity of the Spirit in every authentic prayer is mediated as such through the rituals of the world religions. The focus was in each instance on what is happening in the heart of the person praying. Still, given that such rituals have been constructed to give expression to that prayer activity, this cannot be closed out.

The most important document by the pope on the Holy Spirit has been his encyclical, *Dominum et vivificantem* (1986). In n. 53 of this encyclical, he pointed out that the Spirit has been active "even before Christ—*even from the beginning*, throughout the world."[25] Of course, this activity is "closely linked with the mystery of the Incarnation and Redemption," and the pope concludes that "grace . . . bears within itself both a Christological aspect and a pneumatological one, which becomes evident above all in those who expressly accept Christ." He thereby seems to accept a principle akin to Rahner's "anonymous Christian." He expanded the perspective beyond the period prior to Christ and, citing *Gaudium et spes* and *Lumen gentium*, "we need to look further and go further afield, knowing that 'the wind blows where it wills.'" The activity of the Spirit "outside the visible body of the Church" associates non-Christians with the Paschal Mystery.

Dupuis focuses solely on the relation of the Spirit to the world religions in Pope John Paul II's thought and does not reflect on the relation between the Spirit and the Church. Some consideration needs to be made of this if one is to situate the pope's thoughts with regard to the necessity of the Church for salvation. In this regard he evoked the scene with Nicodemus and "the need for a new birth '*of water and the Spirit*' in order to 'enter the kingdom of God'" in n. 1 of his encyclical (emphasis added). The Spirit is "the vital principle of the Church, in which He works in union with the Head of the Mystical Body, Christ."[26] He is "the soul of the Church."[27] "The *Redemption accomplished by the Son* in the dimensions of the earthly history of humanity—accomplished in His 'departure' through the Cross and Resurrection—is at the same time, in its entire salvific power, *transmitted to the Holy Spirit*"[28] (emphasis added). "In the power of the whole Paschal Mystery of Jesus Christ, the Holy Spirit comes in order to remain *from the day of Pentecost onwards* with the Apostles, to remain with the Church and in the Church, and through her in the world"[29] (emphasis added). The references can be multiplied. There remains an ecclesiocentric understanding of redemption even of non-Christians that will have to be taken into account in the next synthetic section of this paper.

The encyclical *Redemptoris missio* (1990) continued the theme of the activity of the Spirit throughout the world but also of the central importance of the Church. Jesus Christ "is the one Savior of all, the only one able to reveal God and lead to God"[30] and as the opening line of the letter makes clear, "the mission of

Christ the Redeemer . . . is entrusted to the Church." The various aspects of the mystery of Christ are unitary. "In the process of discovering and appreciating the manifold gifts—especially the spiritual treasures—that God has bestowed on every people, we cannot separate those gifts from Jesus Christ, who is at the center of God's plan of salvation."[31]

> Christ won the Church for Himself at the price of His own blood and made the Church His co-worker in the salvation of the world. Indeed, Christ dwells within the Church. She is His Bride. It is He who causes her to grow. He carries out His mission through her.

> The Council makes frequent reference to the Church's role in the salvation of humanity. While acknowledging that God loves all people and grants them the possibility of being saved, the Church believes that God has established Christ as the one mediator and that she herself has been established as the universal sacrament of salvation. . . . It is necessary to keep these two truths together, namely, the real possibility of salvation in Christ for all humanity and the necessity of the Church for salvation. Both these truths help us to understand the *one mystery of salvation*, so that we can come to know God's mercy and our own responsibility. Salvation, which always remains a gift of the Holy Spirit, requires man's cooperation, both to save himself and to save others. This is God's will, and this is why He established the Church and made her a part of His plan of salvation.[32]

John Paul went on, noting that salvation is concretely available to everyone, "not only to those who explicitly believe in Christ and have entered the Church."[33] He acknowledged the various reasons why many, without guilt, do not enter the Church. "For such people salvation in Christ is accessible by virtue of a grace which, while having a mysterious relationship to the Church, does not make them formally part of the Church but enlightens them in a way which is accommodated to their spiritual and material situation."

Dupuis cites this letter in support of the notion of a universal activity of the Spirit:

The Spirit manifests Himself in a special way in the Church and in her members. Nevertheless, His presence and activity are universal, limited neither by space nor time . . . . The Spirit . . . is at the very source of humanity's existential and religious questioning, a questioning which is occasioned not only by contingent situations but by the very structure of his being.

The Spirit's presence and activity affect not only individuals but also society and history, peoples, cultures and religions.[34]

But the pope goes on:

This is the same Spirit who was at work in the Incarnation and in the life, death and resurrection of Jesus, and who is at work in the Church. He is therefore not an alternative to Christ, nor does He fill a sort of void which is sometimes suggested as existing between Christ and the Logos. Whatever the Spirit brings about in human hearts and in the history of peoples, in cultures and religions serves as a preparation for the Gospel and can only be understood in reference to Christ, the Word who took flesh by the power of the Spirit . . . .

Moreover, the universal activity of the Spirit is not to be separated from His particular activity within the body of Christ, which is the Church. Indeed, it is always the Spirit who is at work, both when He gives life to the Church and impels her to proclaim Christ, and when He implants and develops His gifts in all individuals and peoples, guiding the Church to discover these gifts, to foster them and to receive them through dialogue. Every form of the Spirit's presence is to be welcomed with respect and gratitude, but the discernment of this presence is the responsibility of the Church, to which Christ gave His Spirit in order to guide her into all the truth.[35]

There are several things to note about this passage. First, the activity of the Spirit in the world religions is understood as a *preparatio evangelica*. In this he has not departed from the continuous tradition of the Church. Second, this activity of the Spirit is inseparable from His activity in the Church. The evangelistic dynamic of the Church is the flip side, as it were, of the same coin in which the Spirit manifests Himself in the religions of the world. This provides the context for the genuine advance that John Paul makes over previous documents—the manifestations of the Spirit outside the visible confines of the Church are to be fostered and received. Still, it is the Church who exercises the gift of discernment in this case. The text can only be characterized as highly ecclesiocentric.

Dupuis delays his treatment of these ecclesiocentric aspects of this letter until his later treatment of the kingdom, though he notes even in this earlier treatment of John Paul's thought that there is this sort of emphasis in later documents. He cites *Tertio millennio adveniente* (1994): "Jesus does not in fact merely speak 'in the name of God' like the Prophets, but He is God Himself speaking in His Eternal Word made flesh. Here we touch upon the essential point by *which Christianity differs from all the other religions by which man's search for God* has been expressed from earliest times. Christianity has its starting-point in the Incarnation of the Word"[36] (emphasis added). The contrast that is here drawn between the search for God which characterizes the religions of the world and God's entry into the world which characterizes Christianity is reminiscent of the distinction between the natural and the supernatural which marks what Dupuis refers to as the "fulfillment theory" and which characterized the thought of Paul VI.[37] He is disappointed "because this seems to leave no room for recognizing in the other religious traditions themselves a first divine initiative towards human beings, no matter how incomplete, and for attributing to the religious traditions a positive role in the mystery of salvation of their followers."[38] The pope showed awareness of current discussions of the theology of religions in *Redemptoris missio*. He wrote:

> There are also conceptions which deliberately emphasize the Kingdom and which describe themselves as "Kingdom-centered." They stress the image of a Church which is not concerned about herself, but which is totally concerned with bearing witness to and serving the Kingdom. . . .

> Together with positive aspects, these conceptions often reveal negative aspects as well. First, they are silent about Christ: the Kingdom of which they speak is "theocentrically" based, since,

according to them, Christ cannot be understood by those who lack Christian faith, whereas different peoples, cultures and religions are capable of finding common ground in the one divine reality, by whatever name it is called. . . .

Furthermore, the Kingdom, as they understand it, ends up either leaving very little room for the Church or undervaluing the Church in reaction to a presumed "ecclesiocentrism" of the past, and because they consider the Church herself only a sign, for that matter a sign not without ambiguity.[39]

There are a variety of schemes available categorizing the various theological approaches to the religions of the world. One influential effort was that of J. Peter Schineller, S.J., who set out to study the correlation between diverse ecclesiological and Christological positions in an article entitled "Christ and Church: A Spectrum of Views."[40] He found that positions tended to fall into one of four classifications: (1) an ecclesiocentric universe with an exclusive Christology; (2) a Christocentric universe with an inclusive Christology; (3) a theocentric universe with a normative Christology; and (4) a theocentric universe with a non-normative Christology. It is against this and similar conceptual schemes that John Paul II's thoughts must be understood. Dupuis himself is clearly sympathetic with the second position.

Still, Dupuis is, quite rightly in my opinion, critical of many such categorical schemes because they presume incompatibilities where none necessarily exist. He argues with others that "the dilemma between inclusivism and pluralism, or equivalently, between Christocentrism and theocentrism, must be transcended."[41]

We have noted above that in Christian theology, Christocentrism, if correctly understood, must not be viewed as contradicting theocentrism; on the contrary, it presupposes it and calls for it. The same is true where the various binaries discussed above are concerned: Christocentrism and soteriocentrism, Christocentrism and regnocentrism, Christology and Jesuology, Christology and Logology, Christology and pneumatology—all are and ought to be viewed as interrelated aspects and complementary elements of the indivisible, whole, and entire reality;

they can only wrongly be set in opposition to one another.

> The integral model we are searching for in view of a Christian interpretation of religious pluralism can best be expressed in terms of a Trinitarian Christology.[42]

One notes that ecclesiocentrism is not included in this list of "complementary elements." His fear is that, the condemnation of Leonard Feeney notwithstanding, a number of magisterial documents provide considerable moral support for a rigid ecclesiocentrism that he finds objectionable. He is more than sympathetic with Congar's suggestion "that the axiom *Extra Ecclesiam nulla salus* should be abandoned" since it cannot "be understood without long explanations."[43]

How does he work around the ecclesiocentrism of the various magisterial documents that we have been examining? He accomplishes this through a "paradigm shift" to regnocentrism. He notes that until recently "the Church was identified quite simply with the Reign of God; on the other hand, the Roman Catholic Church was well and truly thought to be identical with the Church itself."[44] The latter was certainly the view of Pius XII's *Mystici Corporis*. Vatican II, however, was led "to distance itself quite clearly from the identification of the mystery of the Church with the Roman Catholic Church" and the reason was the desire to acknowledge ecclesial elements in other Christian churches.[45] At the same time there had been development in the understanding of the kingdom of God and particularly with regard to its eschatological dimension. The effect of these studies was to establish a distance between the historical reality of the Church and the kingdom.

Dupuis acknowledges that Vatican II and a number of post-conciliar documents continue, in large measure, to identify the Church with the kingdom.[46] *Redemptoris missio*, however, significantly modified the earlier view. On the one hand, it clearly affirmed that a kingdom-centered perspective could not be opposed to a Christ-centered view. On the other hand, although the kingdom cannot be detached from the Church, it is not identical with the Church:

> It is true that the Church is not an end unto herself, since she is ordered towards the Kingdom of God of which she is the seed, sign and instrument. Yet, while remaining distinct from Christ and the Kingdom, the Church is indissolubly united to both. . . . The result is a unique and special relationship which, while not

excluding the action of Christ and the Spirit outside the Church's visible boundaries, confers upon her a specific and necessary role; hence the Church's special connection with the Kingdom of God and of Christ, which she has "the mission of announcing and inaugurating among all peoples."[47]

It is true that the inchoate reality of the Kingdom can also be found beyond the confines of the Church among peoples everywhere, to the extent that they live "Gospel values" and are open to the working of the Spirit who breathes when and where He wills. But it must immediately be added that this temporal dimension of the Kingdom remains incomplete unless it is related to the Kingdom of Christ present in the Church and straining towards eschatological fulness.[48]

These texts are decisive for Dupuis since they establish distinctions "on the one hand, between the Reign in time and its eschatological dimension and, on the other hand, between the Reign and the Church."[49]

It is easy to establish the "continuity between the Kingdom-centered character of Jesus's proclamation and the Christocentrism of the kerygma of the apostolic times."[50] Dupuis briefly argues, following Oscar Cullmann, that the relation between the Church and (the kingdom in) the world should be understood as "concentric circles whose common centre is Christ."[51] This allows him to conclude, then, that "the universality of the Reign of God consists in that Christians and the 'others' share the same mystery of salvation in Jesus Christ, even if the mystery reaches to them through different ways." He adopts a kingdom-centered approach that is interconnected, not mutually exclusive, with a Christocentric one. It follows that interreligious dialogue can proceed in a more mutual fashion than is possible under an exclusive, ecclesiocentric perspective.

Concomitant with this Dupuis must narrow the meaning of the doctrine of the necessity of the Church. This, in his judgment, has not been precisely spelled out in the relevant magisterial documents. He would resist placing "the necessity and universality of the Church on one and the same level with that of Jesus Christ" because this would yield the excessively rigid interpretation of the principle *extra ecclesiam nulla salus*. One must also avoid reducing the necessity of the Church to the salvation of its own members since this would introduce "two parallel ways of salvation without any mutual relationship."[52] He seeks a middle position.

In this regard the notion introduced by Vatican II of the orientation of graced non-Christians to the Church which is not a formal membership provides a grounding for the necessary ecclesial relationship. In line with this Dupuis will narrow the doctrine of the mediation of salvation by the Church.

> The council affirms the necessity of the Church for salvation (LG 14), as the "universal sacrament of salvation" (LG 48). This necessity does not, however, imply a universal mediation in the strict sense, applicable to every person who is saved in Jesus Christ. On the contrary it leaves room for "substitutive mediations". . . , among which will be found the religious traditions to which the "others" belong. From this one may infer that the causality of the Church in relation to the "others" is of the order not of efficiency but of finality.[53]

To this finality Dupuis will also add an intercessory mediation which is likewise not of the order of efficiency; it is of the moral order.

The sacramentality of the Church is set out in a similar fashion:

> The Church, in its visible aspect, is the sacrament (*sacramentum tantum*); the reality signified (*res tantum*), which it both contains and confers, is the belonging to the Reign of God which is being conferred; the intermediate reality, the *res et sacramentum*, is the relationship to the Church which is realized in the members of the ecclesial community, by virtue of which they share in the reality of the Reign of God. Nevertheless, as the sacramental theory implies, God is not bound by the sacraments (*Deus non alligatur sacramentis*). That means that one can attain to the reality of the Reign of God without recourse being had to the sacrament of the Church and without belonging to the body of the Church. The "others" can thus be members of the kingdom of God without being part of the Church and without recourse to its mediation.[54]

Dupuis is quite right to argue that the various perspectives under which the theology of religions is pursued are not necessarily incompatible with one another. Regnocentrism, theocentrism, Christocentrism, and so on, all can be seen as different elements of a single mystery. The only perspective, apparently, that he sees as incompatible with this synthetic view is an ecclesiocentric one. I think he is mistaken in this judgment. To be sure an ecclesiocentric perspective can be taken to the sort of extreme to which Feeney went. It does not follow that an ecclesiocentric view must involve such exclusionism. In what follows I will first examine the case for an ecclesiocentric view and then suggest ways in which such a view can adequately address many of the concerns which Dupuis (or James L. Fredericks mentioned in Bracken's paper) has voiced.

There are at least two intertwined presuppositions that underlie many of these discussions and certainly Dupuis's. The first is the widespread presumption that human efficient causality can only operate in a temporally forward direction and in terms of some sort of physical contact, however attenuated. The second is that the Lord remains sovereign over the Church and is able to operate outside the context of the Church. The first would rule out any other than final or moral mediation on the part of the Church in the salvation of those outside the Church, certainly for those whom she has never physically encountered; the second would assure that salvation is nonetheless available to them.

The problem with the first presupposition is that it also rules out efficiency in salvation on the part of the crucified Christ with regard to those who have preceded Christ. The solution that is sometimes tried, that graces are given to those individuals proleptically in view of Christ's sacrifice, does not really work. This merely establishes Jesus's passion and death as a final cause. The efficient causality for those graces does not pass through that human event itself. This, however, would undermine Dupuis's case for saying that Christ's mediation is qualitatively different from the mediation of the Church.

Thomas's discussion is apposite here. He distinguishes a twofold efficient agency—the principal and the instrumental. God is the principal agent of salvation but Christ's humanity is the instrument of the Godhead, "therefore all Christ's actions and sufferings operate instrumentally in virtue of His Godhead for the salvation of men. Consequently, then, Christ's Passion accomplishes man's salvation efficiently."[55] He clarifies the distinctness of Christ's human and divine operations: "in Christ the human nature has its proper form and power whereby it acts; and so has the Divine."[56] Yet, the two distinct operations are united: "the proper work of the Divine operation is different from the proper work of the human operation.

Thus to heal a leper is a proper work of the Divine operation, but to touch him is the proper work of the human operation. Now both these operations concur in one work, inasmuch as one nature acts in union with the other."[57]

This analysis is brought to bear on the question of the redemption in Christ: "hence in so far as His human nature operated by virtue of the Divine, that sacrifice was most efficacious for the blotting out of sins."[58] In response to the objection that since "no corporeal agency acts efficiently except by contact" and "Christ's Passion could not touch all mankind," Thomas responds that "Christ's Passion, although corporeal, has yet a spiritual effect from the Godhead united, and therefore it secures its efficacy by spiritual contact—namely, by faith and the sacraments of faith."[59]

There is a related issue that Thomas brings out in his discussion of the efficiency of Christ's resurrection and this is God's power to effect the graces of salvation, here the resurrection of the dead, apart from Christ's action. God's power to save, abstractly considered, is not limited to Christ's action in His passion, death, and resurrection; concretely, in view of the divine decree:

> God's justice is the first cause of our resurrection, whereas Christ's Resurrection is the secondary, and as it were the instrumental cause. But although the power of the principal cause is not restricted to one instrument determinately, nevertheless since it works through this instrument, such instrument causes the effect. So, then, the Divine justice in itself is not tied down to Christ's Resurrection as a means of bringing about our resurrection: because God could deliver us in some other way than through Christ's Passion and Resurrection, as already stated. But having once decreed to deliver us in this way, it is evident that Christ's Resurrection is the cause of ours.[60]

The next objection makes it clear how this is effected. Christ's resurrection is the efficient cause of ours because His humanity is the instrument of His divinity and operates in conjunction with the divine power:

> therefore, just as all other things which Christ did and endured in His humanity are profitable to our salvation through the power of the Godhead, as already stated, so also is Christ's

> Resurrection the efficient cause of ours, through the Divine
> power whose office it is to quicken the dead; and this power by
> its presence is in touch with all places and times; and such virtual
> contact suffices for its efficiency.[61]

This union of the humanity with the divinity allows Christ's human actions to have an effect that transcends space and time even though His humanity, considered in itself, has no such power.

It is clear that if one holds that Christ's sacrificial death is effective of salvation for the entire world this can only be understand in terms of the union of Christ's divinity to His humanity. Obviously this precise argument will not work with regard to the Church. The question remains, however, whether or not God is not able to use a created instrument such as the Church in such a way that the effect of actions by the Church transcends space and time.

A better starting point for answering this question, better because the issues become very simple, is to ask the same question with regard to Mary. I do not have in mind, at least primarily, the doctrine of Mary as the mediatrix of all grace. Does Mary exercise any causality with regard to the salvation of the world and if so what is it? If she does not answer "Yes!" to the angel's proclamation, there is no Incarnation and without an Incarnation there is no salvation of the world. The question is not whether God has the power to save the world in some other way. Of course He does. But what has God decreed? If Mary answers "No!," there is no salvation for the world.

It will not do to claim that God would simply ask someone else. All have sinned. If Mary answers "No!," no one else will answer "Yes!" They will not have access to the grace which makes a "Yes!" possible. What is at issue in, for instance, the doctrine of the Immaculate Conception? Is it not that God has chosen to make salvation infallibly available to the world? Mary's "Yes!" was assured by grace, she was full of grace from the first moment of her existence, even as it remained an utterly free response on her part. Mary's grace, to be sure, has its source in the redemptive death and resurrection of her Son. No grace is independent of that sacrifice. And yet that sacrifice is inseparable from the grace given to Mary. Absent the grace given to Mary, there is no sacrifice.

This paradox, this mystery itself flows from the nature of the Triune God. The Father's outpouring that is the generation of the Son infallibly generates the Son. In dealing with the world, should we then expect that God's outpouring will be anything other than effective, that it would not be, by someone, by the mother of God's Son, infallibly received? All of her graces, including this one, are caused by her Son's redemptive act which by the power of God transcends space and time.

What sort of causality does Mary exercise toward the whole world? Her very human "Yes!" is causally related to every offer of grace made through the subsequent sacrifice of Christ. It is not a final cause; it is not a moral cause; motherhood is brutally efficient—brute fact and womanly struggle to bring forth a child. Here is the mystery. How is it possible for one woman's response, itself constrained under the conditions of space and time, to have this sort of causal linkage to every place and every time? Such a causality is not native to human nature, not even to Christ's human nature. That Christ's human action in laying down his life is causally efficient in the salvation of the entire world is dependent upon the power of God who is not limited by space and time. Mary enters the causal chain which produces world salvation because the Spirit overshadowed her, making her mother of God. One can argue that Mary's action does not have an efficiency that transcends space and time only by arguing that Christ's action lacks such efficiency.

If this is true of Mary's action, what of the action of the Church? If Mary's mission was toward her Son and through this toward the world, the Church's mission from the Son is toward the world. The Church too has infallibly received the Spirit of God. Because Mary received the Spirit, because the Church received the Spirit, the world, which does not infallibly receive the Spirit, has access to that Spirit. One cannot divorce the sacrifice of Christ from the Church. His body, His blood was given "for you." This New Covenant between Christ and the Church transcends space and time not because of any causality native to the human Church but because of the power of God. The justifying Spirit that non-Christians receive outside the visible bonds of the Church is nonetheless the Spirit that was infallibly given to the bridal Church, the Church of the New Covenant. Apart from this donation of the Spirit to the Church, there is no salvation for the world. "Where the Church is, there is the Spirit of God," Irenaeus wrote, "and where the Spirit of God is, there is the Church and all grace."[62]

More is involved than moral mediation or final causality. God efficiently saves the world only by means of the covenant established by Christ in His blood and that covenant was with His Church. Without the Bride of Christ, there is no Spirit in the world because the Spirit in the world is Christ's gift to His Bride. The mediation of the Church, its infallible reception of the Spirit of her Lord in her Eucharistic worship, is necessary with the necessity that is rooted in the Trinitarian nature of God. This is not a relative necessity. It has about it the absoluteness of the divine decree.

It is a mistake to limit the grace of the Eucharist to "the unity in the Spirit of its own members."[63] Dupuis cites the prayer of epiclesis in support of this contention. This is surely among the graces of the Eucharist, but the institution narrative makes it clear that the Eucharist itself is "My body which will be given up for you"; "My blood . . . shed for you *and for all so that sins may be forgiven.*" One cannot separate the salvation of non-Christians from the graces of the Eucharist any more than one can separate it from the death and resurrection of Jesus. To do this is to sunder the unity between the Eucharist and Christ's death and resurrection. And the Eucharist, while primarily the action of Christ the Priest, is also the action of the Church. That joint action, in which the bridal Church rejoices in the Spirit given to her by the Bridegroom, is the efficient cause of the salvation of the world.

The second presupposition, the sovereignty of the Lord to act outside the Church, likewise has serious consequences. The issue is not the power or the absolute right of the Lord to act apart from the Church. The issue is the divine decree. Has God committed Himself to act through the Church for the salvation of the entire world? The Lord Jesus has given Himself to the Church body and soul, humanity and divinity. Are we to understand that this self-gift of Himself is only a partial gift, that something of the Lord has been reserved to be given to the world religions apart from the Church? A similar question can be asked of the Spirit. Was God's self-donation of Himself in the gift of the Spirit to the Church only a partial gift of the Spirit? Or rather, is the activity of the Spirit outside the visible confines of the Church to be understood nonetheless as the activity of the Church's Spirit—hers not by nature but by divine decree. It is possible so to stress the divine sovereignty over and against the Church as to deny the reality of the New Covenant in Christ's blood in which He takes His Church to Himself as His Bride and gives to her His most precious Gift. Any Christocentric perspective which prescinds from this concrete self-gift of the Bridegroom is by that fact distorted.

What does this do to interreligious dialogue? First, the Spirit of God is active in the religions of the world, both in their members and in the religious traditions which peoples have developed, at least in part, in response to that activity. That Spirit is the Church's Spirit, rushing out, as it were, ahead of the Church "preparing" individuals and peoples for the proclamation of the Gospel which the Church brings. All graces in non-Christians are, at their most fundamental level, a *praeparatio evangelica.* They are intended to create hearts responsive to the Gospel message. This has been affirmed repeatedly by the magisterium down to the present day.

Second, even granting this most fundamental structure, it does not follow that the relation between the Church and other religions must be one-sided. It is true that the Church possesses all truth and grace, at least in principle, because she possesses the Spirit of truth, the Giver of life. This does not mean that those graces and insights are active in the consciousness of the Christian community at any given time. The graces given to Cornelius in Acts 10 outside of the Church were indeed preparatory, leading him to baptism, but they were also revelatory for the Church. The recognition of the Spirit active in the unbaptized Cornelius led the Church to realize that "God has granted life-giving repentance even to the Gentiles" (Acts 11:18). There was a comparable recognition that the Word of God was present in pagan philosophy as the Church went out into the Gentile world.

One might reasonably expect similar results from the dialogues with world religions. As the activity of the Spirit is recognized in them, the Church will come to know more about herself and her mission and how she is to exist in the world. In recognizing the Spirit active in the world religions she will recognize herself because it is her Spirit. Such a spiritually discerned recognition can take place, however, only in the context of authentic dialogue, only on the presupposition that both sides have something to learn from the other. John Paul was aware of the possibility of this sort of exchange when he wrote in *Redemptoris missio*, and I repeat: "Indeed, it is always the Spirit who is at work, both when He gives life to the Church and impels her to proclaim Christ, and when He implants and develops His gifts in all individuals and peoples, guiding the Church to discover these gifts, to foster them and to receive them through dialogue. Every form of the Spirit's presence is to be welcomed with respect and gratitude, but the discernment of this presence is the responsibility of the Church, to which Christ gave His Spirit in order to guide her into all the truth."[64] What is it that is being discerned? Vatican II introduced the notion of "ecclesial elements" present in non-Catholic Christian churches as a way of recognizing authentic traditions and developments in those Churches. Perhaps it is time to extend this notion to include the world religions. If the Spirit is indeed active, not simply in the hearts of individuals, but also in the religious traditions and rituals which those peoples develop in response to the divine initiative, then these things form the kernel for a reality that is at least analogously "ecclesial." It is for the Church to discover and cherish these ecclesial moments. This cannot be done apart from authentic dialogue.

Let me briefly conclude these considerations. There is a twofold purpose to the Church's involvement in dialogues with other world religions. There is, on the one hand, the explicit evangelistic purpose of coming to know the culture, including its religious structure, to which the Gospel message is addressed and in allowing the dialogue partners to come to know the Church and its message of salvation in Christ. All that is good and true in such cultures is to be taken up, purified, elevated, and perfected. On the other hand, there is the self-interest on the part of the Church in observing the activity of the Spirit outside her visible confines because that activity reveals to the Church how she is to grow, how she is to achieve her mission of bringing the kingdom proclaimed by Christ to fulfillment.

NOTES

1. Jacques Dupuis, S.J., *Toward a Christian Theology of Religious Pluralism* (Maryknoll, New York: Orbis, 1997).

2. Dupuis is in part dependent on Francis A. Sullivan, S.J., *Salvation Outside the Church? Tracing the History of the Catholic Response* (New York: Paulist Press, 1992).

3. See, for instance, the *Cohortatio ad Graecos*, 37-38, attributed to Justin Martyr.

4. *Enchiridion symbolorum: definitionum et declarationum de rebus fidei et morum, quod primum edidit Henricus Denzinger, et quod funditus retractavit, auxit, notulis ornavit Adolfus Schönmetzer* (Barcinone: Herder, 1976), hereafter abbreviated as DS. Here, DS 792.

5. DS 802. This and other translations of conciliar documents are from Norman P. Tanner, S.J., ed., *Decrees of the Ecumenical Councils*, 2 vols. (London: Sheed & Ward/Washington, D.C.: Georgetown University Press, 1990).

6. DS 870, 872, 875. This and other translations of non-conciliar documents are from J. Neuner and J. Dupuis, *The Christian Faith in the Doctrinal Documents of the Catholic Church* (New York: Alba House, 1982), unless otherwise indicated.

7. Session 8. DS 75.

8. Session 11. DS 1351. The references to Fulgentius are to his *De fide* 38, 39, found in *Sancti Fulgentii episcopi Ruspensis Opera*, ed. J. Fraipont (Turnholt: Typographi Brepols, 1968), Corpus Christianorum, Series Latina, vol. 91A: 757.

9. Dupuis, *Religious Pluralism*, 111.

10. Ibid., 112-13.

11. Ibid., 114.

12. Ibid., 116.

13. Ibid.

14. *Mystici Corporis*, n. 100; DS 3821

15. DS 3869-72.

16. Dupuis, *Religious Pluralism*, 134.

17. Ibid., 144.

18. nn. 3, 9, 11.

19. Cf. *Evangelii nuntiandi*, n. 53.

20. Dupuis, *Religious Pluralism*, 173.

21. *Redemptor hominis*, n. 6. The translation is that of the Publications Office of the USCC.

22. Ibid, 11.

23. n. 11, cited in Dupuis, *Religious Pluralism*, 175.

24. n. 4, cited in Dupuis, *Religious Pluralism*, 174-75.

25. Vatican translation published by Pauline Books & Media, Boston.

26. n. 2.

27. n. 26.
28. n. 11.
29. n. 14.
30. n. 5, Vatican translation, published by St. Paul Books & Media, Boston.
31. n. 6.
32. n. 9.
33. n. 10.
34. n. 28.
35. n. 29.
36. n. 6; Vatican translation published by Pauline Books & Media, Boston.
37. Dupuis, *Religious Pluralism*, 177-78.
38. Ibid., 178.
39. *Redemptoris missio*, n. 17.
40. *Theological Studies* 37 (1976): 545-66.
41. Dupuis, *Religious Pluralism*, 200.
42. Ibid., 205.
43. Ibid., 351.
44. Ibid., 333.
45. Ibid., 334.
46. Ibid., 335-38.
47. *Redemptoris missio*, n. 18.
48. Ibid, n. 20.
49. Dupuis, *Religious Pluralism*, 340.
50. Ibid., 342.
51. Ibid., 344. He is citing Cullmann, *Christ and Time: The Christian Conception of Time and History* (London: SCM Press, 1952), 187.
52. Dupuis, *Religious Pluralism*, 347.
53. Ibid., 351.
54. Ibid., 354.
55. *ST* III.48.6.corp. Translations are those of the English Dominican Province, 1911, 1920.
56. *ST* III.19.1.c.
57. *ST* III.19.1 ad 5.
58. *ST* III.22.3 ad 1.
59. *ST* III.48.6 ad 2.
60. *ST* III.56.1 ad 2.
61. *ST* III.56.1 ad 3.
62. *Adversus haereses* 3.24.1.
63. Dupuis, *Religious Pluralism*, 350.
64. n. 29.

Karol Wojtyla, Artist;
John Paul II, Theologian of Art

John J. Conley, S.J.

If John Paul II is rightly called "the philosopher pope," he has no less a claim to the title of "the artist pope." Before his election to the papacy, Karol Wojtyla had established himself as a major Polish poet and playwright. During his pontificate, John Paul II has often reflected on the nature and value of art. In his *Letter to Artists* (1999), he provides a systematic theology of art, rooted in the mystery of the Incarnation.

Despite the substantial practical and theoretical artistic canon elaborated by John Paul II, little critical attention has been paid to this part of the pope's work. In part this omission arises from the scandalous ignorance of Slavic cultures that characterizes American academe, otherwise so awash in the multicultural. This omission also arises from the preoccupation with moral and ecclesiastical controversies surrounding the teaching of John Paul II. The media focus on issues of sexuality and authority has obscured the key role which art holds in the pope's theory of culture. In John Paul II's perspective, the artist plays a prophetic role in providing icons of the mysterious. This witness prevents society from enclosing itself in the merely material, the merely economic, the merely scientific.

I. KAROL WOJTYLA, POET[1]

Written under a series of pseudonyms and published primarily in Catholic journals,[2] the poems of Karol Wojtyla are clearly the works of a philosopher. They constitute a series of meditations on spiritual problems, especially those of personal identity and of moral freedom. Often grouped into a cycle organized around a particular theme, Wojtyla's poems frequently use the technique of the monologue to permit different characters to present a particular insight into the question under

173

examination. Several cycles focus on specifically Christian themes: *Song of the Brightness of Water* on the Samaritan Woman; *Mother* on the Blessed Virgin Mary; *Profiles of a Cyrenean* on the Passion of Christ; *Easter Vigil* on the millennium of Poland's evangelization. Other cycles focus on less thematized spiritual issues: *Thought–Strange Space* on language; *The Quarry* on work; *Thinking My Country* on national identity; *Meditation on Death* on hope.

Despite the variety of themes, the poetry of Wojtyla pivots around several recurrent metaphysical concerns. One is the necessity to witness a mysterious, spiritual depth that lies behind the material and the routine. Recurrent images of the well, the abyss, the ocean, and the tree trunk underline the centrality of this epiphany of the spiritual. An allied theme is the difficulty of this witness to the transcendent. Quarried stone and Jacob's struggle with the angel symbolize the ardor of a spiritual witness that always remains a partial failure.

Wojtyla's poems also probe the moral opacity that vitiates the revolt of the just against evil. If the cross manifests God's truth, it is a truth which few can face and which fewer still can bear. Although firmly apolitical (unsurprisingly, since practically all the poems were written under Nazi-Communist regimes), the poems clearly concern the problem of witness to God in an atheistic society, where the path of authentic revolution is at best obscure.

The early cycle *Song of the Hidden God* (1944) indicates the necessity of attention to the presence of the spiritual. However, in the leaden terror of the Nazi-Stalinist occupation, the presence of God has become fragile: a memory, a hint, an offstage whisper:

> He is Your Friend. Your memory always meanders
> back to the morning in winter.
> For many years you believed, knew for certain
> and still you are lost in wonder.
>
> But over a lamp, a sheaf of light in a knot
> over your head. You look up no more,
> not knowing—is he out there, or
> here in the depth of closed eyes?
>
> There, he is there. Only a tremor here,
> only words retrieved from nothingness.

> Oh—and a particle still remains
> of that amazement which will become the essence
> of eternity.[3]

If God's presence remains certain, it remains elusive. The place of God's presence is unclear: neither here nor there. The touch of God is slight, a mere tremor. The memory of God, which grounds the hope of eternity, pivots between a particle and the void.

In the cycle *Song of the Brightness of Water* (1950), Wojtyla studies the encounter between Christ and the Samaritan woman at the well. In a series of monologues, the Samaritan woman recounts and reinterprets the meeting as she ages. In the final poem of the cycle, she describes Christ as the mirror who revealed her to herself just as He had revealed God to her:

> From the depth—I came only to draw water
> in a jug—so long ago, this brightness
> still clings to my eyes—the perception I found,
> and so much empty space, my own,
> reflected in the well.
>
> Yet it is good. I can never take all of you
> with me. Stay then as a mirror in the well.
> Leaves and flowers remain, and each astonished gaze
> brings them down
> to my eyes transfixed more by light
> than by sorrow.[4]

Christ illumines the darkness of this witness to the transcendent. Christ touches an unexpected depth within the soul itself. Through His loving gaze and His interrogation of the soul, He redeems the soul. What began as a comic search for water, and then as an infatuation with the person of this rabbi, now matures into a spiritual quest deepened by a beatitude rooted in grace.

Throughout his poetry, Wojtyla evokes the difficulty of this witness to the spirit, whether the spiritual journey is generic or specifically Christian. In the cycle *Thought—Strange Space* (1956), he frequently alludes to Jacob's battle with the angel. Language itself, the very effort to give verbal flesh to our internal ideas, manifests the pain of witnessing to the Spirit through visible signs:

> If he suffers, deprived of vision,
> he must tear through the thicket of signs
> to the word's very centre,
> its weight the ripeness of fruit.

> Is this the weight Jacob felt,
> pressing him down
> when tired stars sank within him,
> the eyes of his flock?[5]

Like Jacob wrestling with the angel, we struggle awkwardly to show others the ideas that inhabit our minds. Despite our efforts, our words often veil or betray the vision we attempt to communicate.

Nor is the struggle to communicate simply rooted in the formal gap between mental vision and the linguistic (mis)expression of that vision. Our moral life often contradicts the ideals we so ardently contemplate:

> This isn't mere wrestling with images
> carried in our thought;
> we fight with the likeness of all things
> that inwardly constitute man.
> But when we act can our deeds surrender
> the ultimate truths we presume to ponder?[6]

Our Jacob-like struggle is not only the effort to articulate faithfully the spiritual realm of ideas. More gravely it is the effort to conform our actions to our spiritual ideals. The gap between our vision of the good and our actions on behalf of the good are of greater consequence than the daily chasm we experience between our ideas and those stumbling words we keep blurting out.

Numerous other poems stress the difficulty of this witness, symbolic or actual, to the realm of the spirit. The cycle *The Quarry* (1956) draws an analogy between this witness and the effort of the stonemason to transform rock into sculpted form. The climactic poem of the cycle, "In Memory of a Fallen Worker," uses the accidental death of a quarry worker to evoke the dangers of the Herculean effort to subdue matter by force of the spirit. Similarly the cycle *The Church* (1962) uses the images of rock to explore the difficulty of penetrating to the apostolic witness interred beneath the superficialities of religious practice, just as St. Peter lies literally interred beneath the floor of the Vatican basilica.

The cycle *Profiles of the Cyrenean* (1961) explores another central theme in Wojtyla's poetic canon: the dynamics of moral responsibility and moral evasion. Focused on Simon the Cyrenean confronting Christ (simply called "the Man") during the Passion, the cycle is a series of monologues by various characters attracted by Christ crucified. Several characters are biblical: Simon and Mary Magdalene. Most, however, represent general types of human beings: the melancholic, the schizophrenic, the girl disappointed in love, the blind man, the actor, the child, the car factory worker, the armaments factory worker. At the end of the cycle, these types broaden into generic kinds of human beings grouped by faculty: the emotive man; the intellectual man; the volitional man. This moral typology not only structures the monologues, but also permits Wojtyla the phenomenologist to describe the moral essence of each human type, with its characteristic mix of overture to and refusal of the mystery of the cross.

Each human type manifests a distinctive moral opacity. The intellectual man reduces life to an abstraction:

> Robbing your life of charm and variety,
> the taste of adventure, of space, spontaneity.

> How cramped are your notions, formulas, judgments,
> always condensing yet hungry for content.

> Don't break down my defences: they're vital to the human
>> lot;
> each road must take the direction of thought.[7]

The armaments factory worker simply refuses moral responsibility for his lethal work:

> I cannot influence the fate of the globe.
> Do I start wars? How can I know
> whether I'm for or against?
> No, I don't sin.

It worries me not to have influence,
that it is not I who sin.
I only turn screws, weld together
parts of destruction,
never grasping the whole,
or the human lot.[8]

Mary Magdalene's capacity to love has opened her to the suffering of the world and to her own need for redemption. In the shadow of Christ, however, this compassion remains radically imperfect:

At times love aches: there are weeks, months, years.
Like the roots of a dry tree my tongue is dry
and the roof of my mouth. My lips are unpainted.
It takes long: Truth sounding out error.

But it is He who feels
the drought of the whole world, not I.[9]

In each of the monologues, the speaker manifests his or her capacity to witness to the truth of redemptive suffering. This witness is not a matter of words or ideas. It is a practical witness, rooted in the capacity—or often enough in the incapacity—to give oneself to others in sacrificial love.

Forced to carry the cross of this obscure criminal, Simon of Cyrene has the most detailed of the moral profiles. The sight of Christ freely accepting His cross disturbs Simon. At first, he attempts to still the disturbance by an act of the will:

No, don't go beyond, don't touch my thoughts
or my heart—you'll stir nothing there. This rough handling,
this violence—and he dares, he accepts it a beggar![10]

At the end, however, Simon's aloofness turns into revolt at the sight of this injustice. But his revolt at the suffering of the innocent cannot find an issue:

No, I don't want merely to be just.
I stand on a threshold, glimpse a new world.

> A crowd passes by: women, children, soldiers;
> they mill round near the frontier with God.
> Silence. Silence.
> Justice calls for rebellion. But rebellion against whom?[11]

In the monologue Simon moves from moral mediocrity to vague conscientiousness to a final outrage at the injustice of the innocent annihilated. But the moral outcry falls short of redemptive love.

The entire cycle closes with this lonely call to futile revolt. Written at the end of the Stalinist period, this bitter plea for opposition to violent evil echoes the longings of the Polish nation itself. If the cross has traced the path of heroic revolt against totalitarian evil, it also illumines the terrible human capacity for moral evasion when this witness to truth entails a serious price.

If Wojtyla's poetry organizes itself around key metaphors, it remains a metaphysician's poetry. It explores the human vocation to probe, to grasp, and to manifest the kingdom of the spirit. It evokes the difficulties of this quest. In its more prophetic passages, it depicts the recesses of human temperament, which permit the human person to elude this vocation to witness the transcendent in deed as well as in sign. As in his philosophical works, the figure of Christ not only reveals the face of God to humanity; it reveals humanity, especially its hidden reservoir of compassion and cowardice, to itself.

While Wojtyla's poetry treats anthropological issues proper to humanity as such, it reflects a particular social setting for this human drama. The moral amnesia studied in the poems is the amnesia of modern society: that of the factory worker, of the intellectual, of the professional actor. And the ethos of this society is that of totalitarian atheism. It is practical and theoretical atheism that systematically closes access to the transcendent, diverts society from spiritual questions, and punishes any revolt from a materialist routine with violence.

II. KAROL WOJTYLA, PLAYWRIGHT[12]

Like his poems, the plays of Karol Wojtyla reflect the philosophical cast of their author. Short on dramatic action and long on metaphysical analysis, the plays are a type of closet drama, more appropriate to a stark reading than to a fully-staged production. Influenced by the traditions of the Rhapsodic Theatre, the underground theatrical troupe in which Wojtyla participated during the Nazi and

179

Stalinist periods, these plays focus on the inner life, rather than the external acts, of their characters. Often employing long monologues, the dramas explore the suffering of the innocent, the human capacity for self-alienation, and the promise of redemption.

The five dramas emerged at different periods in Wojtyla's life. Written during the Nazi terror, the Biblical dramas *Job* (1940) and *Jeremiah* (1940) evoke the inexplicable suffering of the innocent individual and of the innocent nation, Poland. *Our God's Brother* (1945-50) studies the vocation of Adam Chmielowski, a nineteenth-century playwright turned apostle to the poor. *The Jeweler's Shop* (1960) explores the difficulty of fidelity to the vows of marriage. *Radiation of Fatherhood* (1964) depicts the challenge of physical and spiritual paternity in a culture marked by aching loneliness and by a refusal of one's childhood in God.

Despite the shift from the violent epic scope of the early biblical plays to the intimate domestic dramas of the 1960s, Wojtyla's entire dramatic corpus pivots around the depth of human suffering, easily prone to despair, and the difficulty of accepting the mysterious salvation offered by Christ.

Job perfectly matches the depth of the protagonist's despair with a vision of redemption in Christ. Rejecting the fallacious explanations of his suffering offered by his erstwhile friends, the innocent Job begs God for death:

> Why do You still keep me alive?
> Why do you keep me alive in my misery?
> Kill me—kill—O Jehovah.
> Yours is the Power
> and Yours is the thunder.
> > And what is man?
> And what is man?
> Blessed be Your Name
> > And what is human might?
> Yours is the Will and Yours is the Power.
> > And what is human happiness?
> Yours is the will and the Power,
> O Jehovah—O Jehovah—O Jehovah.[13]

The play is suffused with images of "terror from the sky," paralleling the unbearable torment of Job with the rape of Poland under the Nazis.

Departing from the biblical narrative, Wojtyla tempers this despair by the character Elihu's vision of a redemption to come through Christ. The suffering of Gethsemane is superimposed on the lament of Job:

I am now in a garden of olives;
it is spring, and many trees bloom.
I see men sleeping under them.
Who are they? Behind them is a stone.
I see Him—I see Him—kneeling,
His head against the stone. I see
His face sweating, His forehead bloody.
It is night: the garden of olives blooms;
the night is fragrant all around the men.
There I see Him—my soul welcomes Him.
He speaks to You, Father. I hear;
I hear through the open door.
He speaks in humility, not pride;
he calls You the Master of His life.[14]

The darkness remains unrelieved. It is Gethsemane, not the dawn of the resurrection, that centers the vision. But the redemptive suffering of the innocent, integrated into the service of the living God offering eternal life, supplants the suffering that issues in despair.

In *Jeremiah*, the suffering of the individual is transposed to an entire nation, Poland. Father Piotr Skarga, the Jeremiah figure of the sixteenth century, attempts to awaken Poland to the need for repentance as it desperately fights the Swedish enemy. Assimilating Poland to Jerusalem, Skarga expresses his incapacity to present successfully his religious vision to the Polish people:

O Lord! It is a martyr's vision!
How am I to take it on me, how?
How, O Lord!
O Jerusalem—Jerusalem!
The foe will trample and disgrace us!
Oh, if only You would reveal to them
what You have revealed to me,

> what You have put into my eyes,
>
> into my soul.
>
> They might yet be moved by a vision–
>
> when my words mean nothing to them,
>
> even though I tear out my heart.[15]

God's awakening of the prophet does not guarantee the success of the prophet's mission. Even the field marshal who confesses his sins under Father Skarga's sway goes on to lead his Polish army to a miserable defeat. The redemption wrought by God, while effected against the background of a war-torn society, works its mercy outside the society's logic of gain and loss.

In *The Jeweler's Shop*, Wojtyla presents the struggles of three couples: one serenely celebrating their wedding anniversary; one unhappily married and on the verge of collapse; one recently and tentatively engaged. The mysterious jeweler delivers a long monologue as he contemplates the moral struggles of the quarreling couple:

> Ah, man's own weight,
>
> the proper weight of man!
>
> This rift, this tangle, this ultimate depth—
>
> this clinging, when it is so hard
>
> to unstick heart and thought.
>
> And in all this—love,
>
> which springs from freedom
>
> as water springs from an oblique rift in the earth.
>
> This is man! he is not transparent,
>
> not monumental,
>
> not simple;
>
> in fact he is poor.[16]

The weight of being human is now softer than it was in the earlier apocalyptic dramas. The human burden is that of freedom itself. It is a specific freedom: the capacity to give oneself to another in an unbreakable commitment of love. The sacrament of marriage, symbolized by wedding rings purchased at the jeweler's, discloses the terrible freedom which permits the human person to manifest the mercy of redemption.

Like his poems, the plays of Wojtyla focus on the types of moral evasion which close the human person to the mystery constituting the backdrop of human existence. The friends of Job, the pusillanimous listeners of Father Skarga, and the quarreling couple at the jeweler's shop all refuse to accept the weight of human suffering. Closed into their particular moral opacity, the characters can neither hear nor accept the gospel of salvation by suffering offered from Christ on the cross. A tool of Wojtyla's phenomenology, the dramas' detailed monologues unveil the ethical superficiality and the stunted consciousness which constitute the practical atheism of modernity. It is precisely the mission of both priest and prophet to assault this moral insouciance by their witness to the mysterious depths of both God and humanity. But this witness will be stoutly resisted, because awakening to the mystery entails an acceptance of suffering, which frankly we would rather avoid.

III. JOHN PAUL II, THEOLOGIAN OF ART

In his *Letter to Artists*[17] (1999), John Paul II provides his most systematic treatment of art. The purpose of the letter is clearly apologetic: to celebrate the history of art's service to the Church[18] and to restate the contemporary Church's need of artists.[19] However, the letter is more than an encomium. In it the pope sketches a comprehensive theology of art. It also permits the pope to present the artist as a privileged witness to the transcendent. This prophetic evocation of the artist echoes the longstanding concerns of Wojtyla in his poetry and his drama.

John Paul II uses the theological categories of creation and incarnation to present the vocation of the artist. Like God, the artist creates a new material reality expressing spirit. Although there is a clear difference between the Creator and the craftsman,[20] the artist's special vocation is to participate in the creative activity of God and to imitate the God-created cosmos as the norm of artistic production.

John Paul II places a distinctively idealist spin on artistic creativity. In artistic creation, the artist expresses certain qualities of his or her own personality. The spiritual and moral qualities of the artist's soul hold a central place in the inner life of the work produced:

> The distinction between the moral and artistic aspects is fundamental, but no less important is the connection between them. Each conditions the other in a profound way. In producing a work, artists express themselves to the point where their work becomes a unique disclosure of their own being, of what they are

183

and of how they are what they are. And there are endless
examples in human history. In shaping a masterpiece, the artist
not only summons his work into being, but also in some way
reveals his own personality by means of it.[21]

According to this perspective, every work of artistic creation is simultaneously an act of the artist's spiritual/moral self-disclosure. This expressionist view of artistic creation refuses to reduce the artistic act to a matter of simple technique or to a simple imitation of an external reality.

Complementing that of creation, the category of incarnation holds a central place in John Paul II's theology of art. Shattering the Hebraic strictures against representation of the divine, Christ's Incarnation presents God Himself.[22] Christ gives a face to the invisible, a voice to the silent divinity. The Incarnation becomes the inspiration for the history of Christian art, vividly offering visual, musical, and literary images of God. John Paul II lends special attention to the iconoclast controversy, where the artistic right to make images of the divine beauty trumps the impulse to ban icons of God out of fear of idolatry.[23]

The artist's relationship to the Incarnation transcends the production of religious images for the Church. In a limited way, the artist is called to incarnate his or her own vision of the mysterious in concrete works of beauty: "Every genuine artistic intuition goes beyond what the senses perceive and, reaching beneath reality's surface, strives to interpret its hidden mystery. The intuition itself springs from the depths of the human soul, where the desire to give meaning to one's own life is joined by the fleeting vision of beauty and of the mysterious unity of things."[24] Just as Christ perfectly expresses the mystery of God, the artist very imperfectly expresses the mystery that transcends the sensate. The pope explicitly recognizes the value of the artistic "epiphany" of the mysterious, even when this epiphany focuses upon the evil or the twisted rather than upon the divine."[25]

John Paul II underscores the suffering of the artist: the experience of the chasm between the vision of the mystery and the imperfect artistic work expressing the vision. The pope parallels this dichotomy with the mystic's painful experience of the gap between the God experienced in vision and the halting symbols used to communicate this experience:

All artists experience the unbridgeable gap which lies between the
work of their hands, however successful it may be, and the

dazzling perfection of the beauty glimpsed in the ardor of the creative moment: what they manage to express in their painting, their sculpting, their creating is no more than a glimmer of the splendor which flared for a moment before the eyes of their spirit.

Believers find nothing strange in this: they know that they have had a momentary glimpse of the abyss of light which has its original wellspring in God. Is it in any way surprising that this leaves the spirit overwhelmed as it were, so that it can only stammer in reply? [26]

As in his poetry and drama, the pope's theology of art dwells upon the suffering central to any act of artistic creation and of prophetic witness. The divide between vision and expression constitutes the crux of this artistic suffering.

Although the pope insists on the reciprocal need of the Church and the artist for each other, the artist's role is not confined to the pedagogy of faith. In its global role of manifesting the ineffable in sensate form, art witnesses to the transcendent. It broadens and deepens human vision. God's Spirit guides all artistic creation: [27]

Overseeing the mysterious laws governing the universe, the divine breath of the Creator Spirit reaches out to human genius and stirs its creative power. He touches it with a kind of inner illumination which brings together the sense of the good and the beautiful, and he awakens energies of mind and heart which enable it to conceive an idea and give it form in a work of art. It is right then to speak, even if only analogically, of "moments of grace," because the human being is able to experience in some way the Absolute who is utterly beyond.[28]

By the power of his or her creative intuition, every artist unveils the transcendent being bearing the traces of God. Explicitly baptized or not, this witness to the transcendent is the religious heart of every artistic vocation.

IV. CONTRIBUTION AND LIMITATION

In his poetic practice and his aesthetic theory, John Paul II defends a concept of art with its characteristic strengths and weaknesses. Both the contributions and the limitations of this theory of art flow from the metaphysical framework in which the pope considers the vocation of the artist.

The first limitation concerns the relative lack of attention to the material conditions of art. The pope stresses the primacy of vision, idea, and witness in his account of art. But the role of matter and the technical mastery of matter in the artistic enterprise remains in the shadows. The use of color in painting or the mastery of rhythm in poetry receives little attention in an approach to art that assimilates the artist to a prophet. When *The Letter to Artists* argues that Gothic architecture reflects the spirit of medieval society and of Christendom, it accurately identifies one of the determinants of artistic creation. However, this approach to art as the expression of idea in matter provides little explanation of how particular types of stone, glass, engineering, and craft guilds made possible the emergence of the Gothic cathedral.

A second limitation in this aesthetic theory is the omission of treatment of art as a virtue. Thomistic philosophy, brilliantly retrieved by Jacques Maritain in the previous century,[29] had argued that art was a virtue of the practical intellect. Art was the habit of knowing what to make. Further, the Thomistic tradition sharply distinguished the virtue of art from that of prudence, the habit of knowing what to do. The moral and artistic orders were thus clearly demarcated. Despite its Catholic pedigree, the virtue approach to art is absent in the pope's letter and in his own artistic works. John Paul II's approach to art so stresses the role of intellectual vision and expression of vision that the technical dimension of art is eclipsed. A more sober emphasis on the virtue of art might temper the neo-romantic strands of the pope's aesthetics, which seem to canonize the artist as a seer blest.

Despite its limitations, John Paul II's theology of art makes several signal contributions to aesthetic theory and to the Church's artistic practice.

Strikingly John Paul II's concept of art frees it from subordination to moral and ecclesial purposes. While the Catholic Church has long praised and used the work of artists, it has tended to instrumentalize art as a tool for moral edification or for religious instruction. The Second Vatican Council's *Decree on the Instruments of Social Communication* indicates how tenacious this subordination of art has been: "The Council asserts that the primacy of the objective moral order demands absolute allegiance, for this order alone excels and rightly integrates all other fields of human concern, including art, however lofty their value. Only the moral order touches man in his total nature as God's reasoning creature, summoned heavenwards."[30] In John Paul II's perspective, the primary vocation of the artist is to make images of what is mysterious. The artist's purpose is to give shape to what is invisible, to give words to what is silent, to give texture to what has neither weight nor size. It is this miraculous epiphany of the spiritual in the sensate which constitutes the unique vocation of the artist. While the artist may powerfully contribute to the moral and religious enlightenment of the viewer, this is not the artist's primary role. In John Paul II's aesthetic theory, the right and duty of the artist to fabricate icons of the spiritual, even when the icon is areligious or disturbing, is vindicated.

Finally, John Paul II celebrates the prophetic role of the artist in society, especially in contemporary society marked by its particular brand of practical atheism. The prophecy of the artist is not the production of religious propaganda cleverly disguised in pleasing images or catchy music. Rather, the prophetic role of the artist is the creation of works manifesting what cannot be reduced to a message, a slogan, an argument. The artist prophetically challenges society by flooding society with images of the transcendent. The artist forces society to contemplate what cannot be measured or quantified. Even without explicit religious symbolism, the artwork initiates its public into depths of the soul and of the Spirit which a materialist society would prefer to suppress. Although this prophetic portrait of the artist obscures the technical dimension of art, it attractively presents the artist as one who incarnates the invisible into material form, rather than reducing the artist to a catechist with spray paint.

NOTES

1.   For an English translation of the poetry of Karol Wojtyla, see Karol Wojtyla, *Collected Poems*, trans. Jerzy Peterkiewicz (New York: Random House, 1982). This book is subsequently cited as *CP*.
2.   The majority of poems were published in two Catholic journals: *Znak* and *Tygodnik Powszechny*.
3.   "Shores of Silence" in *Song of the Hidden God*, *CP*, 5-6.
4.   "Song of the Brightness of Water" in *Song of the Brightness of Water*, *CP*, 39.
5.   "Words' Resistance to Thought" in *Thought–Strange Space*, *CP*, 55.
6.   "Thought's Resistance to Words" in *Thought–Strange Space*, *CP*, 53.
7.   "Man of Intellect" in *Profiles of a Cyrenean*, *CP*, 87.
8.   "The Armaments Factory Worker" in *Profiles of a Cyrenean*, *CP*, 85.
9.   "Magdalene" in *Profiles of a Cyrenean*, *CP*, 86.
10.   "Simon of Cyrene" in *Profiles of a Cyrenean*, *CP*, 88.
11.   "Simon of Cyrene" in *Profiles of a Cyrenean*, *CP*, 89.
12.   For an English version of Karol Wojtyla's plays and dramatic criticism, see Karol Wojtyla, *The Collected Plays and Writings on Theater*, trans. Boleslaw Taborski (Berkeley: University of California Press, 1987). The work will be subsequently cited as *CPWT*.
13.   *Job* in *CPWT*, 44.

14. *Job* in *CPWT,* 69.
15. *Jeremiah* in *CPWT,* 109.
16. *The Jeweler's Shop* in CPWT, 289.
17. Cf. John Paul II, *Letter to Artists* (4 April 1999). This work is subsequently cited as *LA*. Numerous Internet versions of LA are available: for example, www.ewtn.com/ library/ PAPALDOC/ JP2ARTIS.HTM
18. See, *LA*, nn. 6-10.
19. See *LA*, n. 11.
20. See *LA*, n. 1.
21. *LA*, n. 2.
22. See *LA*, n. 5.
23. See *LA*, n. 7.
24. *LA*, n. 6.
25. See *LA*, n. 10.
26. *LA*, n. 6.
27. See *LA*, nn. 14-16.
28. See *LA*, n. 15.
29. See Jacques Maritain, *Art and Scholasticism*, trans. Joseph W. Evans (Notre Dame: Univ. of Notre Dame Press, 1974) 10-22. *Letter to Artists* only provides a passing reference to art as a virtue in footnote 2.
30. Vatican Council II, *Decree on the Instruments of Social Communication*, n. 6, in *The Documents of Vatican II*, ed. Walter M. Abbott, S.J. (New York: America Press, 1966), 322.

A Response to John J. Conley, S.J.

Dennis McNally, S.J.

John Conley's remarks about the pope's wonderful *Letter to Artists* are very clear and rather encouraging. Although I am neither a theologian nor a philosopher, I find great support from the Holy Father's letter, for I read it as a priest whose hyphenate-occupation brings me to look to this letter more for professional encouragement as painter than as priest. I read this letter not so much to see what the pope thinks about art but to learn what art the highest official in the Church is seeking from us. What should I be doing for the Church? We will consider a little later that the Church must also see herself as patron (if not as matron) if artists are to produce their best for her.

Jesuits and Churchmen

As Jesuits, we have found from our earliest time in the Society that our documents at least suggest that the Holy Father's encouragement is not new nor contradictory. Indeed, there were many statements in the General Congregations that met during our earliest years in the Society which encouraged artists personally to regard our particular academic interest and, more critically, our professional calling as something to pursue for "the greater glory of God and for the good of souls." The sixth decree of the 32nd General Congregation (on formation) suggests that Ours should be engaged in "studies leading not only to a living knowledge of man and his modern world, but also suited to expressing ourselves to the people of our times. . . . Hence training in the sciences, in languages, in literature, in the classic 'liberal arts,' in modern media of communication, and in the cultural traditions of the nation, must be undertaken with much greater care" (n. 27). Revisiting the thought of Father General Janssens and Decrees Nine and Thirty of the 31st General Congregation ("The Training of Scholastics Especially in Studies," esp. nn. 158-59, and "Cultivating the Arts in the Society") led, I believe, to the Society's fostering of the "other vocations" of so many Jesuit artists. This kind of thinking about the arming of Jesuits for the battle against atheism ratified the call we were hearing within and made it acceptable for artists to say, "Here I am, Lord; is it I?"

Decree Eleven of the 34th General Congregation ("On Having a Proper Attitude of Service in the Church") recommends that "the new culture" (n. 11) of communication must be learned in order to proclaim the faith and to pursue justice—within that culture. It also suggest that for Jesuits: "Though we remain always loyal to the truth, our Ignatian sense of *sentire cum ecclesia* will lead us to present what is praiseworthy in the Church, revealing the bonds of affection that make us love the Church and cleave to it as a source of life, solace, and healing, as an internal authority for genuine religious experience, as a nurturing matrix of our deepest values" (n. 26). Father General Arrupe spoke eloquently in his 1974 address to artists about the "heart which speaks to heart" when the artist works. I personally remember meeting him at the Jesuit Artists Institute in the Villa Mondragone just outside Rome in 1972. That saintly man expressed an inspired and inspiring understanding of the risks involved in putting one's inside out on public display and of the necessity to do so for us as *artists* and specifically as *Jesuit artists* if we were to serve the Lord who called us with the gifts which the Father gave us in the work of the Church.

ARTISTS AND PHILOSOPHERS

Now, there is a way that artists, I must tell you, find all philosophical and theological statements about what we do pretentious—at least when the statements are made by philosophers and theologians. But we seem quite willing to go on and on and we take seriously the "philosophical" and "theological" goings on and on of our colleagues—as long as it is an artist who is talking. If I may invert Susanne Langer's understanding (in *Philosophy in a New Key*) of how the non-discursive, non-verbal, or non-linear thinking of artists is not easily accepted by more structural thinkers, artists do not seem to appreciate discursive "artwork"—but this is, after all, what a philosophical or theological construct is (in our sense of making art with materials). In this case, thoughts, words, and logic are used about experience—*fides quaerens intellectum*. Indeed, the Holy Father and Father General could have been talking about the necessary risks to be taken by thinkers who engage their creativity in much the same way as artists do who make art.

However, unless writing novels, plays, or poetry, the artist (one must always remember) does not customarily use words. Words and logic are not the usual tools of artists. We use our experience and our senses to express something beyond the problem in paint, bronze, movement, sound, and image. We express more what we *feel* than what we *think*. In *Art as Experience*, John Dewey talked of "aesthetic problem solving" as the essential work of the artist. This is one of those statements that we usually reject with venom because the mystery we are trying to express, or even communicate, is not something solvable, not a problem (in the sense of "problem" articulated by Gabriel Marcel's distinction between problem and mystery in *The Mystery of Being*). The real mystery is other: ultimately all human endeavor yearns toward God. The artist seeks to interpret the divine. In the words of Pope John Paul II: "Every genuine artistic intuition goes beyond what the senses perceive and, reaching beneath reality's surface, strives to interpret its hidden mystery. The intuition itself springs from the depths of the human soul, where the desire to give meaning to one's own life is joined by the fleeting vision of beauty and of the mysterious unity of things" (*Letter to Artists,* n. 6). Pope Paul VI spoke most apologetically to artists a quarter of a century before Pope John Paul II's own remarkable *apologia*—I use that term because he seems to be speaking of the artistic experience as one he himself shares. Pope Paul VI's apology was, however, something that was even more extraordinary. He actually implied that the institutional Church, and particularly the Apostolic See, had for a very long time been the antithesis of a patron of the arts when he said: "We have insisted on this or that style or tradition being followed; we have set up these canons from which you must not deviate; we have oppressed you at times as it were with a cloak of lead. . . . For this we beg your pardon."[1] Now, this statement from Paul VI must be looked at as the papal backdrop against which the statement from John Paul II is played. Essentially, the comment that I would like to make in response to John Conley is a suggestion that these papal encouragements, coming at a later date in their papacies, amount to a mature realization that the Church needs the arts more than is immediately evident, more than we can know. The Church needs to hear the voice of her heart.

Patronage of the arts will necessarily become more important than is presently true in our culture, according to Bran Ferren, President of Disney Imagineering R&D, Inc., who speaks for many others in the field of popular entertainment when he writes: "In a future when intelligent machines will reason and do our donkey-work, human artists will become the most valued and irreplaceable of professional—unique in an automated world. Painters, sculptors, writers, actors, architects, animators, and even people who can decorate a decent Easter egg will achieve unprecedented fame and fortune" (*New York Times Magazine*).

CHURCH BUILDINGS AND BUILDING CHURCHES

There are some churches built during the twentieth century with great fanfare. Constantly written about and critiqued in architectural journals as the most important things built in Christendom in the modern era, churches will afford a wonderful education to one who looks at them to see who we (the Church who built them) have become. Consider these gems of architectural genius: August Perret (Notre Dame du Raincy), Domenikus Bohm (Church at Nordeney), Rudoph Schwarz (Maria Königen in Saarbrucken), Karl Moser (Saint Anthony in Basle), le Corbusier (Notre Dame du Haut in Ronchamp), Oscar Niemeyer (San Francisco in Pampulha), Kenzo Tange (St. Mary's Cathedral in Tokyo), Marcel Breuer (St. Louis Priory), Pietro Belluschi (St. Mary's Cathedral in San Francisco), Aarnu Ruusuvoric (Church at Hyrinkaa), Alvar Aalto (Church at Riola di Vargato).

The example of these significant "designer churches" (by which I mean churches built under the aegis of the literati, the intelligentsia, the avant garde over the last century) is an example of high architecture, produced for worship in the post-Christian era in such a way as to express the drive toward mystery that architects *feel*. The art of architecture is, of course, more demanding of the resources of a community. More people are involved in producing the product than there would be in making any other artform. Architects build, moreover, within an international community of artists. Their products are compared worldwide, their dialogue about the mystery is global. There are precious few priests among them. One might even propose that there are precious few Catholics engaged in that dialogue.

In building a church there is both a backward-looking urge that finds itself expressed in church buildings which remind us of an earlier comfort and a forward-looking demiurge which would express something new in those buildings. Perhaps architecture is a medium of communication where the Church and the Society of Jesus have been enjoying inculturation because the specifically Christian dimension is so lacking in both of these spiritual edifices. At any rate, it is troubling that there has been such success in producing a significant body of post-Christian churches, those without spiritually commanding images of the Lord Christ for those congregants who think visually. This group would include the non-literarily, non-philosophically, non-theologically inclined, the foreign-born, the pre-literate, the illiterate, the dramatic and artistically driven young, and a whole host of Carl Jung's "sensate" people who perceive before they judge.

These latter churches have been designed by architects in dialog with church leaders, to be sure. Both architects and churchmen have been searching for a non-derivative idiom—the church of the modern world, as it were. Until just yesterday, it has been quite acceptable to build churches that hearken back to an earlier era. Those Byzantine, Romanesque, Gothic, Renaissance, and Baroque Revival churches that we all know and love from our childhood are, in the minds of architectural professionals, revisited answers to ancient problems. The architects may not be aware that the ancient problems are not always the modern problems.

Those revival buildings which have been built in recent decades have been populated often enough with statues chosen from a catalog. The designer churches, on the other hand, do not have statues from the rack, but often they do not have religious sculptures at all. Moreover, painting has become extremely rare. Here we take to mind Paul Tillich's distinction between sacred subject matter and religious intention in making true artwork. It seems that inauthentic artwork, even if it is about "sacred subject matter," is not really artwork because it is not done authentically and is not therefore "religious."

It may be helpful here to note a motivation for the National Council of Catholic Bishops' statement on the necessity of seeing "the hand of the artist" in work done appropriately for the Church. Spiritual content in artwork has the power to evoke spiritual attention in the pilgrim. In his "Origin of a Work of Art," Martin Heidegger says that an artwork "preserves a world" and that this is what makes it different from a "tool." In this sense, the world of the Spirit is "preserved" or even "invoked" in the pilgrim who is able to participate in the mystery that comes through the artwork.

There is a conflict here that needs to be addressed. I do believe that the end of a long run as pope might give a man the insight that there is an abyss between derivative church buildings with endless copies of Raphael's paintings or mail-order statues and empty church buildings which have been constructed in the search for a new sacred space for our time. Recent history has given us almost two different catholic churches, one with non-art (because done not authentically but mechanically or totally by mimicry), the other with no art (because constructed with pristine, protestant spaces, with no messy devotional pieces to *distract* the faithful).

In this latter instance we might even recognize the confused rejection of modern art as a righteous refutation of "modernism."

NOTES

1. Quoted in C. J. McNaspy, S.J., *Our Changing Liturgy* (New York: Hawthorn Books, 1966), 128.

John Paul II on the Priesthood

Cardinal Avery Dulles, S.J.

1. INTRODUCTION

John Paul II is preeminently a priest. He has written a deeply appreciative account of his own priestly vocation on the golden jubilee of his ordination.[1] His entire adult life offers a striking example of priestly ministry lived out to the full. Since becoming pope, he has written annual Holy Thursday letters to priests expressing his affection and concern. These letters, notwithstanding their predominantly hortatory and devotional tone, contain important doctrinal elements.

The pope presents his teaching on priesthood most comprehensively in the apostolic exhortation *Pastores dabo vobis*, issued in 1992 on the basis of the 1990 synod on priestly formation, and in the 18 catecheses on priesthood presented at General Audience talks in 1993. Other apostolic exhortations, such as *Catechesi tradendae* (1979), *Reconciliatio et paenitentia* (1984), and *Vita consecrata* (1996), contain significant passages dealing with priesthood. Additional materials are provided by presentations to priests given on the pope's apostolic journeys, such as the talk given at Philadelphia on 4 October 1979. In all this documentation there is inevitably a certain amount of repetition.

2. THE MINISTERIAL AND THE COMMON PRIESTHOOD

Vatican II, reacting against the clericalism of the preceding centuries which seemed to isolate priests from the rest of the Church, gave a more ecclesial and pastoral interpretation, situating priesthood among the many charisms bestowed by the Holy Spirit for the service of the community. The Council revived the concept of the universal priesthood of the faithful, but it continued to insist, with the whole Catholic tradition, that the priesthood of the ordained is distinct in kind, and not simply in degree, from the priesthood common to the baptized (*LG,* n. 10).

Since the Council some "progressive" Catholic theologians have tried to advance further, as they see it, in the direction taken by Vatican II. They depict the ministerial priesthood in merely functional terms, as a particular way of exercising the baptismal priesthood. They deny that the ministerial priesthood is distinct in kind and in particular they reject the doctrine of the so-called priestly character as a medieval fabrication. Hans Küng, going still further in the direction of Protestant theology, questioned the very idea that ministers of word and sacrament should be called priests.[2]

John Paul II stands by the teaching of Vatican II on all these points. "The ministerial priesthood conferred by the sacrament of holy orders," he writes, "and the common or 'royal' priesthood of the faithful, which differ essentially and not only in degree, are ordered to one another—for each in its own way derives from the one priesthood of Christ" (*PDV,* n. 18; cf. *SR,* nn. 221-31). The sacramental character of ordained priesthood involves a special configuration of the ordained to Christ the Priest, enabling them to exercise ministerial powers in the name of Christ as head and shepherd of the Church (*PDV,* nn. 16-17; *Church,* 303).[3] By virtue of this consecration, the priest participates ontologically in the priesthood of Christ and becomes "a man of the sacred" (*Church,* 304).

In a commentary on the pope's Holy Thursday letter of 1990, Father Edward Kilmartin, S.J., remarked on the pope's neglect of the pneumatological dimension of priesthood and Eucharist.[4] Even in this letter, however, the pope holds that eucharistic worship is directed to the Father through Jesus Christ in the Spirit, so that priesthood cannot be understood without the gift of the Spirit (*DC,* n. 3). Elsewhere he asserts that the Holy Spirit confers the mysterious power for the completion of the eucharistic consecration, as the Church acknowledges at the *epiclesis* in her eucharistic prayers (*Spirit,* 354). A similar intervention of the Holy Spirit occurs in priestly ordination. "Just as in the Mass the Holy Spirit brings about the transubstantiation of the bread and wine into the Body and Blood of Christ, so also in the Sacrament of Holy Orders He effects the priestly or episcopal consecration."[5]

3. THE ORIGINS OF THE PRIESTHOOD

The historical origins of the ministerial priesthood have become a topic of intense discussion in recent years. Some hold that it was a creation of the apostolic

Church or even of the sacerdotalism that overlaid the gospel in the third century. Such views, long in vogue in the churches of the Reformation, have recently been popularized in Catholic theology.

John Paul II, following Vatican II, holds that in calling the Twelve Jesus made a decisive choice whereby they became "a special, distinct socio-ecclesial reality" (*Church*, 202). From the Gospels the pope finds evidence that Jesus gave the apostles a share in His own authoritative mission of evangelizing, forgiving sins, and shepherding the community (*Church*, 203-04). On the basis of the command of Jesus, "Do this in memory of Me" (Lk 22:19; 1 Cor 11:24), he concludes that the priesthood was effectively established at the Last Supper and indeed at the very moment of the institution of the Eucharist (*DC*, n. 2; cf. Trent, *DS*, 1752). The gift of the Holy Spirit at Pentecost enabled the apostles to fulfill their mission (*Church*, 204).

The apostles, according to John Paul II, understood that they were commissioned to provide for successors to continue the Church's ministry to the end of time. The hierarchical structuring of the Church's ministry can therefore be traced to Christ's institution of the apostolic office (*Church*, 205).

In the New Testament itself one cannot easily distinguish between the status of bishops and presbyters, but the distinction becomes clear in the subapostolic period (*Church*, 302). As Vatican II authoritatively taught (*LG*, nn. 21, 28), bishops enjoy the fullness of the priestly office, and presbyters are their co-workers (*Church*, 299-302). When I use the term "priest" in the present paper, I shall be speaking primarily of presbyters.

4. WHO CAN ORDAIN?

Following the Council of Trent (*DS*, 1777), Vatican II spoke of the bishops as "dispensers of sacred orders" (*LG*, n. 26). In the rite of priestly ordination, as revised after the Council, the bishop is informed of the Church's request that he ordain the candidate, and the people express their consent by applause or some such appropriate sign.

These efforts to involve the laity might seem to suggest that ordination is the work of the entire community, with the bishop "presiding" as an official witness. Some in fact contend that all the baptized have the radical capacity to ordain and that in an emergency, where a regularly ordained priest is lacking, the congregation can designate one of its own members to exercise the office of priest, at least temporarily, so as to celebrate a true Eucharist.

In opposition to these trends, John Paul II insists that the sacramental priesthood does not take its origin from the community, "as though it were the community that 'called' or 'delegated'" some of its members to take on priestly functions.[6] The Church must always retain its apostolic structure, which enables the bishops, as successors of the apostles, to impart the sacrament of holy orders.[7]

5. WHO CAN BE ORDAINED?

Insisting as he does that the call to priesthood is a free gift of God, John Paul II goes on to affirm that no one has a right to it. In calling only men as apostles, he says, "Christ acted in a completely free and sovereign manner" (MD, n. 26). Although he involved women in many aspects of His mission, He did not give them the sacramental charge that is joined to the institution of the Eucharist. After teaching many times that women cannot receive priestly orders (as had Paul VI and other popes before him), John Paul II in May 1994 declared that all the faithful are to hold definitively that the Church has absolutely no authority to confer priestly ordination on women.[8] The Congregation for the Doctrine of the Faith on 28 October 1995, in a document approved by the pope, declared that this doctrine, based on a longstanding consensus of the hierarchical magisterium, was infallibly taught and pertained to the deposit of faith.[9]

While maintaining that Christ acted freely in reserving ordination to men, the pope sometimes gives a theological explanation of the reason for Christ's decision. Following a well-established theological tradition, he holds that the priest must represent Christ precisely in His capacity as Bridegroom of the Church. This is notably the case at the Eucharist, when the priest acts in the person of Christ the Head (in persona Christi capitis). At the consecration the priest speaks the very words uttered by Jesus with reference to the sacrifice by which He offered His life for the Church, His beloved Bride (cf. Eph 5:25-26). The pope spells out this argument most extensively in Mulieris dignitatem, where he speaks of the Eucharist as "the sacrament of the Bridegroom and of the Bride" (MD, n. 26).

In answer to the objection that Christ or the Church discriminates against women, the pope points out that the ministerial priesthood is not a position of social privilege or dominative power. It consists in humble service toward Christ and the entire People of God.[10] The ministry of the priest exists for the sake of building up the whole Church in holiness and promoting the common priesthood of the faithful

(*PDV*, n. 16). In his teaching on the family, the lay apostolate, and the religious life, John Paul II maintains that women play an indispensable role in Church and world. In the person of Mary, who is without spot or wrinkle, the Church has already reached its perfection. The "Petrine" or hierarchical aspect of the Church exists in order to strengthen the Church in its "Marian" aspect—the ideal of sanctity exemplified in the Mother of Jesus (*MD*, n. 27).

6. FUNCTIONS OF THE PRIESTHOOD

John Paul II frequently refers to the teaching of Vatican II on the three offices of Christ: the prophetic, the priestly, and the regal. The whole Church participates in the threefold office, but in a special way this is true of the ministerial priesthood, which receives what the pope calls a "threefold ministry of word, sacrament, and pastoral charity" (*PDV*, n. 26). Although it would be wrong to separate these three functions by allotting some of them to some priests and others to others, there can be a certain division of labor since individual priests and groups of priests may receive different charisms. Paul, for example, was sent primarily to proclaim the gospel rather than to administer the sacraments (1 Cor 1:14, 17; *Church*, 312-13).

(a) The proclamation of the word, according to Vatican II, is the first and most fundamental task (*LG*, n. 28; *Church*, 305). Not limited to the pulpit, this ministry may consist in activities as diverse as teaching, writing, publishing, radio, and television (*Church*, 309). The *Catechism of the Catholic Church* is entrusted above all to priests as pastors of God's people.[11] The Church expects them "to neglect nothing with a view to a well-organized and well-oriented catechetical effort" (*CT*, n. 64).

Priestly ministry, according to John Paul II, is missionary to its very core.[12] It means being sent out for others, in order to bring the good news to all strata of humanity. As evangelist, the priest must proclaim that salvation is to be found in Jesus Christ, the Son of God. "It is His name, His teaching, His life, His promises, His kingdom, and His mystery that we proclaim to the world."[13] The priest is not the author or proprietor of the word, but a minister and witness. To be an effective witness, he must be a faithful disciple, docile to the living tradition of the Church (*PDV*, n. 26). "Continuing theological study is necessary if the priest is to faithfully carry out the ministry of the word, proclaiming it clearly and without ambiguity, distinguishing it from mere human opinions" (*PDV*, n. 72).

(b) The second major task of the priest, which presupposes the ministry of the word, is that of sacraments and sanctification. Quoting the final message of the Synod of 1990, John Paul II declares that the principal task of ordained priests is to be "ministers of the Eucharist and ministers of God's mercy in the sacrament of penance" (*PDV*, n. 4). Let me expatiate a little on these two sacraments.

Following Vatican II, which depicted the eucharistic sacrifice as "the center and root of the whole priestly life" (*PO*, n. 14; cf. *PDV*, n. 23), the pope declares: "The priest cannot be understood without the Eucharist."[14] "The presbyter," he writes, "is above all the man of the Eucharist" (*Church*, 320). The priesthood and the Eucharist presuppose each other. On the one hand, the Eucharist could not exist without the priest, and on the other, priesthood would be reduced to a lifeless shadow without the Eucharist.[15]

The Eucharist, as seen by John Paul II, has three dimensions: sacrifice, communion, and real presence (*RH*, n. 20). Against the recent tendency to insist almost exclusively on its character as a meal, the pope moves in a contrary direction. In his Holy Thursday letter of 1980, *Dominicae cenae*, he declares: "The Eucharist is above all else a sacrifice," one that restores humanity to its right relationship with God. He warns against the false opinion that the Mass is "only a banquet in which one shares by receiving the body of Christ in order to manifest, above all else, fraternal communion" (*DC*, n. 11). While the congregation join in the offering by virtue of their royal priesthood, the priest alone effects the holy sacrifice, as he can do by virtue of the powers conferred through sacred ordination (*DC*, n. 9).[16] At the consecration he acts in union with Christ, the author and principal subject of the sacrifice. Distinguishing between his own part in the sacrifice and that of the congregation, the priest asks the people to pray "that my sacrifice and yours may be acceptable to God, the almighty Father" (*DC*, nn. 8-9).

While everything possible should be done to gather the faithful for the Eucharist, situations may arise in which there is no congregation. It would be a mistake, says the pope, to omit celebration on that account. "Even if the priest is alone, the Eucharistic offering which he performs in the name of Christ has the effectiveness that comes from Christ and always obtains new graces for the Church" (*Church*, 337-38).

In the aftermath of Vatican II some theologians minimized devotion to the Blessed Sacrament outside of Mass. To counter this tendency, Paul VI in his encyclical *Mysterium fidei* (1965) defended the solemn exposition of the sacrament and the carrying of consecrated hosts in procession (n. 56). John Paul II likewise recommends personal prayer before the Blessed Sacrament, hours of adoration, eucharistic benediction, eucharistic processions, and eucharistic congresses (*DC*, n. 3). He assures priests that the time they spend in adoration of the Blessed Sacrament will contribute to the dynamism of their ministry (*Church*, 339).[17]

Ever since his days as a seminarian, the present pope has had a great devotion to St. John Mary Vianney, the Curé of Ars, who would often hear confessions for more than ten hours a day. "My encounter with this saintly figure," he writes, "confirmed me in the conviction that a priest fulfills an essential part of his mission through the confessional—by voluntarily making himself a prisoner of the confessional."[18] Of all priestly ministries, says the pope, "this is undoubtedly the most exhausting and demanding . . . , but also one of the most beautiful and consoling (*RP*, n. 29). Here, as in the Eucharist, the priest acts in the person of Christ (*in persona Christi*), in Whose name he absolves the sinner (ibid.).

(c) The third aspect of priestly ministry, in the view of the pope, is that of governance (*munus regendi*). This ministry is at once hierarchical and ministerial. It is hierarchical because connected with the power of forming and governing the priestly People of God, and ministerial because it is a service exercised in the name of Christ, who came not to be served but to serve.[19] In carrying out this ministry, the priest must be guided by pastoral charity, imitating Christ in His self-giving and service (*PDV*, n. 22). As a pastor the priest has the task of coordinating all the gifts and charisms that the Spirit raises up in the community (*PDV*, n. 26). Gathering the family of God about its Lord, he builds up the community over which he presides.[20]

7. RELATIONALITY IN THE PRIESTHOOD

From the standpoint of his dialogic personalism, John Paul II welcomes the new emphasis of Vatican II on the relational quality of the priestly office. Priestly ministry is meaningful, he holds, only within the community of faith and in relation to the various components of the Body of Christ—the pope, bishops, fellow priests, and lay persons.

(a) In accepting ordination the priest enters into an organized community in which the bishops, as successors of the apostles, have the task of teaching and governing in the name of Christ. In the ordination rite the new priest promises filial respect and obedience to ecclesiastical superiors (*PDV*, n. 28). The entire pastoral activity of the priest is an extension, as it were, of the ministry of the bishop. The grace of orders creates a special bond among priests and bishops, described by Vatican II as "hierarchical communion" (*Church*, 373; cf. *PO*, n. 7).

(b) Priestly obedience is necessarily exercised in solidarity with the presbyterate, which is called as a body to cooperate harmoniously with the bishop and, through him, with the pope (*PDV*, n. 28). Christ's prayer for unity at the Last Supper is a reminder to priests that they must live out their ministry in fraternity and friendship.[21] Structures such as senates or councils of priests give concrete expression to the unity of bishop and priests in shepherding the flock of Christ.[22] John Paul II favors common life for priests, access to a common table, and fraternal gatherings for rest and relaxation (*Church*, 381-82).

(c) Besides being related to various groups of clergy, priests have a crucially important relationship to the laity, since they are ordained for service to the entire People of God. Pastors have the duty to recognize the dignity of the lay faithful as persons raised by baptism to divine adoption (*Church*, 384-85). The Church develops organically according to the principle of the diversity of gifts, all of which are bestowed for the sake of the common good.[23] With ample quotations from Vatican II, the pope recalls the importance of developing and utilizing the distinctive gifts of lay Christians and making use of their prudent advice.[24] The laity have an indispensable role, since they can bring the Gospel to bear upon areas of life not ordinarily accessible to priests, such as the family, civil society, professional life, and culture. It is the task of priests to discern, acknowledge, and foster the charisms of the lay faithful (*CL*, n. 23; *Church*, 385).

John Paul II dwells by preference on certain groups of the laity to whom priests must relate themselves. One of these is youth. Thinking perhaps of his own experience in Poland, he remarks that the priest must make himself accessible to young people and be their companion in tourism, sports, and cultural interests. He should know how to listen and answer, giving guidance about the most fundamental questions that young people will ask. In such contexts the pope refers repeatedly to the conversation between Jesus and the rich young man in the Gospels who asked about the way to salvation and perfection.[25]

In his 1995 annual letter to priests, the pope chose as his topic, "Women in the Life of the Priest." He there repeats the exhortation of Paul to Timothy: "Treat . . . older women like mothers, younger women like sisters, in all purity" (1 Tim 5:2). In our ministry, he says, we priests must give scope to the participation of women as well as men in the threefold mission of Christ—prophetic, priestly, and royal.[26] In this connection the pope recalls the significant role played by women in the public life of Jesus, at the Cross, and in bearing witness to the resurrection.[27]

8. PRIESTLY IDENTITY

The primary office of priests, according to the pope, is to represent Christ the priest (*DC*, n. 11). Configured as they are to Christ by the sacramental character received in ordination, priests are called "to prolong the presence of Christ, the one high priest, embodying His way of life and making Him visible in the midst of the flock entrusted to their care" (*PDV*, n. 15).

John Paul II emphatically denies that the ministerial priesthood should take on a more "secular" style so as to draw closer to the laity. On the contrary, he maintains, the person of the priest must be a clear sign of his specific identity and mission. Only by way of exception should priests involve themselves in professional or cultural activities that are not directly Church-related. Worker-priests run a particular risk of reducing their spiritual ministry to a secondary role or even eliminating it (*Church*, 359).

Even more specifically, John Paul II warns that priests should abstain from political activism (*Church*, 362-67). They must certainly share in the concern of all Christians for truth and justice, but as priests they must perform this service in the perspective of eternal salvation. "Our brethren in the faith, and unbelievers too, expect us always to be able to show them this perspective, to become real witnesses to it, to be dispensers of grace, to be servants of the word of God. They expect us to be men of prayer."[28]

On many of his pastoral visits to foreign countries, the pope has urged priests to render their own specific service and to avoid involvement in partisan politics, which is contrary to their particular calling.[29] When priests become enmeshed in political struggles or run for electoral office, an element of ambiguity is introduced into their ministry. It becomes unclear whether they are speaking and acting as witnesses to the Gospel or submitting to the practicalities of politics and the demands of party discipline. By taking stands on purely secular issues, priests can alienate lay persons who may have different economic or political positions. Besides, says the pope, the clergy should not infringe on the proper territory of the laity, whose responsibility it is to apply Christian principles to social situations through the mechanisms of the economy and government. The lay faithful, by reason of their "secular" vocation, have a particular obligation to work for the Christian animation of the social order (*CL*, n. 36).

Some recent proposals for bringing priestly life up to date are, in the estimation of John Paul II, inadequate and ill-conceived. The holiness and zeal that characterized priests such as St. Vincent de Paul, the Curé of Ars, St. John Bosco, and others are as relevant today as they ever were. "In practical terms, the only priest who will always prove necessary to people is the priest who is conscious of the full meaning of his priesthood: the priest who believes profoundly, who professes his faith with courage, who prays fervently, who teaches with deep conviction, who puts into practice in his own life the program of the beatitudes . . . ."[30] John Paul II contends that priestly service, included in the "today" of Christ the Redeemer (cf. Heb 13:8), is never in danger of falling "behind the times."[31]

9. PRIESTLY VOCATION

In his exhortation on priestly formation, John Paul II devotes an entire chapter to the subject of the call that comes from Christ. He is convinced that any priestly vocation begins with a living dialogue between the Lord who calls and the individual who freely responds.

Freedom, however, implies the possibility of a negative response, such as that given by the rich young man in the Gospels, who went away sorrowful because he had great possessions (Mt 19:22; *PDV*, n. 36; cf. *VS*, nn. 19-21). In the affluent societies of our day, which urge young people to make an absolute out of personal satisfaction and riches, there are many obstacles to the hearing and acceptance of God's call. The Church must strive mightily to create an environment in which young people can make a full and free commitment to Christ in faith. Priests have a special responsibility to pray to the Lord of the harvest to send more laborers into the field (Mt 9:38; *PDV*, n. 38; *Church*, 389-90).

The freedom of the priestly vocation is demonstrated in an outstanding way by the full and irrevocable self-disposition that it demands and elicits. For John Paul II, the priesthood is permanent not only because the sacramental character of ordination is indelible, but also because of the quality of the call and the response. Since priesthood involves a total gift of self, it cannot be merely temporary or provisional. "The priesthood," he writes, "cannot be renounced because of the difficulties that we meet and the sacrifices asked of us. Like the apostles, we have left everything to follow Christ; therefore we must persevere beside him also through the cross."[32]

10. Prayer and Holiness.

In his first Holy Thursday letter to priests (1979), John Paul II linked priestly identity with prayer and holiness. He wrote: "Perhaps in these recent years—at least in certain quarters—there has been too much discussion about the priesthood, the priest's 'identity,' the value of his presence in the modern world, etc., and on the other hand there has been too little praying. . . . It is prayer that shows the essential style of the priest; without prayer this style becomes deformed."[33]

Since prayer is so essential to the beginning and growth of every priestly vocation, and to the observance of celibacy, it is imperative for the priest to be a man of prayer. By their prayer in the offering of the Eucharist and in the Liturgy of the Hours, priests offer the voice of the Church which intercedes on behalf of all humanity (*Church*, 334). The faithful commonly look to priests for instruction in the art of prayer. "The priest," writes the pope, "will only be able to train others in this school of Jesus at prayer if he himself has been trained in it and continues to receive its formation" (*PDV*, n. 47).

Although there are no limits to the holiness to which lay Christians can be called, the priest, specially consecrated through ordination, has a particular vocation to holiness. In the rite of ordination, the Church prays that the new priest will be enriched with God's Spirit of holiness. This communion with the Spirit, as the pope told a group of priests, "calls for your personal sanctification."[34]

Priestly spirituality is the cultivation of the specific form of holiness that flows from the very identity of the priest as a sacramental representation of Christ, whom he makes visibly present in the midst of the people (*PDV*, n. 15). To be a competent preacher of the word, a guide of souls, and a pastoral leader the priest must excel in pastoral charity. The priesthood of Christ, whose headship coincides with His character as servant, must be the model of every priest (*PDV*, nn. 12, 21). Because Christ's servanthood comes to its fullest expression in His death on the cross, the priest is required to make a total gift of himself to the service of the Lord and of the Church, His Bride (*PDV*, nn. 22-23). As Christ's instrument the priest must be, like him, a victim (*sacerdos et victima*) (*Church*, 330).

Jesus invites all priests to share in the intimacy enjoyed by the first apostles.[35] As His close companions, they may hear as addressed to themselves the words, "No longer do I call you servants . . . but . . . friends, for all that I have heard from My Father I have made known to you" (Jn 15:15; *PDV*, n. 46).

11. Evangelical Counsels in the Life of the Priest

Tracing the origins of the priesthood to Christ's call of the Twelve, John Paul II speaks of the "radicalism of the gospel," which holds forth the ideals of the evangelical counsels to all who are called to follow Jesus in His ministry. The evangelical counsels of obedience, chastity, and poverty, by inserting priests more deeply into the mystery of Christ, give particular fruitfulness to their ministry.

(a) Reference has already been made to the obedience owed by the priest to ecclesiastical superiors. In his exhortation on priestly formation, John Paul II points out that this obedience is apostolic and pastoral in character (*PVD*, n. 28). It is based on a readiness to be consumed by the demands of the flock, setting the needs of the Church ahead of any personal preference or convenience.

(b) John Paul II attaches great importance to priestly celibacy. At the Synod of Bishops in 1971, Cardinal Wojtyla strongly defended the discipline as a sign of priestly commitment. Confirming the expressed will of the Synod of 1990, he reiterates in *Pastores dabo vobis* that no doubt should be left in anyone's mind regarding the Church's firm will to maintain the current discipline, which he describes as a precious charism maintained in the Western Church. This practice, he holds, harmonizes with the meaning of sacred ordination, which configures the priest to Christ as spouse of the Church. Celibacy "for the sake of the Kingdom" is both an eschatological sign and a significant help in enabling the priest to make himself totally available for the service of the People of God.[36] Celibacy, therefore, is to be welcomed and continually renewed with a free and loving decision to accept it as a precious gift (*PDV*, n. 29). The gift does not, however, dispense the individual from personal effort to remain faithful to it and carry it out generously and joyfully (*PDV*, n. 50).

In an address to the presidents of the European episcopal conferences, the pope took note of challenges to priestly celibacy arising, as he said, from the general climate of secularization. He appealed to the bishops not to give in to these pressures or surround this vocation with an atmosphere of discouragement.[37]

(c) Priestly poverty, which the pope generally treats last among the three evangelical counsels, is expressed in "detachment toward money, in renunciation of all greed for possessing earthly goods, in a simple lifestyle," and abstention from luxury (*Church*, 360). It enables the priest to stand in solidarity with the poor and makes him more available to be sent wherever he is most needed, even at the cost of personal sacrifice. In consumerist societies, priestly poverty takes on prophetic significance inasmuch as it expresses trust in God's providence rather than excessive reliance on money and material possessions (*PDV*, n. 30).

12. THE CONSECRATED LIFE

As is well known, the young Wojtyla seriously considered entering the Carmelite order. His apostolic exhortation *Vita consecrata* evinces deep esteem for the religious life. The priestly and religious vocations, according to the pope, are mutually supportive. Consecration to the evangelical counsels can dispose a man to accept the grace of priestly ordination. Conversely, commitment to the demands of the ministry prompts significant numbers of diocesan priests to join religious institutes (*Church*, 597-600).

Some religious institutes quite properly enjoy exemption in order to govern themselves according to their own constitutions and pursue the apostolate on a universal scale. But when religious priests engage in ministry within a diocese, they should obtain a mandate from the bishop. Like diocesan priests, religious priests are to that extent co-workers of the bishop (*Church*, 374).

John Paul II's theology of the religious life lies beyond the scope of the present paper. It may suffice to note his conviction that the consecrated life, as an eloquent testimony to the beatitudes, fosters a deeper awareness of the demands of the Gospel and has an objective superiority in relation to other states of life (*VC*, nn. 18, 32). Both the priestly and religious vocations belong inalienably to the mystery of the Church and effectively serve her mission. Where the two vocations are united in the same person, as is usually the case with Jesuits, the pope obviously approves.

CONCLUSION

In his teaching on the ministerial priesthood, John Paul II does not seek to be original. His originality, if the term is appropriate, consists in showing that Vatican II permits, and indeed demands, a high doctrine of priestly ministry. While gladly accepting the collegial and pastoral emphases of the council and its esteem for the laity, the pope, practicing a "hermeneutics of continuity," integrates these features with traditional Catholic teaching. Vatican II, he insists, does not require a repudiation of earlier models of priesthood. The council did not desacralize the priesthood. Nor did it diminish the links between priesthood and Eucharist or between priesthood and prayer. Nor did it cast doubt on the value of the evangelical counsels. Nor did it exalt marriage at the expense of consecrated celibacy. If John Paul II is right, the efforts of some post-conciliar theologians to secularize or demythologize the priesthood are misreadings of the council, very harmful to the life of the Church.

John Paul II's doctrine of priesthood is admittedly countercultural in the American context, but perhaps for that very reason it needs to be boldly asserted if the Church is to maintain its distinctive identity. The future vitality of Catholicism is inseparable, I believe, from a correct and traditional understanding of priestly ministry.

ABBREVIATIONS

Church - John Paul II, *The Church: Mystery, Sacrament, Community. A Catechesis on the Creed* (Boston: Daughters of St. Paul, 1988).

CL - John Paul II, Apostolic Exhortation *Christifideles laici* (1988)

CT - John Paul II, Apostolic Exhortation *Catechesi tradendae* (1979)

DC - John Paul II, Letter to Bishops, *Dominicae cenae* (1980)

DS - *Enchiridion symbolorum . . .* , ed. H. Denzinger, rev. A. Schönmetzer (Freiburg: Herder, 1976)

LG - Vatican II, Dogmatic Constitution *Lumen gentium*

MD - John Paul II, Apostolic Letter *Mulieris dignitatem* (1988)

PDV - John Paul II, Apostolic Exhortation *Pastores dabo vobis* (1992)

PO - Vatican II, Decree on Priestly Formation, *Optatam totius*

RH - John Paul II, Encyclical *Redemptor hominis* (1979)

RP - John Paul II, Apostolic Exhortation *Reconciliatio et paenitentia* (1984)

Spirit - John Paul II, *The Spirit: Giver of Life and Love. A Catechesis on the Creed* (Boston: Pauline Books & Media, 1996)

SR - John Paul II, *Sources of Renewal: The Implementation of Vatican II* (San Francisco: Harper & Row, 1979)

VC - John Paul II, Apostolic Exhortation *Vita consecrata* (1995)

VS - John Paul II, Encyclical *Veritatis splendor* (1993)

NOTES

1. John Paul II, *Gift and Mystery: On the Fiftieth Anniversary of My Priestly Ordination* (New York: Doubleday, 1996).

2. Hans Küng, *Why Priests? A Proposal for a New Church Ministry* (Garden City, N.Y.: Doubleday, 1972), 41-42.

3. Under Paul VI, the Congregation of the Doctrine of the Faith had strongly insisted on the permanent priestly "character" in *Mysterium Ecclesiae*, n. 6; text in *Origins* 3 (19 July 1973): 97-100, 110-12, at 112. Under John Paul II, this doctrine was reaffirmed by a letter to bishops from

the Congregation of the Doctrine of the Faith, "The Minister of the Eucharist," in *Origins* 13 (15 Sept. 1983): 229-33.

4. Edward J. Kilmartin, *Church, Eucharist and Priesthood* (New York: Paulist, 1981), 7.

5. *Gift and Mystery*, 44. Since this paper was written, John Paul II has strongly emphasized the *epiclesis* in his encyclical *Ecclesia de Eucharistia*, nn. 17 and 23.

6. John Paul II, "A Letter to Priests (1979)," n. 4; text in *Origins* 8 (19 Apr. 1979): 696-704, at 698.

7. Under John Paul II, the Congregation of the Doctrine of the Faith in 1983 declared that the opinion that the community can designate its own president and confer on him the faculties needed to preside at the Eucharist "undermines the entire apostolic structure of the Church and distorts the sacramental economy of salvation itself." See "The Minister of the Eucharist," III/1, p. 231.

8. John Paul II, Apostolic Letter on Ordination and Women, *Ordinatio sacerdotalis*, n. 4; text in *Origins* 24 (9 June 1994): 49-52, at 51.

9. Congregation for the Doctrine of the Faith, "Response to the Dubium," *Origins* 25 (30 Nov. 1995): 401-03, at 401.

10. John Paul II, "Women in the Life of the Priest," n. 7, *Origins* 24 (20 Apr. 1995): 749-55, at 754. In *Gift and Mystery* (44-46) the pope explains that the ultimate meaning of all priestly spirituality is expressed by the rubric in the rite of ordination requiring the ordinand to lie prostrate on the floor in the form of a cross. Priests, he says, must become a "floor" for their brothers and sisters.

11. John Paul II, "1993 Holy Thursday Themes: Catechism, Celibacy," n. 2; text in *Origins* 22 (8 Apr. 1993): 746-48, at 747.

12. John Paul II, "Dimensions of the Priesthood," n. 3; *Origins* 9 (18 Oct. 1979): 281-84, at 283.

13. Ibid.

14. John Paul II, "Priests and the Eucharist," *The Pope Speaks* 29 (1984): 197-99, at 198.

15. Ibid.

16. In holding that the ordained priest alone confects the eucharistic sacrifice, John Paul II is following the teaching of Vatican II (*LG,* n. 10, and *PO,* n. 2) and that of many other official documents. Since this paper was completed, John Paul II has reaffirmed the same teaching with added emphasis in his encylical *Ecclesia de Eucharistia* n. 32.

17. See also "Priests and the Eucharist," 198.

18. *Gift and Mystery*, 58.

19. John Paul II, "A Letter to Priests" (1979), n. 4, p. 698; "To All Priests," *The Pope Speaks* (1985): 166-73, at 166.

20. "Holy Thursday Letter to Priests," n. 6; text in *Origins* 18 (6 Apr. 1989): 729-34, at 733.

21. "Dimensions of the Priesthood," n. 4, p. 283.

22. Ibid., n. 1, p. 281.

23. John Paul II, "Holy Thursday Letter to Priests," n. 4, p. 732.

24. Ibid., n. 7. p. 733, with references to *LG,* nn. 30 and 37, and *GS,* n. 43.

25. "To All Priests," 168-73.

26. "Women in the Life of the Priest," n. 7, p. 754.

27. Ibid., n. 6, p. 754.

28. "A Letter to Priests" (1979), n. 7, p. 700.

29. See in this connection his address "Be Mediators, Not Politicians," to the assembly of priests in Zaire on 4 May 1980, *Origins* 10 (22 May 1980): 10-12, at 11; also his address on "Communion, Participation, Evangelization," to the bishops of Brazil on 10 July 1980, *Origins* 10 (31 July 1980): 129-36, at 136.

30. "A Letter to Priests" (1979), n. 7, p. 700.

31. *Gift and Mystery*, 84.

32. "A Letter to Priests" (1979), n. 4, p. 698.

33. Ibid., n. 10, p. 703.

34. These words, from a homily of John Paul II to priests given in October 1984, are quoted in *Pastores dabo vobis*, n. 33.

35. "Dimensions of the Priesthood," n. 4, p. 283.

36. "A Letter to Priests" (1979), n. 8, p. 701.

37.   Reflections at conclusion of meeting with presidents of European episcopal conferences, *Origins* 22 (8 Apr. 1993): 747-48, at 748.

A Response to Cardinal Dulles

Lucien F. Longtin, S.J.

Since I am a catechist by mission, and not a theologian, and since my knowledge of Pope John Paul II's writings cannot hold a candle to the author of this paper, my response should largely be to note some of the striking points in this presentation, to raise a number of questions, and to offer some ideas about promoting vocations to the priesthood. In the effort to think about how we may "create an atmosphere in which young people might be led to make a full and free commitment to Christ in faith," I will mention one point of the pope's thought in *Pastores dabo vobis* that is, perhaps, underdeveloped in this paper.

Dulles's presentation is a thorough and splendid synthesis. I can hardly think of any other aspect of priesthood that Pope John Paul II might have treated that he did not, except perhaps the signs of sexual/affective maturity that are needed for priesthood. And I cannot think of a better scheme for organizing a presentation of his ideas than the twelve-point grid that is used here. Studying this paper gave me the Isaian feeling of awe . . . and of dread too, like the feelings I often experience in retreats—the feelings we all have when we know that God is addressing us at the core of our being.

Especially consoling for me—to use the word as Ignatius did—were the sections which developed these themes: the pope's rich exposition of the three functions of the priesthood; the positive dimensions of the pope's thoughts about priestly identity; the presentation of Pope John Paul II's ideas about the importance of prayer and personal holiness to the ministry of the priest; and the presentation of his thoughts about the importance of the three evangelical counsels in the life of the priest. At one point, for instance, he writes: "In practical terms, the only priest who will always prove necessary to people is the priest who is conscious of the full meaning of his priesthood: the priest who believes profoundly, who professes his faith with courage, who prays fervently, who teaches with deep conviction, who puts into practice in his own life the program of the beatitudes." He complements that insight with this comment: "Our brethren in the faith, and unbelievers too, expect us always to be able to show them [the] perspective of eternal salvation. . . . They expect us to be men of prayer."

While personally I judge it pointless for me to compare or contrast my capacity for holiness to that of others, no matter what their state of life, it nonetheless seems right to me to say, as the pope does, that a priest, in virtue of his calling, has a special duty to strive to become a person in whom the life of God and Jesus is clearly manifest, and that therefore the priest's call to serve and to lead God's people imposes obligations on him to become a person of deep prayer as His Master was and to open himself to suffering for the sake of his pastoral mission as Jesus did. For this reason the evangelical counsels, which call for complete and generous giving of oneself to one's mission, seem appropriate. As Pope John Paul II writes in *Pastores dabo vobis*, "Jesus Christ, who brought His pastoral charity to perfection on the Cross with a complete exterior and interior emptying of self, is both the model and source of the virtues of obedience, chastity, and poverty which the priest is called to live out as an expression of his pastoral charity for his brothers and sisters."

The pope's treatment of these matters moved me deeply. But there are several areas of his writings on priesthood where I need better understanding: (1) I do not grasp the probative theological significance of the bridegroom-bride image drawn from Ephesians. How does it explain the permanent option by Jesus to choose only men for the priesthood? (2) While I agree with the pope's admonition that priests should avoid political activism and roles more properly assumed by lay people, does the clarity of priestly identity called for in his writings frown upon the kind of prophetic stances taken by Rupert Meyer, Oscar Romero, or Rutillo Grande? Would not each of them have been accused of inappropriate political activism by their violent enemies? Was not such ambiguity of identity at times the very lot of the Galilean whose cross bore the scornful emblem "King of the Jews"? (3) If mothers can and should sometimes influence their sons to consider the priesthood, perhaps we should engage in further study of *Mulieris dignitatem* so as to reassure ourselves that, in recommending that they urge their sons to consider priestly service in the Church, they will not be teaching them to perpetuate injustice.

Let me also ask whether Dulles's paper has taken sufficient note of what the pope wrote in *Pastores dabo vobis,* n. 30: "The interior freedom which is safeguarded and nourished by evangelical poverty will help the priest to stand beside the underprivileged, to practice solidarity with their efforts, to create a more just

212

society, to be more sensitive and capable of understanding realities involving the economic and social aspects of life, and to promote a preferential option for the poor. The latter, while excluding no one from the proclamation and gift of salvation, will assist him in gently approaching the poor, sinners, and all those on the margins of society, following the model given by Jesus in carrying out His prophetic and priestly ministry. Nor should the prophetic significance of priestly poverty be forgotten, so urgently needed in affluent and consumerist societies. A truly poor priest is indeed a specific sign of separation from, disavowal of, and non-submission to the tyranny of a contemporary world which puts all its trust in money and in material security."

The experience which most deeply touches the youth that I work with is direct experience of the sorrowful and unjust plight of the poor. This face-to-face experience of their suffering opens the hearts of students to a greater reality than their usual affluent surroundings, which blind their vision and dull their spiritual imaginations. We should capitalize on this experience together with Jesus's concern for the poor and for the transformation expressed in His prayer "Thy Kingdom come." The call to promote justice in the world is a tangible, meaningful goal for students which can open them to the life of the spirit. For it is precisely when one finds oneself powerless, vulnerable, and frightened before the mountain of suffering of the poor that one is most ready to be led to embrace the deeper realities of daily prayer and vocational discernment, to weigh seriously the question: "How can I best serve?"

The Desire for Fulfillment: Comments on an Issue Raised in Pope John Paul II's *Letter to Families*

Peter F. Ryan, S.J.

This paper will focus on an issue that arises in Pope John Paul II's *Letter to Families,* n. 9. God creates man for divine life, yet also wills man for his own sake. The pope makes it clear that he finds no incompatibility between the two kinds of willing, and I agree. However, I believe that further explanation is needed to clarify what is at stake. A closer look points to the necessity of addressing a problem that theologians have been grappling with for centuries: how can the beatific vision be both a fitting fulfillment for human nature and an utterly gratuitous gift? I will argue that traditional efforts to resolve the problem cannot be sustained, and that its solution requires a more radical approach.

The pope raises the issue as a quandary in need of resolution: "Does affirming man's ultimate destiny not conflict with the statement that God wills man 'for his own sake'? If he has been created for divine life, can man truly exist 'for his own sake'? . . . It might appear that in destining man for divine life God definitively takes away man's existing 'for his own sake' [*Gaudium et spes,* n. 24]. What then is the relationship between the life of the person and his sharing in the life of the Trinity?"[1]

John Paul is asking how God can will human beings for their own sake, that is, how He can will them not just to exist but to find the human fulfillment for which they naturally yearn—if He creates them to share in divine life. He attempts to resolve the quandary as follows:

> Saint Augustine provides us with the answer in his celebrated phrase: "Our heart is restless until it rests in You" [*Confessions* I, 1]. This 'restless heart' serves to point out that between the one finality and the other there is in fact no contradiction, but rather a relationship, a complementarity, a unity. By his very genealogy, the person created in the image and likeness of God, exists *"for his*

own sake" and reaches fulfillment precisely *by sharing in God's life*. The content of this self-fulfillment is the fullness of life in God, proclaimed by Christ (cf. Jn 6:37-40), who redeemed us precisely so that we might come to share it (cf. Mk 10:45).[2]

The pope seems to identify the human fulfillment we naturally desire with the beatific vision. This enables him to regard fulfillment in the beatific vision as entirely fitting for human persons. It is important to establish that fittingness, for otherwise we could not be fulfilled by the vision. Without a natural reason to seek it, the beatific vision could only be viewed as an alien imposition.

However, as it stands, the pope's explanation seems vulnerable to the following objection: The beatific vision is a supernatural gift. Scripture makes this clear by teaching that to find this fulfillment we must be "born anew" (Jn 3:7) and become "children of God" (1 Jn 3:1). Indeed, the pope's statement that we are called to share in *divine* life indicates that he regards the beatific vision as a supernatural gift. But such a gift is by definition a gift over and above the gift of our being created in the first place. To preserve the gratuity of the beatific vision, we must be able to say that God need not have offered it. But how can we say that God need not have offered us fulfillment in *divine* life if we are by nature "restless" for it?

One might attempt to solve the problem by pointing out that God did not need to offer the beatific vision to sinful human beings. In the sixteenth century, Baius claimed that until they fell, human beings were owed fulfillment in the beatific vision.[3] The Church firmly rejected that claim, and I know of no theologian who defends it today. Thus, it is necessary to show that even if they had not fallen, human beings would need grace to receive the beatific vision.

Theologians responded to Baius by arguing that our existence would make sense even in "pure nature," a hypothetical state without sin and grace, and thus also without the offer of supernatural fulfillment. They maintained that it would be absurd for God to create us, yet make it impossible for us to find the fulfillment we naturally desire. These pure-nature theorists therefore concluded that our natural desire is not directed to the beatific vision but to a perfect happiness that is entirely natural. Their thought experiment allowed them to regard the offer of supernatural fulfillment in the beatific vision as truly gratuitous, a fulfillment over and above what God commits Himself to in creating us. Although they denied that we have an unconditional natural desire for such fulfillment, they argued that we do desire it conditionally, and they claimed that human nature has the "obediential potency" to be raised up by God and made capable of receiving that fulfillment.[4]

The pope apparently rejects this solution, for he says "the person created in the image and likeness of God, exists *'for his own sake'* and reaches fulfillment precisely *by sharing in God's life.*" I take that to mean that we find the fulfillment we naturally desire by sharing in divine life. By contrast, pure-nature theorists assume that the fulfillment we naturally desire is superseded by our fulfillment in the beatific vision.

Henri de Lubac offers a devastating critique of the pure-nature theory.[5] He denies that the concept of obediential potency can account for the fittingness or even the possibility of our being fulfilled by the beatific vision. He argues that if we have only obediential potency for the beatific vision, we cannot "feel it as a blessing."[6] He claims that concrete nature is to some degree defined by the innate desire for whatever fulfills it, and that a nature can find true fulfillment only in what is naturally desired. So, de Lubac draws the inevitable conclusion that if our natural desire were for perfect *natural* fulfillment, it would be impossible for us to be fulfilled by the beatific vision.

Although the pope does not mention de Lubac, what he does say suggests that he concurs with de Lubac's critique of the pure-nature theory. I agree that the pure-nature theory is fatally flawed because it fails to show how the beatific vision is a fitting fulfillment. However, rejecting that theory means that we must face anew the problem it purports to solve: sustaining the gratuity of the beatific vision.

De Lubac attempts to solve the problem by denying that natural desire is efficacious. He argues that God can never be a debtor and that under no circumstances could we ever have rights before God. He therefore concludes that the beatific vision is an utterly gratuitous gift. Unfortunately, that explanation does not hold up. Of course, it is true that everything we have, including our very existence, is a gift from God. But it is one thing to affirm that God was not obliged to create us, and quite another to say that even if we had retained our innocence, he could have denied us the only thing that could possibly fulfill us. Yet that is what de Lubac maintains.

Because he holds that we naturally desire the beatific vision itself, his effort to preserve its gratuity is reduced to the claim that God is sovereign and therefore could withhold that vision. Thus, de Lubac's argument wrongly assumes that God could act in a capricious manner.[7] Charles Boyer offers a telling critique of that assumption:

To say that the creature does not have rights before God can have a religious sense, if by that one means that it has nothing that it has not received, or again that it has been well made and that He has lovingly provided for its interests; but if one means to say that God could treat the work of His hands in any way whatsoever, that He could put a just person in hell, or simply deprive an innocent human person of the final good proportioned to him, that would be irreconcilable with a correct idea of the divinity. It is numbered among those things that God, according to Augustine, is too powerful to do: "*potenter non potest.*" It is traditional to say that in such a case, God owes it to Himself not to act in a certain manner.[8]

How then are we to solve the problem of the gratuity of the beatific vision without, like the pure-nature theorists, finding it impossible to account for its fittingness? Although a proper answer to that question would require a much fuller treatment than can be offered here, I will sketch out the main lines of a solution that seems to me correct.[9] Although I do not assume that the pope would agree with the following analysis, his statement that "between the one finality and the other there is in fact no contradiction, but rather a relationship, a complementarity, a unity," taken by itself, is certainly compatible with this solution. In order to speak fruitfully about these two finalities, I am convinced that we must clearly distinguish the fulfillment of our human nature as such from our fulfillment in the beatific vision, and that we can do so without compromising the requisite unity of these finalities.

To what is our desire for human fulfillment directed? We naturally seek fulfillment in the human goods that pertain to our nature: for example, we seek to stay alive and healthy, to learn new things, to be at peace with ourselves, with other people, and with God. Our desire is not for absolutely perfect fulfillment in some single good; rather, we desire unimpeded fulfillment in the whole range of human goods.[10]

The view that human nature is not called to natural but to supernatural fulfillment—fulfillment directly in God—fails to do justice to our natural desire for these fundamental goods of our nature. Of course, St. Thomas Aquinas argues that in the beatific vision, these goods will be virtually present in God who is their source.[11] However, his argument does not solve the problem, for natural and supernatural fulfillment are different in species.[12] If human nature is called to fulfillment in the beatific vision, there seems to be no room for human goods precisely as such to fulfill us. Conversely, if human nature is oriented to natural fulfillment, it is not clear how it could be fulfilled directly in the beatific vision.

Yet God not only offers us fulfillment in human goods, but also calls us to supernatural fulfillment in the beatific vision. The problem dissipates once we see that the latter gift need not be interpreted as referring to the fulfillment of our human nature as such. Indeed, Scripture does not describe our fulfillment in the beatific vision as the fulfillment of our human nature. Rather, it suggests that being born again and becoming "partakers of the divine nature" (2 Pt 1:4) is the condition for our sharing in divine intimacy: "Beloved, we are God's children now; it does not yet appear what we shall be, but know that when He appears we shall be like him, for we shall see Him as He is" (1 Jn 3:2).

The following consideration supports this view. Natures are fulfilled when they are fully actualized. But "beings that share the same complete reality must be of the same nature, and beings different in nature cannot share the same complete reality." Since enjoying divine goodness is natural to divine persons insofar as they are divine, it cannot fulfill human persons as human. Therefore, human persons can be fulfilled in divine goodness only insofar as they are given a share in the divine nature.[13]

If this proposal is sound—if sharing in Trinitarian intimacy does not fulfill human persons precisely insofar as they are human but insofar as, having been born of water and the Spirit, they have been divinized—then the problem of gratuity is resolved. For, insofar as we are human, we are called to fulfillment in the human goods we naturally desire and, at least in principle, nothing more is required for our specifically human fulfillment. If we nevertheless are offered a share in the divine nature by which we reach the beatific vision, it obviously would be a gift over and above the gift of our natural being.

What about the problem of the fittingness of the beatific vision? If the beatific vision is not the *per se* fulfillment of human persons precisely as human, then there obviously is no need to account for its fittingness as such. Still, the problem of fittingness is not resolved simply by identifying the beatific vision as the fulfillment of human persons insofar as they are given a share in the divine nature. For unless we have some natural reason to accept that share in divine life and the beatific vision to which it leads, it can only be regarded as an alien imposition.

What natural reason might we have to accept the offer of the beatific vision? People naturally recognize that they depend on God for all the goods for which their nature yearns. So, they naturally desire to be at peace with Him. In fact, people recognize harmony with God as being itself one of the humanly fulfilling goods they seek. They therefore recognize the fittingness of accepting whatever gifts God may offer. Christians believe that God offers us a supernatural relationship with Himself—a relationship, that is, that goes beyond anything He commits Himself to offer in deciding to create us. Indeed, Christians believe that God offers us a share in his very nature. Our natural interest in remaining in a harmonious, cooperative relationship with God gives us reason to accept that gift even if no other reason to do so is evident to us.

Another argument from faith further supports the appropriateness of our accepting the share in His nature that God offers us. Faith and experience both make it clear that we are enslaved to sin and death. We naturally want to be freed from this yoke of slavery, but we cannot free ourselves. Faith tells us that God offers to free us from sin and death, but only by also giving us a share in his divine nature. He offers the healing grace we need, but only in the context of his offer of elevating grace. If we can find the answer to our human problems only by receiving the share in divine life that God offers, then we have a particularly strong reason to accept that gift.

Although this analysis goes far beyond anything the pope committed himself to in his *Letter to Families*, it does support his claim that "between the one finality and the other there is in fact no contradiction, but rather a relationship, a complementarity, a unity." For I have argued that as human, we naturally seek humanly fulfilling goods, and insofar as we have been given a share in the divine nature, we are called to fulfillment in the beatific vision. Those two finalities do not contradict each other but are related and indeed complementary. Again, fallen human beings receive the healing grace that enables them to find ultimate human fulfillment only if they also accept the gift of a share in divine life. Moreover, these two aspects form a unity, for the same human person who, as human, seeks humanly fulfilling goods is, insofar as he has been given a share in the divine nature, oriented to fulfillment in the beatific vision. Like the divine and human natures in the person of Christ, these aspects are distinct but not separate, united but not confused in the human person who has received the grace of divine adoption.

How can God will human beings for their own sake if He creates them to share in divine life? God's purpose in creating is to extend His divine family—to call others into Trinitarian intimacy. But in doing so, He does not instrumentalize our human nature. Human nature must retain its own intrinsic meaning and intelligibility, so that there will exist persons able to receive the participation in divine life that God wants to give. Human beings must be able to find fulfillment in what they naturally desire, so that they also can receive, as a completely gratuitous gift, their share in the divine nature and the beatific vision to which it leads.

Are human fulfillment and the beatific vision the same reality? The pope seems to suggest that they are when he quotes Augustine's famous cry, "Our heart is restless until it rests in You." But the pope also says that the content of our fulfillment "is the fullness of life in God, proclaimed by Christ." The life Christ proclaimed is life in the kingdom. Although the vision of God is the kingdom's chief constituent, it also includes properly human goods. Vatican II makes this clear in teaching that those who obey the Lord will find in heaven all the good fruits of their nature and effort.[14] If we follow Jesus's exhortation to seek the kingdom above all else, we will find both integral fulfillment in the human goods that our restless hearts naturally desire, and the utterly gratuitous yet entirely fitting gift of the beatific vision that God promises to His children.

NOTES

1. Pope John Paul II, *Letter to Families,* n.9.

2. Ibid. (emphasis in original).

3. See Baius, *De meritis operum,* chs. 1-3; also see Jansenius, *De statu naturae purae,* Bk.1, ch. 15, and Bk. 2, ch. 1.

4. Although some anticipation of this theory is already evident before Baius in the work of theologians like Thomas de Vio Cajetan, Sylvester of Ferrara, and Domingo Bañez, the theory's full development came only later. See, for example, Victor Cathrein, "De naturali hominis beatitudine," *Gregorianum* (1930): 398-409. For a more detailed exposition, see Garrigou-Lagrange, *De revelatione per Ecclesiam Catholicam proposita,* vol. 1, 4th ed. (Rome: Libreria Editrice Religiosa, 1945), 180-204, 315-76; *De beatitudine de actibus humanibus et habitibus: Commentarius in Summam theologicam S. Thomae Ia IIae qq. 1-54* (Turin: Marietti, 1951), 164-66; and *De Deo uno: Commentarium in primam partem S. Thomae* (Turin: Lega Cattolica, 1950), 244-69.

5. See de Lubac, *The Mystery of the Supernatural,* trans. Rosemary Sheed (New York: Herder and Herder, 1967).

6. Ibid., 78, note 16.

7. See ibid., 308-10. In *Augustinianism and Modern Theology,* trans. Lancelot Sheppard (New York: Herder and Herder, 1969), 13-14, de Lubac praises Ockham for preserving "the idea of a sovereignly independent God" through the concept of "*potentia absoluta.*"

8. Boyer, "Nature pure et surnaturel dans le 'Surnaturel' du Père de Lubac," *Gregorianum* 27 (1947): 391 (my translation). "Dire que la créature n'a pas de droits vis-à-vis Dieu peut avoir un sens religieux, si l'on veut signifier par là qu'elle n'a rien qu'elle n'ait reçu ou encore qu'elle a été bien faite et qu'il a été amoureusement pourvu à ses intérêts; mais si l'on entendait dire que Dieu pourrait traiter n'importe comment l'oeuvre de ses mains, mettre un juste en enfer, ou

simplement priver une personne humaine innocente du bien final qui lui est proportionné, c'est cela qui serait inconciliable avec une juste idée de la divinité. Cela appartient au nombre de ces choses que Dieu, selon Augustin, est trop puissant pour les faire: 'potenter non potest.' Il est traditionnel de dire qu'en pareil cas, Dieu se doit à lui même de ne pas agir d'une certaine façon."

9.   For a fuller exposition of this approach, see Peter F. Ryan, S.J., "How Can the Beatific Vision Both Fulfill Human Nature and Be Utterly Gratuitous?," *Gregorianum* 83 (2002): 717-54; *Germain Grisez,* "Natural Law, God, Religion, and Human Fulfillment," *Gregorianum* 82 (2001): 20-36; and Peter F. Ryan, S.J., "Fulfillment as Human in the Beatific Vision? Problems of Fittingness and Gratuity," *American Journal of Jurisprudence* 46 (2001): 153-63. I believe that the view that I shall set out is faithful to Scripture and compatible with the teachings of the Catholic Church. However, I am prepared to accept the Church's judgment on the matter.

10.   St. Thomas Aquinas employs the notion of fundamental human goods at *ST* 1-2, q. 10, a. 1, c., where he teaches that human beings naturally desire as ends the human goods that correspond to the various aspects of their nature, and at ST 1-2, q. 94, a. 2, c., where he teaches that natural law has not just one but several principles that direct human action to diverse human goods. But he does not explain how these diverse basic goods are related to the single ultimate end in which he says we expect to find perfect happiness and for which he says we necessarily act. For an argument that challenges the view that we necessarily seek absolutely perfect happiness in some single ultimate end, see Peter F. Ryan, S.J., "Must the Acting Person Have a Single Ultimate End?," *Gregorianum* 82 (2001): 327-55.

11.   See ST 1-2, q. 3, a. 3, ad 2.

12.   See ST 1-2, q.5, a. 5, c. and ad 3.

13.   Grisez, 25.

14.   See *Gaudium et spes,* n. 39.

Nature and Grace after the Baroque

Stephen Fields S.J.

Fides et ratio makes an important contribution to contemporary understandings of the relation between nature and grace. It is implicitly critical of the position that, since the sixteenth century, has become a common understanding of this relation. Based on interpretations of Aquinas, this position contends that theology can discern a state of human nature that is purely independent of grace. Grace, available to humanity as a result of Christ's work in history, is added onto this pure state of nature, thus elevating it beyond its postlapsarian capacities.[1] Although it is doubtful that Aquinas himself holds this position, aspects of his thought can be seen as contributing to it.[2] In offering an alternative, John Paul conceives nature as sacramental—as the symbol that intrinsically mediates the divine life. The following study will situate his position within the modern development of the problem. This, as the contemporary philosopher of culture Louis Dupré tells us, begins in the Baroque, whose passing lost for the West its last great harmony between nature and grace. [3]

I.

According to Dupré, the Baroque achieved this harmony by a dynamic understanding of the human person in its intrinsic relation to its transcendent source. In this understanding, human creativity is appreciated, not only because it follows its own rules and standards, but precisely because, in the complexity of these, it symbolizes the divine.[4] Baroque culture is essentially representational: the divine immanence in creation and the divine transcendence to creation are harmoniously yet dynamically fused.[5] This fusion is capitulated in aesthetic productivity. In the plastic arts, Roman and Bavarian churches, for instance, are filled with forms and shapes, like saints and angels, that mediate between the merely earthly and the

223

purely heavenly. They are brightened with light and color and displayed in motion in order to radiate the transcendent glow of nature redeemed.[6] In the theater, a recurring theme shows life alternating between truth and illusion. What is represented on stage, either in character or plot, occludes and hides reality, as well as manifesting and revealing it. The great dramatists of the age, like Shakespeare (1564-1616) and Calderón (1600-81), turn the theater into a metaphor for existence: representation belongs simultaneously to both appearance and reality.[7] As a result, the theater, like the plastic arts, depicts reality as ever expanding, as ever in the process of being created by its immanent spiritual impulse.[8]

In the realm of spirituality, Ignatius Loyola best exemplifies how nature harmoniously and dynamically represents grace. His mystical vision is the principal articulator of the centrifugal movement of the Baroque. Grounded in the vocation of the human person, this movement fills the mundane order with symbols that reflect the subject's own divine immanence.[9] More than any other creature, the human person, as the image of God, represents its Creator, especially in the use of its freedom. Through the mystical gifts of discernment given in prayer, this freedom becomes real and authentic.[10] It is liberated from the false appearances of freedom conjured up by what Ignatius calls "the enemy of our human nature."[11] So freed, human volition can recreate the world according to its own immanent divine image by positing the highest form of symbols: acts of charity that make God transparent. According to Ignatius, grace is thus the *sine qua non*, the very condition without which true human freedom cannot obtain. For this reason, Dupré argues that Ignatius effects "a more radically God-centered view of reality" than had heretofore been possible.[12] In filling Renaissance humanism with mystical content, this view brings the dynamic sacramentality of the Baroque to its pinnacle: God becomes the foundation of the person, even while Creator and creature each retains its appropriate autonomy. Having prayerfully met the divine in its own powers, and having been reformed in the way of Christ, the human person actively responds to the ineluctable attractiveness of grace.[13] The genius of Ignatian mysticism is embodied in the paradox that, as Dupré says, "the way down [into the person is] the way up [to God]."[14]

But the Baroque synthesis between nature and grace onto which the plastic arts, the theater, and mysticism open a window is a product of a homogeneously God-centered culture.[15] The fracturing of this homogeneity leads to what is perhaps the hallmark of modernity: secularization—culture's loss of its religious attitude. This loss results from a restricting of the mind's dialectical drive toward its transcendent term. When the mind fails directly to experience the sacred reflected in the natural order but nonetheless radically different from it, the mind not only compromises its sense of the divine, it forfeits its sense of the profane. Perceived only as the antithesis of the sacred, the profane is the sacred's parasite. The loss of both the sacred and the profane constitutes the secular: a world whose symbols fail to cohere because the transcendent universal that alone is capable of reconciling their diversity has evanesced.[16]

Sensitive to the complex development of secular modernity, Dupré focuses on language as a touchstone. Once humanity gives up its belief that it is God's living image, it is ultimately unable to sustain a symbolic world of meaning. He cites as emblematic of this belief a doctrine of Nicholas of Cusa, the Renaissance prelate and Neoplatonic thinker: Just as God creates natural forms that represent His mind, so humanity actively creates concepts, images, metaphors, and symbols that represent its own. Although important nuances have to be made, this doctrine typifies a God-centered culture. Language is at once the result of human genius and a remote representation of divine creativity, whose principal representation is human intelligence.[17]

With the advent of the secular, however, language eventually becomes detached from representation. With the loss of the transcendent, language devolves first into a representation merely of the human subject. Symptomatic of this devolution, the novel arises as modernity's premier literary form. A narrative whose development becomes more and more privatized, the novel is unable to offer the elevated ethical vision of tragedy or epic. In fact, its increasing idiosyncrasy approaches nihilism.[18] As it becomes solipsistic, the novel disengages language, not only from the transcendent, but from generally understood communication.[19] Thus becoming the fetish of individual writers, language finds itself "at war with the established reality structures" of culture.[20] Now evoking doubt and insecurity instead of representing the true, the good, and the beautiful, speech continues to be formulated, but its meaning is more and more reduced to silence.[21]

Dupré's analysis of modernity reveals that the essence of the harmony between nature and grace achieved by the Baroque is grounded in the intrinsic link between the creative dynamism of human rationality and God's own dynamic engagement with human history. This link renders the human person a representation of its transcendent source. As a divine microcosm, humanity fashions a macrocosm of symbolic meaning. In reflecting the genius of its human creator, this world necessarily reflects its infinite archetype. When language, the touchstone of humanity's symbolic potential, is sundered from this link, it devolves into mere human meaning. Thus unable to exercise the plenitude of its symbolic capacity, it collapses into confusion. Alas, as Dupré argues, Christian theology over most of the next three centuries was unable to reestablish the lost harmony. It retreated into forms of rationalism whose sterile concepts of human nature suppressed reason's relation to the existential life of faith.[22] In confirming this analysis, Michael Buckley points out the unfortunate irony: theological rationalism paved the way for modern atheism. By confining religion to an intellectual defense of creed and code, theology neglected cult, thereby excoriating religion's driving energy in personal religious experience.[23]

II.

The first notable effort to restore the lost harmony between nature and grace came with the theologians of the Catholic School of Tübingen. Johann Adam Möhler (1796-1838), Johann Sebastian Drey (1777-1853), Franz Anton Staudenmaier (1800-56), Johannes Evangelist Kuhn (1806-87), and Johann Baptist Hirscher (1788-1865) were conscious of theology's need to counter-balance the rationalism of the Enlightenment.[24] Owing a special debt to Goethe (1749-1832), they incorporated into Catholic thought insights especially from Schleiermacher (1768-1834), Hegel (1770-1831), and Schelling (1775-1854). These three thinkers, by positing the transcendent as the core of human reason, understand religion and history as suffused with dynamic intelligence.[25] Nonetheless, despite the Tübingen School's creative dialogue with German Romanticism, its influence in the short term remained localized. Regrettably, it was overshadowed by the Thomistic revival occurring in mid-century Rome, the center of ecclesiastical prominence.[26] Although Karl Rahner (1904-84) came under its influence in the longer term, this was indirect.[27]

Only with Maurice Blondel (1861-1949) did a significant advance obtain. Like the Tübingen thinkers, he saw incisively that for the harmony lost in the Baroque to be regained, the seeds of the graced order had to be found planted firmly in the natural order without in any way violating the integrity of either order. He approached this problem from below, as it were, by undertaking a philosophical analysis of reason's natural capacity. In so doing, he demonstrated humanity's need for a divine revelation without thereby making such a revelation necessary.[28] At the heart of his demonstration lies what he calls the "superstition" of reason. This obtains when reason falls into a delusion, mistakenly believing that its own object will fully satisfy the demands of its own method. In fact, as his principal work *Action* (1893) argues, philosophy's autonomy is driven by a dynamic exigency that, although rationally immanent, requires a heteronomous and infinite object fully to explain.[29] Because this object is congenial with reason's autonomy, philosophy points to faith as reason's consummation without subsuming faith within reason.[30] He thereby avoids the absolute idealism of Hegel and other German Romantics.

Blondel's philosophical account of the relation between nature and grace spurred Catholic theology to reconsider the problem. Because philosophy showed that natural reason was not free-standing, but was constituted by a transcendent exigency that made a divine revelation both reasonable and likely, it became difficult for theology to assert that grace was merely added onto nature in order to elevate its self-contained capacities. Blondel made it apparent to theology that vestiges of the graced order were required precisely in order to constitute reason's natural capacities. If this were the case, then theology needed to ask itself how these capacities could be considered natural. The most significant answers to this question were given by Rahner and Hans Urs von Balthasar (1904-84) who, bringing the work of Henri de Lubac (1896-1991) to full flower, reconceive nature as a moment within the order of grace.[31]

III.

In developing his position, Rahner, like Blondel, approaches the problem philosophically from below, but he also provides a theological consideration from above. He delineates two types of revelation that show how knowledge of God can be correlated to the faculties of the human person. First, independently of theology, he undertakes a philosophical analysis of reason's capacities. This shows that humanity is constituted by a "general" revelation of the absolute and infinite Being. Developing the thought of Blondel and the Belgian thinker Joseph Maréchal (1878-1944), general revelation hinges on what Rahner calls the "preapprehension of absolute Being."[32] This power is the foundation and summit of human thought. In a dim and unobjectified way, it grasps in the human intellect's knowledge of finite realities the unconditioned existence of God as the intellect's necessary and sufficient explanation.[33] In addition to general revelation, a "categorial" revelation comes to humanity in history. Access to it is given by the act of faith. This manifests Christ as the Absolute's definitive Word who reveals the Trinity and the other data mediated by Scripture and the tradition of the Church.[34]

According to Rahner, general and categorial revelation function reciprocally. On the one hand, general revelation is the condition for the possibility of categorial revelation. The person's assent to the grace of the Absolute's self-revelation in Christ represents a development of the natural openness to the Absolute, which philosophy shows as constituting the human intellect.[35] On the other hand, categorial revelation is the condition for the possibility of general revelation. Although reason can investigate and affirm humanity's necessary openness to the Absolute independently of grace, still general revelation actually belongs to the graced order.[36] Because the cosmos is created through the divine Logos, the grace of the Incarnation operates implicitly from the very dawn of time and space. Although a distinction can be drawn between the orders of nature and grace, only one concrete order exists, that of grace. According to Rahner, therefore, the notion of a pure nature ontologically separate from grace is fictitious. Because the historical world of creation incarnates the world of grace, grace both constitutes and suffuses nature.[37]

Nonetheless, the concept of nature continues to be theologically significant. Rahner calls it a "remainder concept." Although nature lacks an objective theological reality, it serves as a useful hypothesis. It explains what humanity would be like were there no categorial revelation in Christ. But since faith shows that such a revelation obtains, faith makes it clear that general revelation exists within the "supernatural existential." This means that categorial revelation shows human intelligence to reach its full term, not in reason's grasp of the absolute Being as its ground, but in faith's assent to the God whom Christ reveals.[38] The supernatural existential means that through the Incarnation Christ embodies the general revelation of the Absolute in time and space. Christ becomes a mirror in which humanity can see the historical fulfillment of reason's orientation to the unconditioned Cause of all reality.[39]

Rahner's analysis of the relation of nature and grace means that the "natural" method of philosophy actually belongs within the world of grace. No qualitative difference obtains between reason's assent to general revelation and faith's assent to categorial revelation.[40] This does not make Christ's work any the less gratuitous on the part of God. Nor does it mean that reason's grasp of the Absolute in any sense logically entails the categorial revelation. It does mean that faith and reason are part of a continuum whose origin lies in grace. It is through the preexistent Word that nature is fashioned and through this Word's Incarnation that it is redeemed. Nature is therefore born of grace, oriented to grace, and refashioned by grace. Although reason may seem to function by its own laws, the theologian knows that their root lies, not merely in general revelation, but in the Absolute's freely issued utterance. Rahner's concept of nature as a remainder concept thus develops from above what Blondel develops from below. From a theological perspective that respects philosophy's integrity, Rahner shows that the graced order subsumes the natural order even while he recognizes nature's distinctiveness and revelation's gratuity.

IV.

The premise that nature is a remainder concept is also asserted by von Balthasar, who warrants it principally from above. Under the influence of the German Catholic thinker Erich Przywara (1889-1972), his concept of nature enters into dialogue with the later position of Karl Barth (1886-1968).[41] According to Barth, the theological concept of nature is equivocal. Original sin causes so radical a breach between God and humanity that the powers of the soul to know the true, the good, and the beautiful are virtually destroyed. Because of the fall's damage to the image and likeness of God in the soul, no viable concept of nature can exist after it. Nature's pre- and post-lapsarian states are thus equivocal. Only Christ's redeeming entry into history can restore the soul's divine image and likeness and revivify the human faculties. So utterly gratuitous is this event, and so dim is post-lapsarian nature of divine reflection, that after Christ only one concrete order exits, that of grace.[42]

In responding to Barth, Balthasar uses the Council of Chalcedon (AD 425) as his point of departure. Its doctrine, he argues, contains a more elevated conception of post-lapsarian nature than Barth's position seems to acknowledge. Chalcedon defines Christ as the union in one Person of two natures, one human and created, one divine and infinite. The Council thus contends, von Balthasar asserts, that even after the fall a viable concept of nature continues to exist. Since Chalcedon is a definitive explication of the Christian faith, it follows that nature cannot be an equivocal concept. It must be analogous.[43] As I interpret Balthasar, this analogy entails three senses.

According to the first sense, the states of pre- and post-lapsarian nature are analogous. To justify this claim, von Balthasar, like Rahner, returns to the Christian datum that creation is spontaneously fashioned by God. Nature's origins are divine because they flow forth out of nothing from the divine essence, whose omniscience contains the archetypes of all created forms. These forms, as a result, must be vestigially graced. Not so cataclysmic as to eradicate these vestiges, the fall means that post-lapsarian nature retains some continuity with its former state.[44] The soul's divine image is sufficiently intact so as to form in Christ the basis of the Incarnation.[45]

As a consequence of the Incarnation, a second analogy emerges. In the Incarnation, divinity has irrevocably impregnated post-lapsarian creation. It has raised nature to a dignity higher than its pre-lapsarian state, which ensued from its being made in the divine image. Nature's post-lapsarian and redeemed states are thus analogous, because both manifest the divine life, although in markedly different degrees.[46] Because of this manifestation, nature is analogous in yet a third sense. As Chalcedon teaches, in Christ humanity and divinity, although distinct, are inseparably united. Because the single Person fuses both natures into a unity-in-diversity, the being of the divine nature and the being of the human nature are similar within their uniqueness. The analogy between these natures is evinced in the doctrine of the "exchange of predicates" (*communicatio idiomatum*). This allows Christ's properly human acts to be applied to his divinity. It is proper to say that, in Christ, God is born, suffers, and dies, because in Christ humanity is divinized. As a consequence of Chalcedon, Balthasar thus concludes that there can be "no slice of 'pure nature' in this world."[47] Created through the Logos, nature originates in God's life, retains this life after the fall, and in Christ is perpetually shot through by it.

In sum, von Balthasar, like Barth, posits only one concrete order, the order of grace. But unlike Barth, he affirms the continued existence of post-lapsarian nature, since the Incarnation is not imposed by strict necessity on humanity. Created nature must exist, at least theoretically, in order for it to constitute the bare minimum pre-supposed by a gratuitously given Revelation.[48] Agreeing with Rahner, von Balthasar thus defines nature as the remainder after the revealed contents of grace are subtracted from the one concrete order. But neither this remainder nor these contents can be precisely delimited.[49]

The preceding overview of the problem of nature and grace since the Baroque provides the context for appreciating *Fides et ratio*. The heart of the Baroque's synthesis lies in its link between the dynamism of human rationality and God's own dynamic engagement within human history. As the verbalizer of symbolic meaning, reason brings to light the immanent presence of God in the depth and diversity of the created order. In no small measure, this synthesis was lost because theology over-rationalized the divine, causing it to lose its footing in an unabashed celebration of nature as grace's necessary medium. The worlds of human experience, matter, history, and culture received less consideration from theology as divine symbols. In turn, a growing separation ensured between nature and grace that the Tübingen School, Blondel, Rahner, and von Balthasar endeavor to rectify. No one supposes that their thought can of itself produce a new pan-cultural synthesis. But if there is a direction sketched out by these thinkers, it begins in their recovery of the intrinsic reciprocity between nature and grace. Whereas nature implicitly originates in grace and is suffused by it, nature is nonetheless the essential medium in and through which grace manifests itself. The one concrete order of grace contains nature as its inner moment; it harnesses nature in ways that defy precise description to reveal the divine life. If this intrinsic reciprocity defines the current state of the problem, then one of theology's immediate tasks requires reclaiming for humanity the power to articulate the graced symbolism of the natural order.

V.

Boldly committed to this task, *Fides et ratio* is structured on a paradox. Exploiting the creative tension between nature and grace, the encyclical contends that nature realizes its own autonomy only when it recognizes that it mediates a higher order. Nature's integrity is grounded in its sacramentality. In order for this recognition to obtain, reason must properly understand itself. John Paul hearkens to the theme of reason's dynamism seminally developed by Blondel, thus distancing himself from those post-Baroque theologians who depict nature as statically independent of grace.[50] Modeling reason as incomplete and restlessly eager for its own fulfillment, he argues that, despite humanity's poignant sense of finitude, reason "yearns for the infinite riches" beyond it.[51] The source of this yearning is a nostalgia for God that, constituting reason, defines the human person's essence as a seeker of truth (*FR*, nn. 24, 28). Reason's infinite goal thus occupies at least a virtually immanent presence in the human person.

The encyclical does not explain how this presence obtains, declining to canonize specific philosophical concepts, such as Rahner's preapprehension of the Absolute. But the Pope does affirm that finite realities can mediate reason to itself by bringing this virtual presence more fully to consciousness (*FR*, n. 22). This mediation is possible because, although the fullness of truth transcends all finite realities, it is immanent in them even as it is in reason (*FR*, n. 20). Through them, reason seems, ironically, "almost to surpass [its] natural limitations" (*FR*, n. 22). By discoursing on the knowledge that it acquires from the sensory faculties, reason realizes an intuition of its own self-transcending capacity. It grasps the power and divinity of the ultimate Cause (*FR*, nn. 22-23). If reason fails to acknowledge this Cause as the fullness of truth, it is not because reason is incapable but because the will impedes it (*FR*, n. 17). Thus opposed to the reduction of reason to the utilitarian ends of mere power and pleasure, John Paul links reason's search for ultimate meaning with "the religious impulse innate in every person" (*FR*, nn. 47, 81).

Creating in reason the nostalgia for God, this impulse is anterior to all of reason's yearnings. Because it is the cause that drives these, they become the sacrament of the religious impulse. Humanity's pluriform searchings for meaning are the outward sign of the restlessness for the divine that initiates them in an effort to obtain satisfaction. This sacramentality makes it clear for John Paul, as for the Tübingen thinkers, Blondel, Rahner, and von Balthasar, that the divine is ingredient in nature, which it originates, stimulates, and brings to completion. In a telling footnote, *Fides et ratio* exemplifies this divine ingredience. Reiterating the teaching of Vatican I on the unity of truth in the orders of nature and grace, John Paul alludes to Galileo, who sensed in his scientific research the Creator's presence stimulating his ingenuity and assisting his inquiry (*FR*, nn. 9, 34, 53).[52] This allusion underscores the need of God's dynamic immanence to bring the created order to full integrity. It shows that the divine, which is the source of reason's searching, is also discovered by reason in the objects of its search. On the one hand, God inspired the questions that Galileo asked of nature, whereas on the other Galileo found God in the answers that nature supplied. According to John Paul, therefore, objective reality mediates a fuller consciousness of God to human intelligence. When it does, the order of nature attains the fullness of its own truth. Nature is thus sacramental, not only because it is an outward sign of its creating Cause, but more especially because it is an efficacious sign that causes what it signifies. Nature brings knowledge of God to light in reason.[53]

If the Pope posits that reason's engagement with empirical reality is epistemically fruitful because it is religiously grounded, he further argues that Christian Revelation is the lens that uniquely opens for reason its potential to see the full sacramentality of creation. In order for reason to make use of this lens, however, it must critically assess both its limit and its capability. In defining reason's limit, the encyclical, without explicitly mentioning Blondel, seems nonetheless to caution against the superstition that he diagnoses. This obtains when reason mistakenly believes that any finite object or idea will satisfy its innate yearning. According to John Paul, reason must admit its own contingency, question its own sufficiency, and even move beyond its natural goal, which is grasping the existence of an ultimate Cause (*FR*, n. 79). "[A]t the summit of its searching," he says, "reason acknowledges that it cannot do without what faith presents[:] the person of the Word made flesh" (*FR*, nn. 41-42). Only this reveals the "fullness of the seminal plan of love which began with creation" (*FR*, n. 15). Only this gives a foretaste of the "definitive vision of God"–the unique surcease of reason's yearning, the single cure for its nostalgia (*FR*, n. 15).

If the encyclical shows that reason's limit leads ineluctably to Revelation, it also contends that Revelation strengthens and enhances reason's capability. Consisting of the "boldness" of human intelligence to perceive and articulate "universally true propositions," this capability is grounded in the knowledge of Being that conforms to and is evinced from objective reality (*FR*, nn. 48, 59). Attested to by the history of human cultures, this boldness, when exercised, generates wisdom, the contemplation of goodness, truth, and beauty (*FR*, nn. 70, 81). Because Revelation embodies a divinely inspired source of wisdom, it augments reason's potential (*FR*, n. 56). "[W]ithout the stimulus of the word of God," asserts John Paul, "a good part of modern and contemporary philosophy would not exist" (*FR*, n. 76). Such ideas as creation and original sin have been appropriated from Revelation by philosophy, which has then developed them according to its own object and methods (*FR*, n. 76). So fecund a union, the marriage between Revelation and reason "cannot be separated without diminishing" humanity's capacity to know itself and its world (*FR*, n. 16).

In short, for John Paul Revelation is the sacrament of reason's integrity. Graciously incarnating the divine in history, it is an outward sign that manifests to reason its limit and its boldness, which reason can nonetheless discern through a critical self-examination. Moreover, Revelation is an efficacious sign, because it answers the question of ultimate meaning that reason's limit generates, even as it expands reason's bold capacity to know universally true propositions about wisdom. Because of this sacramentality, Revelation enjoys a circular relation to reason. Sensing its limit as a result of the divine nostalgia that constitutes it, reason appropriates Revelation, which then stimulates reason's universal power "to explore paths which of itself it would not have suspected it could take" (*FR*, n. 73). New syntheses in the empirical disciplines and in philosophy and theology thus ensue for the benefit of human culture.

In sum, *Fides et ratio* advances the post-Baroque understanding of the relation of nature and grace by evolving within the Church's magisterium strains of thought developing in philosophy and theology since the early nineteenth century. Indebted to the Tübingen thinkers, it posits the transcendent as ingredient in reality. On this basis, it positions reason's integrity and autonomy squarely within the sacramentality of nature. It defines this integrity as reason's capacity for self-transcendence grounded in a restless nostalgia for God. Thus it is indebted to Blondel, who envisages the divine ingredience in nature as reason's dynamic striving toward a transcendent destiny that nature cannot supply.

The encyclical defines reason's autonomy as its ability coherently to articulate universal propositions about goodness, truth, and beauty that correspond to objective reality. In this articulation, reason uses methods whose validity does not pre-suppose Revelation. Although reason can know autonomously that its striving for self-transcendence is driven by the virtual immanence of the divine, it cannot know autonomously the full message of love that this immanence entails. When reason acknowledges the insufficiency of its own methods to obtain full integrity, it can freely grasp in faith the Revelation thematizing the message of love that reason only dimly adumbrates. This relation between reason and Revelation, which *Fides et ratio* calls circular, strongly echoes Rahner's supernatural existential, which explains the mutuality between general and categorial revelation.

Finally and decisively, for John Paul the order of created nature is the outward and efficacious sign of grace, which nature incarnates in every person in a way analogous to its unique epiphany in Christ. In this he hearkens to von Balthasar, for whom no slice of pure nature exists in this world because, as Chalcedon teaches, in Christ nature and grace, although distinct, conjoin in a redemptive circumincession.

VI.

However boldly *Fides et ratio* makes its case, it does not take into account the current plight of the religious believer who must dwell in a secular world. This world, as Dupré reminds us, is hallmarked by an attenuated sense of representation in which the symbols of art and religion, if not yet moribund, have at least lost much of their lustre "as beacons of meaning [guiding us] on our journey through time."[54] Although agreeing with John Paul that reason is sufficiently capacious to reach a transcendent term, Dupré nonetheless observes that, when reason is restricted, language becomes silent. In such a context, public religious symbols like verbal revelation and ecclesiastical doctrines fail decisively to convey a sacred experience—an existential sense of nature's graced dimension.[55] It is becoming increasingly difficult for the modern person to point to anything in direct experience that is sacred, or even for this person meaningfully to conceive the term.[56] Although contemporary society has witnessed religious revivals, many of these, Dupré opines, are only marginally religious. All too often they merely evoke romantic remembrances and aesthetic imitations of the past.[57]

Dupré therefore endeavors to offer guidance to the modern believer. As a definition of culture, the secular is a uniquely novel phenomenon in the West.[58] As a result of it, anyone who wishes to cultivate the religious attitude today must make a commitment to become separated from public culture and deliberately to turn inward. There, more or less alone, the subject can experience a mediated sense of the sacred that cannot be known directly in the patent symbols of the world. Thus isolated from secular society, the contemporary religious subject lives in a painful state of tension. Caught between culture's impoverishment of the human capacity for transcendence and the interior will to believe, the subject must reconcile the orders of nature and grace in the personal cultivation of religious experience. Only as a result of an enriched inner life can the believer subsequently impose a sense of the sacred on the objects of experience. Although inner conviction has become the genesis of the sacred, the total integration of reality that religion promises is still possible.[59] But in secular modernity, "the center of human piety has moved" from a religiously accessible cosmos to an individual choice.[60] However much this shift might cause us to grieve what culture has lost, still, exhorts Dupré, it should spur institutional religion on to develop structures that mediate the sacred for its adherents. These structures should especially encourage the mystical life.[61] As his analysis of the spiritual doctrine of Ignatius Loyola shows us, it is the direct experience of grace, personally appropriated deep within the human faculties, that, above all, reconnects the order of faith to that of nature.

An assessment of modernity such as Dupré's offers a tempering balance to *Fides et ratio*. Both creatively retrieve the Augustinian tradition. On the one hand, John Paul's view of reason hearkens to Book I of the *Confessions* where the human heart is restless until it rests in God.[62] He develops this metaphor into a model of reason boldly extroverted in its searching for meaning. It is the world of empirical reality that, itself representing grace, answers many of reason's driving questions. On the other hand, Dupré evokes Book IX. In Augustine and Monica's vision at Ostia, we see that the rivulet of divine immanence in the heart can, in prayer, be followed to its source: the fountain of love, the divine Subject itself, that overflows its abundance into humanity, this Subject's image and likeness.[63] By contrast with John Paul, Duprê reminds us that secularity entails a world of impoverished meaning. He is thus less sanguine than the Pope that reason's extroversion will lead it to its transcendent term. Reaffirming humanity's power to articulate the graced symbolism of the natural order, however necessary, is not sufficient to heal the post-Baroque breach between nature and grace. Also needed is reason's inner reappropriation of its own transcendence where the power to generate religious experience is lodged. Prayer creates an inner culture revealing the sacramentality of nature to a public culture ignorant of it. Dupré is thus right to underscore the urgency of individual acts of pious recollection as means of grasping the divine.

Nonetheless, Dupré over-emphasizes private experience as the bridge between nature and grace. For instance, we might wonder how the individual can find the divine life within when the intellect's quest for its transcendent term is so restricted. It is here that *Fides et ratio* offers Dupré a tempering balance. The encyclical guides us to behold the culture of institutional religion as an oasis of meaning for the human heart parched by secularity. If public symbols are sacramentally opaque, the Christian Church remains to radiate its beacon. In its traditions of worship and prayer and its systems of creed and code, the Church mediates reason's transcendence to itself. Moreover, without the Church to guard and regulate religious experience, personal piety easily devolves into delusion and fantasy, as the great doctors of the spiritual and mystical life have reiterated. Such a devolution, far from reconnecting faith to nature, distorts them both into another form of the fetish that Dupré deplores in the modern novel.

In sum, if there is a future hope for refashioning a cultural synthesis between nature and grace analogous to that of the Baroque, it lies in ecclesial religion. This community of meaning is efficacious both for the modern believer and secular culture. For the believer, it stimulates and protects the religion experience that is the fulfillment of reason. For culture, it prophesies against the diminishment of public symbols, thus giving witness that empirical reality is appreciated adequately only when grasped as a moment within its transcendent constitution.

NOTES

1. Louis Dupré, *Passage to Modernity: An Essay in the Hermeneutics of Nature and Culture* (New Haven/London: Yale University Press, 1993) 171-72, citing as an instance the sixteenth-century Thomist Sylvester of Ferrara, *Opera* (Venice, 1535) 1, 39-41. For a recent study defending a position similar to the sixteenth-century interpreters, see Peter F. Ryan, "Moral Action and the Ultimate End of Man: The Significance of the Debate between Henri de Lubac and His Critics," S.T.D. diss., Pontifical Gregorian University, 1996.

2   For Aquinas's understanding of nature and supernature, see *Summa Theologiae* I-II, quest. 62-63 and *Summa contra Gentiles* III, ch. 150, s. 5, and ch. 152, s. 3. See the commentary by Henri de Lubac, *Surnaturel: études historiques* (Paris: Aubier, 1946), ch. 5. For the aspect of Aquinas's thought that contributes to the theory of pure nature, see ST III, quest. 1, art. 2-3. All cited in Dupré, *Passage*, 172.

3. Louis Dupré (1925-) is T. Lawrason Riggs Professor in the Philosophy of Religion Emeritus at Yale University. Holding a doctorate from Louvain, he was Professor of Philosophy at Georgetown University until moving to Yale in 1973. A member of the American Academy of Arts and Sciences and of the Royal Belgian Academy of Letters, Arts, and Sciences, he holds honorary doctorates from Loyola College, and from Georgetown and Sacred Heart Universities. For a study of his thought and a bibliography of his works, see Paul J. Levesque, *Symbols of Transcendence: Religious Expression in the Thought of Louis Dupré* (Louvain: Peeters Press, 1997).

4. Dupré, *Passage*, 237.

5. Ibid., 240.

6. Ibid., 242-43.

7. Ibid., 240-42.

8. Ibid., 239.

9. Louis Dupré, "Ignatian Humanism and Its Mystical Origins," *Communio: International Catholic Review* 18 (Summer 1991): 164-82, at 181.

10. Ibid., 171.

11. Ignatius Loyola, *The Spiritual Exercises of St. Ignatius*, trans. and ed. Louis J. Puhl S.J. (Chicago: Loyola University Press, 1951), "Introductory Observations" 10, p. 4.

12. Dupré, "Ignatian Humanism," 173.

13. Ibid., 178-79.

14. Ibid., 174.

15. Ibid., 180.

16. Louis Dupré, *The Other Dimension: A Search for the Meaning of Religious Attitudes* (New York: Seabury, 1979), 14-18.

17. Louis Dupré, "The Broken Mirror: The Fragmentation of the Symbolic World," *Stanford Literature Review* 5 (Spring-Fall 1988): 7-24, at 11-12.

18. Ibid., 20.

19. Ibid., 21.

20. Ibid.

21. Ibid., 22-24.

22. Dupré, *Passage*, 247-48.

23. Michael J. Buckley, *At the Origins of Modern Atheism* (New Haven/London: Yale University Press, 1987), 362-63.

24. For details on these figures, together with bibliographies, see Donald J. Dietrich and Michael J. Himes, "Introduction," in *The Legacy of the Tübingen School: The Relevance of Nineteenth Century Theology for the Twenty-First Century*, eds. Donald J. Dietrich and Michael J. Himes (New York: Crossroad, 1997), 11-19. This volume also contains individual studies of Drey, Kuhn, Hirscher, and Möhler.

25. For Goethe's influence, see A. Minon, "L'attitude de J. A. Moehler dans la question de développement du dogme," *Ephemerides Theologicae Lovanienses* 16 (1939): 328-82, at 362-67;

see also Edmond Vermeil, *Jean-Adam Möhler et l'école catholique de Tubingue* (1815-1840) (Paris: Librarie Armand Colin, 1913), 1-8.

26. This revival began in the work of Kleutgen (1811-83), Liberatore (1810-92), and the Jesuits who founded the theological journal *La Civiltà Cattolica* in 1849. It received special impetus with *Aeterni Patris*, Leo XIII's encyclical of 1879. For details, see Gerald A. McCool, *Catholic Theology in the Nineteenth Century* (New York: Seabury, 1977), 145-215.

27. Rahner's theory of language bears the influence of Johann Adam Möhler. See Stephen M. Fields, S.J., *Being as Symbol: On the Origins and Development of Karl Rahner's Metaphysics* (Washington: Georgetown University Press, 2000), ch. 5.

28. Henri Bouillard, "Philosophy and Christianity in the Thought of Maurice Blondel," in *The Logic of the Faith* (New York: Sheed and Ward, 1967), 161-85, at 161-62; originally published as *Logique de la foi* (Paris: Éditions Aubier, 1964).

29. Maurice Blondel, *Action* (1893), trans. Oliva Blanchette (Notre Dame: University of Notre Dame Press, 1984); originally published as *L'Action* (Paris: Presses universitaires de France, 1950).

30. Bouillard, "Philosophy and Christianity," 168-72, summarizing the thesis of *Action*, 43-322.

31. Regrettably it is not possible here to consider Henri de Lubac's work. See his major studies on the subject: *Augustinianism and Modern Theology*, trans. Lancelot Sheppard (New York: Crossroad, 2000), originally published as *Augustinisme et théologie moderne* (Paris: Aubier, 1965), and *The Mystery of the Supernatural*, trans. Rosemary Sheed (New York: Crossroad, 1998), originally published as *Le mystère du surnaturel* (Paris: Aubier, 1965).

32. See especially Joseph Maréchal, *Le thomisme devant la philosophie critique*, vol. 5 of *Le point de départ de la métaphysique*, 5 vols. (Brussels and Paris: Desclée de Brouwer and Éditions universelle, 1944-49).

33. See Karl Rahner, *Spirit in the World*, trans. William V. Dych (New York: Herder and Herder, 1968), 387-407; originally published as *Geist im Welt* (Munich: Kösel, 1957).

34 Karl Rahner, "The Theology of the Symbol," *Theological Investigations* 4, trans. Kevin Smyth (Baltimore: Helicon, 1966), 221-52, at 235-36; originally published as "Theologie der Symbols," *Schriften zur Theologie*, 16 vols. (Einsiedeln: Benzinger, 1954-84) 4:275-312.

35. See Karl Rahner, *Foundations of Christian Faith: An Exploration into the Idea of Christianity*, trans. William V. Dych (New York: Crossroad, 1987) esp. ch. 4; originally published as *Grundkurs des Glaubens: Einführung in den Begriff des Christentums* (Freiburg: Herder, 1976).

36. Ibid., 55-57; and Rahner, "Nature and Grace," *Theological Investigations* 4:165-88, at 178-79; originally published as "Natur und Gnade," *Schriften zur Theologie* 4, 209-36.

37. Rahner, "Nature and Grace," 181-83.

38. Rahner, "Concerning the Relationship Between Nature and Grace," *Theological Investigations* 1, trans. Cornelius Ernst (London: Darton, Longman and Todd, 1974), 297-317, at 312-13; originally published as "Über das Verhältnis von Natur und Gnade," *Schriften zur Theologie* 1, 323-46.

39. Rahner, "The Order of Redemption Within the Order of Creation," *The Christian Commitment*, trans. Cecily Hastings (New York: Sheed and Ward, 1963), 38-74, at 49-50; originally published as *Sendung und Gnade* (Innsbruck/Vienna/Munich: Tyrolia, 1961).

40. Rahner, "Anonymous Christian," *Theological Investigations* 6, trans. Karl-H. and Boniface Kruger (London: Darton, Longman and Todd, 1974), 390-98, at 393-94; originally published as "Die Anonymen Christen," *Schriften zur Theologie* 6, 545-54.

41. Hans Urs von Balthasar, *The Theology of Karl Barth*, trans. John Drury (New York: Holt, Rinehart, Winston, 1971), 217; originally published as *Karl Barth: Darstellung und Deutung seiner Theologie* (Cologne: Jakob Hegner, 1962) [Eng. trans. subsequently cited as TKB]. This book is based on two articles in *Divus Thomas*, "Analogie und Dialetik" (1944) and "Analogie und Natur" (1945), which von Balthasar acknowledges "were prompted" by Przywara's work (TKB 307, note 2). These articles are studied in J. Zeitz, "Przywara and von Balthasar on Analogy," *The Thomist* 52 (1988): 473-98.

42. See TKB, esp. 95, 145-47, 164-70.

43. TKB, 221-22.

44. TKB, 227, 229.

45. TKB, 228.

46. TKB, 232.

47. Ibid.

48. TKB, 228-29.

49. TKB, 234-35.

50. For more on Blondel's relation to John Paul II, see Peter Henrici, "The One Who Went Unnamed: Blondel in the Encyclical *Fides et ratio*," *Communio: International Catholic Review* 26 (Fall 1999): 609-21.

51. John Paul II, *Encyclical Letter Fides et Ratio: On the Relationship between Faith and Reason* (Boston: Pauline Books and Media, 1998), n. 17 (hereafter *FR*). All subsequent references to this encyclical are to this edition and are indicated between parentheses in the body of the text.

52. See Vatican I, Dogmatic Constitution on the Catholic Faith *Dei Filius* III (Denzinger-Schönmetzer 3008). See also John Paul II, "Address to the Pontifical Academy of Sciences" (11/10/79): *Insegnamenti* II, 2 (1979) 111-12.

53. For St. Thomas's treatment of sacramental causality, see *ST* III, especially qu. 60-63; for a broad study, see Bernard Leeming, *Principles of Sacramental Theology* (Westminster: Newman, 1960). *Fides et ratio* and Rahner both use the symbolic structure of the Eucharist as an inspiration for their views of reality: see the encyclical, Ch. I, n. 13, pp. 23-24, and Fields, *Being as Symbol*, ch. 3.

54. Dupré, "Broken Mirror," 24.

55. Louis Dupré, *Transcendent Selfhood: The Loss and Rediscovery of the Inner Life* (New York: Seabury, 1976), 29.

56. Ibid., 23-24.

57. Ibid., 26.

58. Ibid., 25. Taking this position puts Dupré at odds with other commentators on contemporary religion, such as Robert Bellah, and aligns him more with Hans Blumenberg, *The Legitimacy of the Modern Age*, trans. Robert M. Wallace (Cambridge: MIT Press, 1987); originally published as *Die Legitimitt der Neuzeit* (Frankfurt-am-Main: Suhrkamp, 1966).

59. Dupré, *Transcendent Selfhood*, 27, 29.

60. Ibid., 29.

61. Ibid., 30.

62. Augustine, *Confessions*, trans. R. S. Pine-Coffin (New York: Viking Penguin, 1987), 21.

63. Ibid., 196-99.

About Our Contributors

Joseph A. Bracken, S.J., retired professor of theology at Xavier University (Cincinnati OH), is the author of five books and the editor or co-editor of two others, all of which deal with the doctrine of the Trinity in such contexts as philosophical cosmology, systematic theology, and interreligious dialogue. His two most recent books are *The One in the Many: A Contemporary Reconstruction of the God-World Relationship* (Eerdmans, 2001) and *World Without End: Christian Eschatology from a Process Perspective* (forthcoming from Eerdmans).

John J. Conley, S.J., is professor of philosophy at Fordham University (Bronx NY). Having received his doctorate in philosophy from the Catholic University of Louvain in 1988, he has focused his research on ethics and modern French philosophy. His recent publications include *The Suspicion of Virtue: Women Philosophers in Neoclassical France* (Cornell University Press, 2002), *Jacqueline Pascal: A Rule for Children* (University of Chicago Press, 2003), and *Madame de Maintenon: Dialogues and Addresses* (University of Chicago Press, 2004).

Christopher M. Cullen, S.J., is assistant professor of philosophy at Fordham University (Bronx NY), where he teaches courses in medieval and ancient philosophy. He is particularly interested in Bonaventure and the Franciscan-Augustinian tradition. He recently contributed an article on Alexander of Hales to the *Blackwell Companion to Philosophy in the Middle Ages* and is currently working on a book on the thought of Bonaventure. His previous publication on Pope John Paul II was "*Familiaris Consortio:* Fifteen Years Since" in *Prophecy and Diplomacy: The Moral Teaching of John Paul II. A Jesuit Symposium* (Fordham University Press, 1999).

Avery Cardinal Dulles, S.J., the Laurence J. McGinley Professor of Religion and Society at Fordham University (Bronx NY), and professor emeritus at The Catholic University of America, is an internationally known theologian and lecturer, and the author of twenty-two books and over 700 articles on theological topics. Past president of both the Catholic Theological Society of America and of the American Theological Society, Cardinal Dulles has served on the International Theological Commission (1992-97) and as a member of the United States Lutheran/Roman Catholic Dialogue (1972-93). Since 1992 he has served continuously as a consultant to the Committee on Doctrine of the United States Conference of Catholic Bishops.

Stephen Fields, S.J., is an associate professor of theology at Georgetown University (Washington, D.C.). He received his Ph.D. in the philosophy of religion from Yale University. He is the author of *Being as Symbol: On the Origins and Development of Karl Rahner's Metaphysics* (Georgetown University Press, 2000) and of articles in *Theological Studies, International Philosophical Quarterly, Philosophy and Theology, American Catholic Philosophical Quarterly*, and *Louvain Studies*. His areas of specialization include Rahner, von Balthasar, Newman, and Neo-Thomism. He is currently working on a book on contemporary Catholicism's notion of human reason.

Raymond Gawronski, S.J., is associate professor of theology at Marquette University (Milwaukee WI). A specialist in the thought of Hans Urs von Balthasar, Fr. Gawronski has long been interested in the spiritual encounter between East and West, both in the broader sense of the dialogue between Buddhism and Christianity, and within Europe itself, where he has long been interested in the Slavic world. His mother was raised in Poland, part of that "greatest generation" that has flowered in Pope John Paul II. His writings are an attempt to glean from these various experiences light for our current situation.

John C. Haughey, S.J., is presently a senior research fellow at Woodstock Theological Center (Washington, D.C.), on leave from Loyola University in Chicago. He is the author/editor of eleven books, of which the most recent are *Housing Heaven's Fire: The Challenge of Holiness* (Loyola Press, 2003) and *Revisiting the Idea of Calling* (Catholic University of America Press, 2004). He is a member of two international dialogue teams sponsored by the Pontifical Council for Promoting Christian Unity, one with Pentecostalism, the other with Evangelicalism. He has been an associate editor of *America* and has held chairs at John Carroll University, Seton Hall University, and Marquette University.

Joseph W. Koterski, S.J., is associate professor and chair, Department of Philosophy at Fordham University (Bronx NY), where he has taught since shortly after his priestly ordination in 1992. He also serves as the editor-in-chief of *International Philosophical Quarterly* and as chaplain and tutor in Queen's Court Residential College for Freshmen on Fordham's Rose Hill campus. He regularly teaches courses in natural law ethics and in medieval philosophy. He has recently produced videotaped lecture-courses on Aristotle's ethics and on human nature and natural law for The Teaching Company and on Spiritual Theology for the International Catholic University. Among his recent publications are *The Two Wings of Catholic Thought: Essays on Fides et Ratio* (Catholic University of America Press, 2003) and *Karl Jaspers on Philosophy of History and History of Philosophy* (Humanity Press, 2003).

William S. Kurz, S.J., is professor of New Testament at Marquette University (Milwaukee WI). He has published over forty professional articles and six books: *The Acts of the Apostles; Following Jesus: A Disciple's Guide to Luke and Acts; Farewell Addresses in the New Testament; Reading Luke-Acts: Dynamics of Biblical Narrative; The Future of Catholic Biblical Scholarship: A Constructive Conversation* (co-authored with Luke Timothy Johnson), and, most recently, *What Does the Bible Say about the End Times? A Catholic View* (St. Anthony/Servant, 2004).

Lucien F. Longtin, S.J., was born in Philadelphia in 1934, entered the Jesuits in 1952, and was ordained in 1965. Fr. Longtin has degrees in classics and education from Fordham University and a Master's degree in religious education from The Catholic University of America. Although he is currently serving as the director of the Jesuit Center for Spiritual Growth at Wernersville PA, he spent most of his ministry in high schools in Baltimore and Washington, where he taught religion. He also served on the Provincial staff of the Maryland Province from 1985 to 1992.

Arthur R. Madigan, S.J., is professor of philosophy at Boston College (Chestnut Hill MA). He works on Aristotle's metaphysics and ethics and on contemporary ethics in the Aristotelian tradition. He currently serves as rector of the Jesuit community at Le Moyne College (Syracuse NY).

John M. McDermott, S.J., is currently adjunct professor at the Pontifical College Josephinum (Columbus OH), where he teaches philosophy of God, dogmatic theology, and New Testament exegesis. He is also a member of the International Theological Commission. Besides editing *The Thought of Pope John Paul II* (Gregorian University Press, 1993), he has published two books and more than one hundred articles in theology and philosophy.

Dennis McNally, S.J., is professor of Fine Arts and chair of the Department of Fine and Performing Arts at Saint Joseph's University (Philadelphia PA). He is also a painter with a markedly academic interest in the history of church architectural environments. Two books, *Sacred Space: An Aesthetic for the Liturgical Environment* (Wyndham Hall Press, 1985) and *Fearsome Edifice: A History of the Decorated "Domus" in Catholic Churches* (Wyndham Hall Press, 2002), discuss his conviction that the environment for mystery is the result, not only of grace, but also of design.

Earl C. Muller, S.J., is a member of the New Orleans province of the Society of Jesus. From 1983 to 1986 he was an instructor in theology at Spring Hill College. In 1987 he received his Ph.D. from Marquette University in Religious Studies, and from 1987 to 1995 was a member of that faculty. From 1995 to 1999 he was an adjunct professor in the faculty of theology at the Gregorian University in Rome. Since 1999 he has been a professor of theology at Sacred Heart Major Seminary (Detroit MI), and in 2004 he was named to the Seminary's Bishop Kevin M. Britt Chair in Christology. He is the author of one book and co-editor of two others. He has published numerous articles and reviews in a variety of professional journals.

Mitchell Pacwa, S.J., entered the Society of Jesus in 1968 and was ordained a priest in 1976. He received his doctorate in Old Testament, with a New Testament minor, from Vanderbilt University in 1984. He taught at Loyola University in Chicago and at the University of Dallas. He is currently the host of two weekly television programs and a radio show at the Eternal Word Television Network (EWTN). He has published two books, *Catholics and the New Age* (Servant Press) and *Father, Forgive Me, For I Am Frustrated* (Servant Press) and many articles. Ignatius Press will soon publish a commentary by him on Proverbs and one on Ecclesiastes.

Peter F. Ryan, S.J., is associate professor of moral theology at Mount St. Mary's Seminary (Emmitsburg MD), where he also does spiritual direction and formation advising. A priest of the Maryland Province of the Society of Jesus, he was ordained in 1987 and received his S.T.D. from the Gregorian University in Rome in 1996. He has written articles on bioethics, academic freedom in a Catholic university, and the relationship between moral action and ultimate human fulfillment. Fr. Ryan is presently working on a book concerned with the significance for the new evangelization of Catholic teaching on heaven and hell.

Martin R. Tripole, S.J., is professor emeritus of theology at Saint Joseph's University (Philadelphia PA), where he taught for over 30 years. He received his S.T.D. from the Institut Catholique in Paris in 1972, and studied three years in Tübingen under Jürgen Moltmann. He directed "Jesuit Education 21," the conference on Jesuit Higher Education held in Philadelphia in 1999, and edited its proceedings (Saint Joseph's University Press, 2000). He also edited *Promise Renewed* (Loyola Press, 1999), a collection of essays by Jesuit educators on the effects of the 34th General Congregation on Jesuit Higher Education. His monograph *Faith Beyond Justice* (Saint Louis: Institute of Jesuit Sources, 1994) critiqued the role of the faith-justice movement in Jesuit life. He has published numerous articles in theological journals.

Indexes

NAMES

Aalto, Alvar, 192
Abbott, Walter, 54, 188
Abraham, 9, 148
Adam, 36, 46, 50
Adophus, L., 32
Aquinas, Thomas, 1, 18, 21-23, 32, 39, 75, 115,
    123, 150, 165-67, 172, 218, 221-23,
    237, 239
Aristotle, 39, 97-98
Armstrong, Scott, 102
Arrupe, Pedro, 190
Attwater, Rachel, 103, 115
Audi, Robert, 113
Augustine, 9, 15, 28, 31, 113, 131, 149, 215,
    218, 221, 235, 239
Baius, 216, 221
Bañez, Domingo, 221
Barth, Karl, 138-39, 229-30, 238
Baruzzi, J., 24
Becker, Joseph, 113
Bellah, Robert, 239
Belluschi, Pietro, 192
Bergner, K., 33
Billot, Cardinal, 150
Biser, E., 33
Blackmun, Harry, 99
Blondel, Maurice, 226-27, 231-32, 234, 238-39
Bloom, Allan, 95
Blumenberg, Hans, 239
Bobola, Andrew, 64
Bohm, Domenikus, 192
Boniface VIII, 149-50
Bouillard, Henri, 238
Bosco, John, 204
Boyack, Kenneth, 116
Boyer, Charles, 217-18, 221
Bracken, Joseph A., x, 135-46, 147-72, 241
Bradley, Gerard, 44
Breuer, Marcel, 192
Buckley, Michael, 226, 237
Burtchaell, James, 101, 114

Buttiglione, Rocco, 14, 38, 53
Cahill, Lisa Sowle, 106
Cajetan, Thomas de Vio, 221
Calderón, 224
Canisius, Peter, 66
Capper, Charles, 112
Caputo, John, 113
Carey, Ann, 54
Casaroli, Agostino, 15, 91
Cassidy, Cardinal, 86
Cathrein, Victor, 221
Cayce, Edgar, 130
Cessario, Romanus, 115
Chaput, Archbishop, 60
Cheever, John, 102
Chesterton, G. K., 122
Chmelnicki, Bohdan, 67
Chmielowski, Adam, 180
Chopin, Frederick, 73
Christ, Jesus, 4, 6-8, 10-12, 18-20, 24-37, 43,
    45-47, 50-52, 57, 78-83, 88, 93, 96-97,
    101, 103, 106, 111, 127, 130-33, 135,
    137-40, 144, 146, 148-50, 152-59, 161-
    69, 174-75, 177-81, 183-84, 190, 192,
    196-98, 200-06, 211-13, 220-21, 223-
    24, 227, 229-30, 234
Ciszek, Walter, 62
Clarke, W. Norris, 115
Clifford, W. K., 113
Cobb-Stevens, Richard, 116
Congar, Yves, 162
Conley, John J., viii-xi, 15, 111, 173-88, 189-94,
    241
Conrad, Joseph Korzeniowski, 69
Cornelius, 170
Crossan, Dominic, 102, 115
Cullen, Christopher M., 117-25, 241
Cullmann, Oscar, 163, 172
Curie, Marie Skladowska, 69
Cyprian, 149
Cyril, 63, 78, 80, 86

☙

PAPAL AND ECCLESIAL DOCUMENTS

SCRIPTURAL REFERENCES

GENERAL CONGREGATIONS OF THE SOCIETY OF JESUS

SUBJECTS